WOMEN AND SPIRITUALITY IN THE WRITING OF MORE, WOLLSTONECRAFT, STANTON, AND EDDY

WOMEN AND SPIRITUALITY IN THE WRITING OF MORE, WOLLSTONECRAFT, STANTON, AND EDDY

Arleen M. Ingham

Materials from The Mary Baker Eddy Collection are used with permission.
Opinions expressed in this book are those of the author and not necessarily approved or endorsed by The Mary Baker Eddy Collection or The Mary Baker Eddy Library.
Materials from The Bristol Record Office are used with permission.

Artwork courtesy of Sharon Winter and used with permission.

First published in 2010 by PALGRAVE MACMILLAN® in the United States—a division of St. Martin's Press LLC, 175 Fifth Avenue, New York, NY 10010

Where this book is distributed in the UK, Europe and the rest of the world, this is by Palgrave Macmillan, a division of Macmillan Publishers Limited, registered in England, company number 785998, of Houndmills, Basingstoke, Hampshire RG21 6XS.

Palgrave Macmillan is the global academic imprint of the above companies and has companies and representatives throughout the world.

Palgrave® and Macmillan® are registered trademarks in the United States, the United Kingdom, Europe and other countries.

ISBN: 978-0-230-10259-0

Library of Congress Cataloging-in-Publication Data

Ingham, Arleen M., 1946-
   Women and spirituality in the writing of More, Wollstonecraft, Stanton, and Eddy / Arleen Ingham.
      p. cm.
   Includes bibliographical references.
   ISBN 978-0-230-10259-0 (alk. paper)
   1. English prose literature—Women authors—History and criticism. 2. American prose literature—Women authors—History and criticism. 3. Women's rights—History—18th century 4. Women's rights—History—19th century. 5. Women's rights—Religious aspects. 6. Women and religion—History. 7. More, Hannah, 1745-1833—Criticism and interpretation. 8. Wollstonecraft, Mary, 1759-1797—Criticism and interpretation. 9. Stanton, Elizabeth Cady, 1815-1902—Criticism and interpretation. 10. Eddy, Mary Baker, 1821-1910—Criticism and interpretation. I. Title.

PR119.I64 2010
820.9'928709033—dc22   2009046430

Design by Scribe Inc.

First edition: July 2010

10 9 8 7 6 5 4 3 2 1

Printed in the United States of America.

I dedicate this book to my mother, Mary, widowed as a young mother, but whose spiritual awareness and representation of the paternal, as well as maternal, nature of the Deity have been an inspirational beacon throughout my life.

She is left a widow, perhaps, without a sufficient provision, but she is not desolate! . . . her heart turns to her children with redoubled fondness, and anxious to provide for them, affection gives a sacred heroic cast to her maternal duties . . . but her imagination, a little abstracted and exalted by grief, dwells on the fond hope that the eyes which her trembling hand closed, may still see how she subdues every wayward passion to fulfil the double duty of being the father as well as the mother of her children . . . I think I see her surrounded by her children, reaping the reward of her care.

—Mary Wollstonecraft, *A Vindication of the Rights of Woman*

Who can feel and comprehend the needs of her babe like the ardent mother? What other heart yearns with her solicitude, endures with her patience, waits with her hope, and labors with her love, to promote the welfare and happiness of her children? Thus must the Mother in Israel give all her hours to those first sacred tasks, till her children can walk steadfastly in wisdom's ways.

—Mary Baker Eddy, *Prose Works*, "Retrospection and Introspection"

Christianity is the great and leading circumstance which raises women's importance.

—Hannah More, *Strictures on the Modern System of Female Education*, Vol. 1

When women understand that governments and religions are human inventions; that bibles, prayerbooks, catechisms, and encyclical letters are all emanations from the brain of man, they will no longer be oppressed by the injunctions that come to them with the divine authority of "Thus saith the Lord."

—Elizabeth Cady Stanton, *Autobiography*

I may be allowed to doubt whether woman was created for man; and, though the cry of irreligion, or even atheism, be raised against me, I will simply declare, that were an angel from heaven to tell me that Moses's beautiful, poetical cosmogony, and the account of the fall of man, were literally true, I could not believe what my reason told me was derogatory to the character of the Supreme Being.

—Mary Wollstonecraft, *A Vindication of the Rights of Woman*

In Natural Law and in religion the right of woman to fill the highest measure of enlightened understanding and the highest places in government, is inalienable . . . This is woman's hour; with all its sweet amenities and its moral and religious reforms.

—Mary Baker Eddy, *Prose Works*, "No and Yes"

Contents

ILLUSTRATIONS

ACKNOWLEDGMENTS

Thanks to the English Departments of York and Hull Universities for the opportunities provided to assist its research students. Special thanks to Professor Valerie Sanders. Without the patience, love, and care of my husband and his culinary skills, this book might have been starved of inspiration and would undoubtedly have been that much more of a challenge. My children have offered cheer and consolation as the occasion has demanded. The little ones have made me laugh, all bringing a wonderful sense of balance to my academic research. They have allowed me to witness that "sheltering wing of maternalism," as referred to by Mary Wollstonecraft, at first hand, so thanks to them all. For their constructive criticism, I should like also to thank friends John and Ray.

I should like to thank Dr. Adam Hart-Davis, descendant of Rev. Richard Hart-Davis, member of Parliament for Bristol from 1812 to 1831. Hannah More wrote three hundred letters to Rev. Richard Hart-Davis. A box of uncataloged manuscript material given to the Bristol Record Office in January 2001 by Dr. Adam Hart-Davis, the property of his deceased father, was made available to me, as a result of contact with Dr. Adam Hart-Davis. This and other manuscript material yielded some valuable and important insights into the mind of Hannah More in her later years. Thanks also to staff at the Bristol Record Office.

Appreciation to staff at the British Library, London and Boston Spa; Bodleian Library, Department of Special Collections and Western Manuscripts and Duke Humphrey's Library at University of Oxford; University of Leeds, Special Collections; University of York, University of Hull Libraries, for their assistance.

Gratitude to the research staff at The Mary Baker Eddy Library in Boston, who assisted in my procurement of copies of Eddy's earliest writings.

Special thanks to Sharon Winter for her artwork.

I am by training a scientist—I think from a background of science—and science is constantly looking to the future. Observation, experiment, and measurement allied to human reasoning have brought impressive progress in the last thousand years. The past, however, can also teach us much, as I have discovered in the process of preparing, presenting, and writing about a hundred history programmes on radio and television. I have less time than I would like for original research, but historical researchers investigating archival material sometimes recover neglected or original manuscripts that offer important ideas for the future. . . . I am happy to have been of assistance, by pointing Dr. Ingham in the direction of correspondence between my ancestor Rev. Richard Hart-Davis and Hannah More. I wish success to her publication.

—Dr. Adam Hart-Davis, English scientist, author, photographer, historian, and broadcaster, presenter of the BBC television series *Local Heroes* and *What the Romans Did for Us*

INTRODUCTION

*The prevailing manners of an age depend more than we are aware,
or are willing to allow, on the conduct of women; this is one of the
principal hinges on which the great machine of human society turns.*

—Hannah More, *The Works of Hannah More*, "Essays on
Various Subjects Principally Designed for Young Ladies," Vol. 2

We are all no doubt familiar with that term "glass ceiling": a situation in which progress, while appearing to be possible, is nevertheless constantly beyond our reach due to restriction or discrimination. It is not uncommon for women to face this "glass ceiling" effect in many areas of their lives, working or otherwise; it has been particularly prevalent in terms of woman and the church. The need, therefore, for a fresh look at the prescribed position of women in the Bible is as necessary now as it was two centuries ago, possibly more so.

This book is overdue. Its innovative challenging of historically accepted perspectives, based largely on centuries of religious and cultural conditioning, allows for the reinstatement of woman at the heart of Holy Scripture. I have spent many years researching the Scriptures, but it was the arguments of four pioneering women, added to my own spiritual glimpses, that proved to be the catalyst for this unique contribution to religious scholarship.

I shall be taking a contemporary look at writings that, though written in a previous century, hold within their pages a religious argument of particular relevance to current feminist theological debate. The women have been featured in many books by many scholars, but the idea of comparing these women in one work is a unique venture. The results are imperative, dynamic, and possibly life-changing.

Elizabeth Schussler Fiorenza writes in *Searching the Scriptures*, "Throughout the centuries, women thinkers who have claimed that the world looks different from the perspective of women have disappeared again and again from historical consciousness and remained unknown"[1] and historian Gerda Lerner adds, "women have not built on the previous intellectual work of women."[2] All the more interesting then are the close links I have discovered between continents and centuries in the arguments of my authors. Throughout this book, I shall work to identify that building "on the previous intellectual work" of the later reformers on their predecessors. Fiorenza notes that feminist Dale Spender believes "historical forgetfulness is fundamental to the perpetuation of patriarchal power."[3] Strengthening the connections, therefore, and acknowledging the historical legacy left by these women thinkers is vital and necessary to future progress.

Introducing the women to the reader is a privilege and will allow me to identify just what makes the arguments so intriguingly convincing. Even today, the book may not sit comfortably with some traditionalists, but at the time these women wrote, their questioning of scriptural interpretation was seen as imprudent, impudent even. Their lives *could* (some might say *should*) have been spent, in keeping with the times in which they lived, quietly within the confines of homestead, subject to tradition and their menfolk. Something, however, led Hannah More, Mary Wollstonecraft, Elizabeth Cady Stanton, and Mary Baker Eddy to step outside these parameters, take control of their lives, and through their attempted reformation of religious tradition, offer new hope to womankind.

It needs to be acknowledged that each woman was of a high intellect. Each woman was a spiritual thinker. Each woman was a pioneer in her field. Each woman faced persecution and distress. As individuals they are powerfully persuasive, but the combined effect of their divine disclosure is calculably convincing.

In *Notorious Voices*, Marla J. Selvidge writes, "There is no text available today which surveys the ways in which women and men have interpreted the Bible between 1500 and 1920," pointing to the many books on feminist interpretation she suggests they mention religion or Christianity "as a factor in the struggle for emancipation but do not analyze the biblical texts which were used by some of the leading feminists."[4]

This book does analyze those biblical texts. When asked what he thought would be the result of "feminism's encounter with religion," David Tracy, the prominent Catholic theologian replied, "The next intellectual revolution."[5]

HISTORICAL IDENTITY FORMATIONS

The historical subjection of women based on patriarchal cultural-religious tradition, alongside a biased scriptural interpretation has for centuries been responsible for the denial of equal status to women. More, Wollstonecraft, Stanton, and Eddy challenged historical identity formations; they pointed to spiritual representations of femininity in Scripture, and textually communicated a spiritual role for women through a language of patriotism and piety. In spite of the parallels in their perspectives, however, there is an exciting diversity. Four authors: two British, two American; two eighteenth century, two nineteenth century; and possibly even more crucial, two feminist and two antifeminist perspectives, all indicate the inevitably complex nature of this topic. It is important to make clear at the outset, however, that the critical interrogatory route will be focused toward the "Woman Question." Because each woman made an indelible mark on the historical landscape, their ultimate achievements will be identified in the first instance, though we will get to know them as individuals more intimately in Chapter 1.

Wollstonecraft was perhaps best known as a political feminist, author, and humanitarian reformer whose most notable text was surely *A Vindication of the Rights of Woman*. More, considered to be a conservative traditionalist, nevertheless wrote in a provocative didactic fashion. Close friend of William Wilberforce and promoter of education and Sunday schools for the poor, her best known text was probably *Strictures on the Modern System of Female Education*. Stanton was one of the founding members of the American suffrage movement, lecturing and writing prolifically for the cause; *The Woman's Bible* was probably her most memorable contribution. Eddy's historic achievement was as founder of a worldwide religious movement, a publishing house, and author of *Science and Health with Key to the Scriptures*.

These writers are connected to each other by ideas that refused to rest with traditional arguments for female subjection and the cult of sensibility rooted their argument for female spirituality. This cultural phenomenon, having achieved a shift in the public consciousness toward appreciation of a more unselfish, sympathetic, and caring nature, assisted in the construction of a "hierarchy" of mental qualities with the maternal becoming highly esteemed.[6] The refined, sensitive thought, more open to divine inspiration, became associated with the feminine, allowing portrayal of the female as an equal spiritual being, worthy of respect. This atmosphere assisted in giving a sense of purpose and authority to women writers; a language of sensibility, language of nature, and ultimately a language of overt spirituality emerged from this "heightened state of consciousness." Eddy writes, "When the heart speaks . . . its language is always acceptable to those who have hearts."[7]

The subjugation of women had been promoted and supported by male authors who were in part responsible for the construction and portrayal of a femininity that emphasized weakness and inferiority. Literature became the means through which women writers could critique a male view of the world that previously had gone largely unchallenged. Wollstonecraft refers to "the fanciful female character, so prettily drawn by poets and novelists," this artificial representation that led to "the sacrifice of truth and sincerity," resulted in virtue becoming simply "a relative idea, having no other foundation than utility." In a condemnatory tone, she concluded that men took it upon themselves to arbitrarily judge that utility, effectively "shaping it to their own convenience."[8]

This period saw the emergence of a number of women who through strong religious convictions evaded cultural silencing. The galvanizing of public opinion was fundamental to their reforming influence. Literature that attempted to dovetail sentimental attitudes with religious ideals served to inspire an appreciation of the feminine. Indeed, a female ideology emerged that, it might be said, became central to a national mission of reform.

Historian Robert Shoemaker suggested that "women had a significant if distinctive role to play in religion, politics, social life and culture." He went on to say that "despite the increasing articulation of the ideology of separate spheres, these opportunities increased over the course of the period." He argued that public behavior was conditioned by religious beliefs, and these reformers saw the potential of women as a stabilizing and regenerating influence.[9] Substantive arguments structured upon a Christian sentiment concluded that, as Wollstonecraft identified, "for men and women, truth, if I understand the meaning of the word, must be the same."[10]

More expected women to exert their powerful influence from the heart and hearth. A discourse that juxtaposed privacy and nationality emphasizes this, contributing toward a portrayal of familial and domestic duty as the utopian model on which social and economic reform could be built: "To you, is made over the awfully important trust of infusing the first principles of piety into the tender minds of those who may one day be called to instruct, not families merely, but districts, to influence, not individuals, but senates. Your private exertions may at this moment be contributing to the future happiness, your domestic neglect, to the future ruin of your country . . . If you neglect this your bounden duty, you will have effectually contributed to expel Christianity from Britain, her last citadel."[11]

More believed that home was the seat of authority, and indeed the powerbase from which emerged all that was good *or bad* in society, and her early writing points to the power and purpose that she understands Christianity confers upon women.

Her later works go further. The year 1811 saw the publication of *Practical Piety: or, The Influence of the Religion of the Heart on the Conduct of Life*. The preface to this text sets a framework for the fresh and innovative insights this work expects to bring to her theological arguments. The natural feminine instinct was given a spiritual authority and to this heavenly disposition she assigned the task of regulating masculine base instincts: "**His** dark understanding is illuminated, **his** rebellious will is subdued, **his** irregular desires are rectified; **his** judgement is informed, **his** imagination is chastised, **his** inclinations are sanctified; **his** hopes and fears are directed to their true and adequate end. Heaven becomes the object of **his** hopes, an eternal separation from God the object of **his** fears. **His** love of the world is transmuted into the love of God. The lower faculties are pressed into the new service."[12]

While it could be suggested that More was simply conforming to grammatical convention, the reader should beware making this assumption. A letter she wrote to her sister in February 1788 gives evidence of her concern at *that* time that her writing tone may offend her influential friends: "I shall expect to find almost every door shut against me."[13] By the time she wrote *Practical Piety*, however, it is clear she means to write without fear of censure: "Those who endeavour to steer clear of all extremes are in danger of being reprobated by both."[14]

Wollstonecraft's dissenting voice made a powerful contribution to the canon of female reforming literature. She was more radical in her vigorous embracing of a feminist position, and certainly caused controversy through her libertine principles and way of life. More considered Wollstonecraft's life to be beneath contempt, suggesting that Wollstonecraft's *Vindication* was "metaphysical jargon," and though she had been much pestered to read the tract, she was "invincibly resolved not to do it."[15] She might have been surprised had she read the work; their thoughts are amazingly consistent and a feminized religious vernacular creates analogous arguments.

Wollstonecraft's political arguments are hedged about with religious implications, and I hope to identify those dissenting theological perspectives as central to her promotion of female equality. A spiritual legitimacy marks her reforming ideal: "The only solid foundation for morality," she writes, "appears to be the character of the supreme Being . . . The High and Lofty One, who inhabiteth eternity, doubtless possesses many attributes of which we can form no conception; but reason tells me that they cannot clash with those I adore—I am compelled to listen to her voice . . . For to love God as the fountain of wisdom, goodness, and power, appears to be the only worship useful to a being who wishes to acquire either virtue or knowledge."[16]

Wollstonecraft pursued an acquisition of both virtue and knowledge, and it is important to note that at the heart of this pursuit was her religious reliance: "Few can walk alone. The staff of Christianity is the necessary support of human weakness."[17]

The works of these women when looked at simultaneously weave a rich tapestry, recording thwarted hopes, dashed expectations, and severe contestation from the masculine world, but alongside this emerges an image of strength, compassion, inspiration, humility, and above all a radical femininity that has contributed to the discursive debate on "the woman question." Wollstonecraft is probably more well known today than More, as her feminist position is one with which women of today can more readily identify.[18]

The writing of two American "sister" reformers will be closely examined in an attempt to identify the pivotal role *their* arguments played in the spiritual authorization of women. The early writing of Eddy and Stanton advanced the humanitarian causes pursued by Wollstonecraft and More. The threads that link their writings are incontestable, but the connections do not end there, it has been suggested that Eddy was related to More.[19]

Nineteenth-century American culture was addressing many of the problems faced by eighteenth-century Britain. The uneasy alliance between Puritanism and capitalism was leading to a secularization of the Protestant ethic resulting, as Keith Stavely suggests, in "an anarchy of individual consciences." Social control, he suggested, should be maintained through "invisible, refined, spiritual ties, bonds of the mind and heart."[20]

Eddy was born into that era referred to as the American Romantic Period, which was marked by literature intended to reestablish an American identity. This period witnessed the emergence of an abundance of female writers who sought to construct a literary form that engaged with American sensibilities. Graceful language that spoke from the heart aroused sympathetic responses in its readership. The cause of abolition was one of the chief beneficiaries of their early literary contributions.

Eddy began writing early: at sixteen years of age she was writing for the leading newspapers, and for many years she wrote for the best magazines in the South and North. Her literary style and argument developed and progressed over the years, as did that of More and Wollstonecraft, resulting in her major polemic in the mid-nineteenth century. Her writing expressed the diversity that was America's history and this was reflected in the company she kept: her associates included A. Bronson Alcott, Frances Hodgson Burnett, and Louisa M. Alcott.

Eddy's awareness and appreciation of contemporary thought are evident in a review of George Eliot's essays, where she wrote, "Her metaphysics purge materialism with a single sentence." Eddy's biographer notes, "In a genuine outburst of sincere appreciation of the great English novelist [Eddy] declares her womanly and heroic with firm, unfaltering adherence to honest conviction and conscientious reasonableness."[21]

Womanly heroics, firm, unfaltering honesty, and conscientious reasonableness were qualities Eddy admired and the very ones needed as she went on to become a staunch supporter of the abolition movement. She was deeply concerned at the plight of women and children, and although not an overt feminist, a letter from Susan B. Anthony[22] to Mary Baker Eddy suggests that Anthony considered Eddy's writing to support the cause of suffrage. Eddy ultimately founded her own publishing house for the purpose of promoting her radical religious ideals. *Science and Health* went through over four hundred editions in her lifetime.

Susan B. Anthony and Elizabeth Cady Stanton worked closely together, publishing profusely on behalf of the antislavery movement and women's rights, their brand of reforming literature contributing to the cause of liberty. Stanton's literary exertions reflected an overt feminist agenda and she was a keen admirer of Wollstonecraft's *Vindication*.

Stanton was an instinctive rhetorician, using language to persuasive and impressive effect, but it was that major polemic *The Woman's Bible*, published toward the latter part of the nineteenth century that provided a platform for her radical religious ideals. She now believed that a masculine interpretation of the Bible was at the root of the subjugation of women. Far from being the word of God, she wrote, "these degrading ideas of woman emanated from the brain of man."[23]

If evidence were needed of the contentious nature of her theological arguments, one need look no further than the split in the suffrage movement that resulted. It caused deep divisions between her and Anthony who believed that women should be discussing with "men and measures on the plane of this mundane sphere, instead of living in the air with Jesus and the angels."[24]

Stanton, however, believed that political rights would follow only in the wake of religious rights, and her argument coincides with and augments those of Wollstonecraft, More, and Eddy, who all sought to recover an equal spiritual status for woman through fresh Biblical interpretations.

Each woman wrote in a particular didactic fashion; indeed, there were only three published novels between them. (Wollstonecraft's second novel being published posthumously.) They wrote to effect reform, denouncing weakness and immorality in whatever guise. They condemned politicians who were deficient in humanitarian sentiments, they reproached bigoted ministers of religion who lacked an innate sense of spirituality and morality. They demanded education for women to equip them as a powerful force for good, championing feminine virtues. The parallels in the literary route these women took to reach their public are notable: as well as producing texts, tracts and essays, three of the women also established worldwide publications.[25]

Each woman was well past middle age when establishing their newspapers: Eddy was aged eighty-seven when she founded *The Christian Science Monitor* as an international daily newspaper.[26] "When the press is gagged," she wrote, "liberty is besieged, but when the press assumes the liberty to lie, it discounts clemency, mocks morality, outrages humanity, breaks common law, gives impulse to violence, envy, and hate, and prolongs the reign of inordinate, unprincipled clans."[27]

A brief historical identification confirms that these women were concerned with liberty, morality and justice for the oppressed, and were prepared to embrace whatever literary genre necessary to press their reformatory ideals.

A Question of Credibility

Julie Melnyk suggests that while religious discourse of the period was "gendered neutral or even slightly feminized, theology, 'the study of or science which treats of God, His nature and attributes, and His relations with man and the universe' (OED), remained a clearly masculine discourse."[28] Add to this the critical neglect of the contribution made by those female authors who *did* attempt to contribute to the canon of theological reforming literature, and it becomes clear that women have been left without a credible alternative to patriarchal argument. Literary critics and historians are becoming aware that through close critical analysis of neglected female texts, an argument can be traced that contributes to a feminized spiritual identity.[29]

The authors in this work adopted a tone of voice and literary form that enabled them to argue with authenticity for a spiritual role for women; they found a language through which coherent *theological* arguments could be pressed. In their own period, and even today, these authors faced severe contestation: misunderstanding, neglect, and outright opposition frequently accompanied authors who spoke ahead of their time.

Disputation of their credibility came in many forms. Robert Hole, in his capacity as editor of More's published works, suggests that her later works "degenerate into decline." He says that "by 1805 More had said everything of interest which she had to say. Her later writings reveal a decline into old age that it is charitable to ignore."[30] Horace Walpole publicly lambasted Wollstonecraft as "that hyena in petticoats,"[31] and Mark Twain swung between overt opposition and outright adulation of Eddy and her writing.[32]

Wollstonecraft spoke to all pioneering women when she wrote, "Those who are bold enough to advance before the age they live in, and to throw off, by the force of their own minds, the prejudices which the maturing reason of the world will in time disavow, must learn to brave censure. We ought not to be too anxious respecting the opinion of others.—I am not fond of vindications.—Those who know me will suppose that I acted from principle.—Nay, as we in general give others credit for worth, in proportion as we possess it—I am easy with regard to the opinions of the *best* part of mankind—I *rest* on my own."[33]

Each woman represented here wrote to influence the "*best* part of mankind"; might that, as suggested in *Paradise Lost*, be woman, "O fairest of creation, last and best of all God's works"?[34] This theory will be explored to discover how these writers advanced an argument for female equality through promotion of woman's spirituality. "Why," asked Stanton, "is it more ridiculous for woman to protest against her present status in the Old and New Testament, in the ordinances and discipline of the church, than in the statutes and constitution of the state? Why is it more ridiculous to arraign ecclesiastics for their false teaching and acts of injustice to women, than members of Congress and the House of Commons? Why is it more audacious to review Moses than Blackstone, the Jewish code of laws, than the English system of jurisprudence?"[35]

Radical Intellectuals

Stanton's style was that of radical revolutionary[36] and there can be little doubt of her disruptive potential, but to discover that Hannah More, that pious eighteenth-century authoress and supporter of conservatism was equally skeptical of scriptural interpretation confirms this is an area that merits investigation: "The religion which it is the object of these pages to recommend," More suggests, "has been sometimes misunderstood, and not seldom misrepresented. What doctrine of the New Testament has not been *made* (my emphasis) to speak the language of its injudicious advocate, and turned into arms against some other doctrine." Exposing the "pious error of holy men" she condemns the "formal religionist who has never obtained any sense of the spiritual mercies of God."[37]

The "Woman Question" clearly cannot be confined to any one period, or defined in any one genre, nor is it the prerogative of any one nation. Different women in different times have approached the question of female subjugation in a number of ways. My purpose is to investigate how four women, apparently quite different, laid claim to a religious rhetoric through which they were able to challenge what they suggested were centuries of mistaken doctrine in terms of female definition. I will also examine how they came to identify a Divinity in the feminine, which in turn, allowed them to proclaim woman's elect status and spiritual purpose. Though their lives did not really coincide, and as in the case of More and Wollstonecraft even seemed to be at severe odds, each woman pointed to a misunderstanding of Scripture that allowed for the subservience of the female sex. What does unite them, however, is their radical Protestantism, and I shall be suggesting it is the threads that link their sometimes diverse perspectives that makes their ultimate arguments for the spiritual autonomy of women so intriguing.

Methodology

I shall compare the authors' religious arguments from a "feminist" and "antifeminist" perspective, and drawing on matriarchal readings will identify, over the chapters, an ascending argument for the undeniable worth of woman, her inviolate right to "revelation."[38] Through *reason* and *revelation*, these women challenge determined doctrine and identify Scriptural authority for the legitimacy of spiritual womanhood.

An image of woman as Eve, tempted or temptress, will be disputed in favor of woman as represented by Mary, mother of Jesus Christ, allowing the moral and spiritual superiority of the "feminine" to be identified.[39] Melnyk suggests, "Recently, literary critics and historians have turned their attention to nineteenth-century women's religious writing. Few, however, have discussed Victorian women's theological writing, perhaps because there isn't supposed to be any."[40]

The later chapters of this book will pay close attention to the women's theological writing. Early writings, however, will be examined in the first instance to identify political and humanitarian arguments, while the heart of the book will investigate the authority the cult of sensibility gave to women. It will seek to discover how overt religious argument pervaded the later works of More, Stanton, and Eddy, highlighting elements of spiritual autobiography. The arrangement will be thematic, and while I am aware this will be the more challenging route, I believe it to be the best means of portraying how the *lives* of these women contributed to the different tropes and genres of their reforming publications.

Throughout this work, and by necessity, substantial amounts of poetry and prose will be subject to close critical analysis. This allows the reader to witness that metamorphosis from social reformer to spiritual pioneer; it allows identification of the part personal trauma and public condemnation played in the spiritual awakening of the authors. It bears witness to the developing literary skills through which they challenged and ultimately reworked patriarchal theological doctrine, their creation of what might be termed a language of spiritual theology.

The authors' texts will be investigated drawing on interpretative investigative strategies that include biographical, historical, political, and feminist, literary critical theory. Because scriptural interpretation becomes a key issue in their arguments for female authority, hermeneutic criticism will assist in understanding the philosophy of language and linguistic structures at work in their theological discourse. Textual interpretations will draw on typology, allegory, semiology, and symbolism; the sociohistorical, political, and cultural issues surrounding the representation of women's spirituality will be examined closely. Orthodox religious tradition has been challenged by many feminist scholars in recent decades and the arguments of Luce Irigaray, Mary Daly, and Sallie McFague all usefully contribute to this work.

Much has been accomplished, but much remains to be done in this field. Fitzgerald notes, "Elizabeth Cady Stanton and her cohorts would likely be pleased to find that the past century of women's struggles has yielded substantial and unequivocal victories, but Stanton would no doubt be the first to claim that these victories are meager compared to the work yet to be done. To live in a world in which essential, absolute, and unequivocal equality on earth for men and women is supported in the home, church, state, and every other walk of life is as yet a compelling and prophetic dream."[41]

I believe the methodology employed in this work allows the uncovering of an argument that uniquely contributes to and furthers even the egalitarian principles at the heart of the "prophetic dream."

SOURCES

The primary sources are the women's published writings. Analysis of key texts and unpublished manuscript material uncovers an aspect of their argument that has been neglected. Personal correspondence from Hannah More to Bart Huber, Rev. Richard Hart-Davis, and a firsthand account of a visit with Hannah More by Anna Victoria Inman all throw fresh light on this remarkable woman.

In support of the women's published works, I shall be examining diaries, essays, and letters; these manuscript sources shed valuable light on some of the more disturbing incidents of their lives.

Figure 1. A likeness of Hannah More by Sharon Winter

Figure 2. A likeness of Mary Wollstonecraft by Sharon Winter

Figure 3. A likeness of Mary Baker Eddy by Sharon Winter

Figure 4. A likeness of Elizabeth Cady Stanton by Sharon Winter

CHAPTER 1

THE FEMALE SUBJECT

FORCEFUL FATHERS, PRESCRIPTIVE PINNIES, AND THE REINFORCING OF FEMALE SUBJECTION

Let us rejoice that we are subject to the divine "powers that be."

—Mary Baker Eddy, *Science and Health with Key to the Scriptures*

CHRISTIAN INDUCTION

Were these young women "subject" to those "divine powers that be," or were they, as is more likely, subject to a hierarchical system of patriarchal power?

In this chapter, I will examine the formative years of these reformers, identifying experiences that may have contributed to their later somewhat unorthodox religious perspectives. I shall pay particular attention to changes in the tone and style of their writing that, as well as responding to political and social issues, may well reflect changes in their "lived experiences." I expect to shed light on the religious and cultural conditioning they were subjected to, through examination of their early writing, including poetry, prose, and letters. I will then chart the effect of this conditioning on their religious attitudes as they questioned the predominant "institutional" faith that they came to believe had allowed, encouraged even, inequalities to flourish. The language used by these women reflects their growing awareness of the need to connect the role of women in society with a sense of moral and spiritual authority.

Religion and Politics in Eighteenth-Century British Culture

The world into which Hannah More and Mary Wollstonecraft were born was structured upon patriarchal values. Literary and cultural historians have argued that the eighteenth century saw a sharpening of the divisions between male and female. As Shoemaker identifies in *Gender in English Society 1650–1850*, this was "a crucial period of change in the history of gender roles . . . there was an increasing separation of spheres, a sharpening of the differences between male and female social roles."[1] The public world of politics and religion was largely inhabited by men, while the private sphere of the home was the focus of women's attention. The decision makers, those with the power to influence affairs of the nation, were thereby masculine.

Prescriptive roles for women were constructed upon a framework of gender differences as described in the book of Genesis. Early Christian teaching justified the subjugation of women, arguing that as God created Adam first, and woman was taken from man, man must be superior. Woman was further castigated as the weaker sex as a result of Eve's role in the fall, taking the forbidden fruit and giving it to her husband. The fundamental inferiority of the feminine was thus established and reinforced on a bedrock of theological tradition.[2] An understanding of the political and religious values that prevailed in eighteenth-century England is necessary to contextualize its radical thinkers.

Hannah More (1745–1833)

Hannah More's early years were spent at the heart of a close knit family. She was born on February 2, 1745, in Fishponds, then part of the parish of Stapleton in Gloucestershire, to Jacob and Mary More. Her background and family connections were of a modest nature. Jacob More, a charity school teacher, had left his home at Norfolk to settle in the West Country, due to a legal dispute that had deprived him of what he considered to be his rightful inheritance. He was a good classical scholar and had intended to take Holy Orders before this dispute. Religion, though, was a contested subject between More and *his* mother who was a zealous nonconformist, while Jacob More was a High Churchman and a Tory. Inevitably, a religious tension existed in the household. He and Mary, who was a farmer's daughter, had five daughters, Hannah being the fourth.

All five daughters benefited from a thorough grounding in the classics, mathematics, and languages. Indeed, so good was Hannah at mathematics that her father stopped lessons, fearing she would become too successful. She learned French, under the tutorship of her sister, and later taught herself Spanish and Italian. During the Seven Years' War (1756–63) her father entertained French prisoners of war while they were on parole in Frenchay, allowing the young More to become a fluent French conversationalist. This background proved to be immensely valuable in her later contribution toward the British Enlightenment.[3] Her translating abilities also allowed a contribution toward European intellectual movements.

In 1758, More's eldest sister, Mary, opened a boarding school for young ladies at 6 Trinity Street, College Green, Bristol. So successful did the school become that, in 1762, larger premises were bought at 43 Park Street. By now, all the sisters were involved in the important task of educating young women as well as young men.

While details of More's early days remain largely obscure, in the light of her father's religious and political beliefs, it is not difficult to establish the sort of influence that would have pervaded her early years. As a High Churchman and Tory, her father would have adhered strictly to a traditional Christian, monarchical, and aristocratic code of conduct. While he clearly encouraged his daughters' education, nevertheless, they would be expected to conform to orthodox and accepted tradition in keeping with religious doctrine and standards of morality.

When More reached her teens, she met Dr. James Stonhouse (1716–95) who was to wield enormous influence in the development of an independence of spirit. Stonhouse had held deeply skeptical religious views until Dr. Philip Doddridge (1702–51), one of the leading nonconformist ministers and writers of the age, caused a conversion to take place in Stonhouse. He subsequently became an Anglican clergyman and physician. More's love of literature, it is said, owes much to the influence of Drs. Stonhouse and Doddridge.

This cultured and intelligent young woman was warmly welcomed into the social and intellectual life that prevailed in eighteenth-century Bristol. She mixed freely with the philosophical thinkers of her day, men such as Rev. Josiah Tucker (1712–99), who became Dean of Gloucester, and philosopher David Hume.

Her fluency in languages was particularly valuable as she worked on a number of translations of contemporary authors' works. At the age of sixteen, she wrote her first acknowledged publication, a pastoral drama, *The Search after Happiness*, which was published in 1773. Her first published work, it is suggested, was the anonymous *Select Moral Tales, translated from the French by a Lady* (1763). Jean Francois Marmontel was the author of the original work, but due to the fact that More disliked the life and work of the Frenchman, it is thought she did not wish to acknowledge authorship of the translation. This piece of work was dedicated to Mrs. Elizabeth Montague, who was to play an important role in the future life of Hannah More.[4]

In 1767, at the age of twenty-two, More became engaged to the wealthy middle-aged squire, Edward Turner of Belmont, of Wraxall, Somerset. His reluctance to marry her, three times delaying the marriage ceremony, resulted in More's calling off the engagement. She regarded this as a humiliating episode and resolved never to marry. Her friend, Dr. Stonhouse, secured an annuity of £200 from Mr. Turner as a sort of compensation, and Turner bequeathed a sum of £1000 to More on his death.

After a period of readjustment, More launched herself among a new circle of friends, who warmly received her into their midst. She quickly became a well known figure among the London theatrical set. David Garrick and his wife became close friends and she was soon found to be an accomplished playwright. A free translation of *Metastasio's Attilio Regalo* became *The Inflexible Captive* (1775) and was presented by Garrick at theatres in Bath and Exeter. This was followed by *Percy: A Tragedy* in 1777 and *The Fatal Falsehood* in 1779. Evidence of More's popularity can be seen in an epigraph inscribed on the walls of The Theatre Royal, "Boast we not a More?"[5]

Five years later, however, years that saw the death in quick succession of her father, Garrick, and close friend Dr. Johnson, More gradually withdrew from the world of the "Great and the Gay," that fashionable world of London society. This withdrawal coincided with a change of location and more notably, the adoption of a more serious literary tone. She had witnessed at first hand the manners and morals of "fashionable society," and they had disturbed her. Disappointed with the irreligious attitudes displayed by the supposedly pious men and women of her London "set," a puritanical zeal surfaced in More, and her writing of this period reflected this change of heart. Religious tracts and moral tales became the vehicles through which she sought to reform the manners and morals of the nation.

More's proselytizing zeal drew her into a new circle of friends known as "The Saints." The genre of her writing in this period was of a politicoreligious and didactic nature. She used elaborate and evocative syntax in an attempt to address the discontent simmering under the surface of British society.

In 1788, More wrote *Thoughts on the Importance of the Manners of the Great to General Society*. In this text, she emphasized the duty of each citizen in contributing toward a cohesive and well-structured society. Great stress was placed on the important relationship between church and state, as the preface to this text notes:

> While Great Britain is exhibiting a glorious energy in the cause of a nation, brave and generous like herself, yet professing an erroneous worship, let her convince that nation that she is actuated in assisting her, by the spirit of religion that is indeed *reformed*: a religion which having the love of God for its motive, has consequently for its end, charity to mankind without distinction of country or of religion.
>
> We are becoming conspicuous like a city set on a hill. We are "the observed of all observers." While the eyes of the whole world are fixed upon us, let the whole world perceive that our active services, our warm benevolence to our suffering fellow-creatures, flow from the only principle which can sanctify right conduct, from the only source which can recommend it to the favour of God.[6]

The rhetoric of this narrative sets an important precedent for More's later writing. The nationalistic fervor is impressive. The epic spirit that is displayed in her discourse reflects a grandeur that parallels the great ceremonial performances of the ancients. The formal and elevated style reflects a masculine topos, but nuanced within its argument are the key themes that are to infuse her later works: the reforming power of a religious sensibility.

More *apparently* grounds her suggestions in orthodoxy and tradition: the above text is not unlike that of John Winthrop, who declared in his famous shipboard sermon that "the eyes of all people are upon us" and that the Puritans were called to erect "a city upon an Hill"—a city that would stand as lesson and beacon to the whole world.[7] This is a powerful invocation, but even at this stage in her writing career, More is identifying and promoting a religion of the heart. As her career progresses, her agenda becomes more overt.

In 1790 when More's text, *An Estimate of the Religion of the Fashionable World*,[8] was published, she was afraid that her influential friends would be dismayed at her criticism of their manners and morals. This fear, however, was largely unfounded as evidenced in a letter she received in July 1791 from John Newton: "There is a circle by which what you write will be read . . . and which will hardly read anything of a religious kind that is not written by you."[9]

More targeted her readers with precision. Robert Hole, in his introduction to *Selected Writings of Hannah More*, suggests that *Thoughts on the Importance of the Manners of the Great (1788)* and *An Estimate of the Religion of the Fashionable World* are "earnest and sincere works addressed to women of society."[10] I would suggest that *An Estimate of the Religion of the Fashionable World* is a pedagogical work directed rather toward a male audience, and witnesses More's careful construction of a didactic platform from which to counsel and restrain negative masculine traits: "Shall we expect then, since men can only be scholars by sedulous labour, that they shall be Christians by mere chance? . . . For the great secret of religious education, and which seems banished from the present practice, consists in training young men to an habitual interior restraint, an early government of the affections, and a course of self-control over those tyrannizing inclinations."

"Moral restraint" she points to as a fundamental virtue, and while "men may, from natural temper, often *do* good," without this vital quality, she suggests "it is impossible that they should ever *be* good." More goes on to identify those Christian character traits that, she suggests, are intrinsic to a truly charitable disposition and that she conspicuously identifies as "the very essence of a man of business."[11]

These two texts, Christine Krueger suggests were "intended to prick the spiritual consciences of the upper ranks . . . No writer manipulated the ideological and rhetoric of evangelicalism to shape social discourse more successfully than Hannah More . . . Her role, like that of women preachers among the Methodist hierarchy, was ambiguous, for the same patriarchal beliefs that made her a powerful evangelist inspired her prophetic rebuke of patriarchal sins."[12]

Further evidence of More's gendered definitions can be seen in *Strictures*, where she turns her attention to women:

> The chief end to be proposed in cultivating the understandings of women, is to qualify them for the practical purposes of life. Their knowledge is not often like the learning of men . . . A lady studies, not that she may qualify herself to become an orator or a pleader; not that she may learn to debate, but to act. She is to read the best books, not so much to enable her to talk of them, as to bring the improvement which they furnish, to the rectification of her principles, and the formation of her habits. The great uses of study are to enable her to regulate her own mind, and to be useful to others.[13]

More's discourse emphasizes the gender divisions inherent in eighteenth-century culture. The mental cultivation and intellectual development of women she considered essential if they were to fulfill their role of educating the next generation of rectifying the manners and morals of society. She clearly emphasizes the interrelation between domestic sentiments and national loyalties in her attempts to authorize femininity.

Admonishing masculine opposition to female improvement, More targets the hostility, so prevalent among eighteenth-century middle-class men, to the improvement of the minds of their womenfolk. She argues that the slight superficial knowledge of women is damaging to both sexes, and appeals for more cooperation between them. She suggests that the "higher minds" of each sex "approximate the nearest to each other," and she appeals to "men of sense" to understand how the contribution of women of intellect will valuably assist in the collective raising of the minds and manners of society. Her strategy is clear as she speaks both individually and collectively to each sex in her attempt to define the roles of each in society. While ostensibly appearing to suggest that the female need not become qualified as an orator, More herself displays all the qualities of a skilled orator as she moves deftly between masculine and feminine discourses.

In the ten years from 1788 to 1798 More wrote prolifically. Her *Cheap Repository Tracts* (1795–98) included moral tales, Bible stories, and instructive ballads, and reached a wide audience with a circulation of two million in the first year. She wrote to influence each section of society from the poor and illiterate to the wealthy upper classes. In 1799 she wrote *Strictures* emphasizing the importance of education for girls, but her suggestion that "Christianity is the great and leading circumstance which raises women's importance"[14] hints at the later connections she will make between Christianity and the feminine. This work was highly regarded, going through thirteen editions and selling more than 19,000 copies, and while Hannah More was viewed as an upholder of traditional values, this text gives a glimpse of the covert radical religious perspectives that were to become an overriding concern.

The foregoing attempts to build an outline of the structure upon which More was to base her reforming literature. The early years, and the influences that shaped her in this period are valuable if one is to understand their contribution to her later writing. Scholarly research of her early writing has been extensive: for whatever reason, interest in her later works has been negligible, though it may have something to do with Hole's suggestion that her later works "degenerate into decline."[15]

It is More's later writing that I am particularly interested in. Her state of mind at this period will be examined in the light of a manuscript copy of an unpublished letter from Hannah More to Rev. Richard Hart-Davis (1821), a richly descriptive letter written by Anna

Victoria Inman after visiting Hannah More in June 1824, and a manuscript copy of an unpublished essay presented to her by More. This essay, written in May 1824 while at Barley Wood, relates specifically to the significance of the Bible, emphasizing that while "other books may teach us the knowledge of the world, the Bible alone can teach us the knowledge of ourselves . . . Other books may teach human Sciences, the Bible alone can teach the Science of Salvation thro' the blood of Christ." The "Science of salvation" and "knowledge of ourselves," I shall be suggesting when critically examining More's later works, have been learned through bitter experience. Other personal correspondence will usefully contribute to the argument.[16]

More wrote, in part, to counter those revolutionary tendencies propounded by Thomas Paine in *Rights of Man* and Wollstonecraft in *Vindication*.

Mary Wollstonecraft (1759–1797)

The formative years of Wollstonecraft were in distinct contrast to those of More. Wollstonecraft was the second of seven children, and the eldest girl. Her father was Edward John Wollstonecraft, a one-time farmer. He had been left a large inheritance on the death of his father, but had dissipated this on various unsuccessful commercial and agricultural ventures. Wollstonecraft's mother was Elizabeth Dixon, of Irish descent. Life in the home became increasingly difficult due to her father's fits of drunken violence. As a child, it is reported, she lay outside her parents' bedroom to prevent her mother being beaten. Her elder brother was most favored by her mother and this situation undoubtedly caused additional distress to the young Wollstonecraft: added to the early view she had of relations between man and wife, it is not difficult to see how these experiences were reflected in her later attitudes to marriage.

From the ages of nine to fifteen Wollstonecraft lived in Beverley, East Yorkshire, in a house in the shadow of the minster, attended the local school, and made some enduring friendships. Letters written during this period reflect her burgeoning interest in literature and the theater. Society in Beverley was lively and a literary club flourished.[17] Cameron notes, "One would gather from Mary's letters that there was a good deal of literary, theatrical, and scientific interest in the town and it may have struck deeper intellectual roots in the young schoolgirl than Godwin seemed to think. Her early letters, in fact, show an almost avid interest in poetry and similar matters."[18]

The patriarchal domination within her home environment, however, left an abiding conviction of the controlling role played by men and the consequential subservience of women. Wollstonecraft reflects on this autocratic and dictatorial masculine ethos in her unfinished novel *Maria, or The Wrongs of Woman* where she suggests, "His orders were not to be disputed; and the whole house was expected to fly, at the word of command . . . He was to be instantaneously obeyed, especially by my mother, whom he very benevolently married for love; but took care to remind her of the obligation, when she dared, in the slightest instance, to question his absolute authority. My eldest brother, it is true, as he grew up, was treated with more respect by my father; and became in due form the deputy tyrant of the house."[19]

The education of his daughters had not been a priority for Edward Wollstonecraft, and his daughter became keenly aware of her short-comings when a new friendship blossomed with Jane Arden. The arrival of this well-educated family in their midst was to prove invaluable to the young Wollstonecraft. Well versed in the sciences, literature, and philosophy, they became a valuable source of intellectual stimulation during this period of her life. She became an avid letter writer at this time. Her letters to Jane, as a schoolgirl of fourteen, gave vent to a variety of emotions and reflected a similar tone to the letters she was to write as a woman of thirty-five on her travels through Scandinavia. A letter written to Arden in June 1773 (or possibly November 1774) represents a sensitive and somewhat fragile temperament: "Dear Jenny I have read some where that vulgar minds will never own they are in the wrong:—I am determined to be above such a prejudice, and give the lie to the poet who says— 'Forgiveness to the injured does belong But they ne'er pardon, who have done the wrong' and hope my ingenuously owning myself partly in fault to a girl of your good nature will cancel the offence—I have a heart too susceptible for my own peace . . . I cannot bear a slight from those I love."

Her reflections mark a sentimental inclination and the inclusion of part of an essay on friendship exposes an emotional nature, an almost desperate need to be loved: "Friendship founded upon virtue Truth and love;—it sweetens the cares, lessens the sorrows, and adds to the joys of life.—It corrects our foibles and errors, refines the pleasures of sense and improves the faculties of the mind."[20]

The overriding impression, however, of Wollstonecraft's early years is of a solitary child who developed a passion for animals and, according to biographer Claire Tomalin, "a detestation of cruelty of all kinds." Her days were spent roaming the countryside "in search of angels."[21]

Possibly the most reliable representation of Wollstonecraft's child-hood can be found in her novel, *Mary.* In this autobiographical "fic-tion," she exhibits a rhetoric of sentimental confession. The preface displays her emotional fervor: "Those compositions only have power to delight, and carry us willing captives, where the soul of the author is exhibited, and animates the hidden springs." *Mary* involved the writer in an extensive exploration into how novels of sensibility could mediate between art and the world at large and she clearly intended to exhibit her own soul.

Writing, which had at its source the emotions, offered women writers an avenue through which to portray women's social experience. This enabled them to depict the effects of gender on the relationship of the individual to society. Wollstonecraft's formative years were clearly not happy ones. Denied parental affection and feeling deeply unappreciated, she records how she "conversed with angels."[22] She suggests that her religious education had been sorely neglected: "Her mother's lukewarm manner of performing her religious duties, filled her with anguish."[23] This text yields sophisticated insights into a mind that was, according to Gary Kelly in his introduction to *Mary* allied to the philosophical method of "necessitarianism" resulting in a religious impulse to self-examination.

While Janet Todd, editor of *A Wollstonecraft Anthology*, suggests that *Mary, A Fiction* "provided an idealized and simplified account of her childhood,"[24] it nevertheless provides useful insights into the issues uppermost in her mind. Clearly religion and the role of women in society were areas of key concern. An apparent desire for death as a release from marital responsibilities was especially revealing: "Mary's delicate state of health did not promise long life. In moments of solitary sadness, a gleam of joy would dart across her mind—She thought she was hastening to that world where there is neither marrying, nor giving in marriage."[25]

Perhaps the "lukewarm" teachings Wollstonecraft had received in religious matters engendered a capacity for freedom of thought that had not been accorded to many of her contemporaries. She professed a religion of sensibility, not unlike that expressed by Hannah More in her poem *Sensibility*, written to "The Honourable Mrs. Boscawen" in 1782. "Sweet Sensibility! Thou secret pow'r."[26] This "secret pow'r" revealed to hearts that were tender and open to divine impressions was in distinct contrast to the restrictive religious practices that claimed the name of Christianity without its nature.

Wollstonecraft's religious passion is evident in her "fiction" where she describes Mary sitting up half the night, studying the Scriptures and preparing to receive the holy sacrament: "The orient pearls were strewed around—she hailed the morn, and sung with wild delight, Glory to God on high, good will towards men. She was indeed so

much affected when she joined in the prayer for her eternal preservation, that she could hardly conceal her violent emotions."[27]

At fifteen, Wollstonecraft had become aware of the deep social
and cultural divisions, not only between male and female, but also
between the poor and their wealthy masters, which prevailed in eighteenth-century society. If one is to accept the autobiographical nature
of *Mary*, this also was a subject that troubled her deeply. The following passage reveals a woman deeply concerned with societal deprivation and inequality: "A little girl who attended in the nursery fell sick.
Mary paid her great attention; contrary to her wish, she was sent out
of the house to her mother, a poor woman, whom necessity obliged to
leave her sick child while she earned her daily bread. The poor wretch,
in a fit of delirium stabbed herself, and Mary saw her dead body . . .
so strongly did it impress itself to her imagination, that every night of
her life the bleeding corpse presented itself to her when she first began
to slumber."[28]

By the time Wollstonecraft was to write *Maria, or The Wrongs of
Woman*, her arguments had become powerfully enshrined in scriptural
metaphor and her heroines accorded names with a biblical resonance.
Wollstonecraft's spiritual affiliations will be examined more closely in
further chapters, but for the purpose of establishing a clear picture
of her early and formative years, a glimpse at the autobiographical
"fiction" has been valuable. This unconventionally religious woman
was a deep spiritual thinker, though her critics have tended rather to
focus on her political and social arguments, neglecting somewhat the
perspective I shall be adopting.

In 1774, Edward Wollstonecraft uprooted the family from Yorkshire and moved once more to London. The bad habits of the father
had made it difficult to live comfortably in the close knit community
that was Beverley and the anonymity that could be found in the capital was considered to be more suitable. Again, Wollstonecraft had to
struggle to find a place in this new community. Her brother, Ned, by
this time a trained lawyer, was a constant source of irritation, torment-
ing, and humiliating his sister, who found it necessary to look beyond
the family circle to find comfort and companionship.

Solace came in the form of a retired clergyman and his wife, Mr. and
Mrs. Clare. In their home, she was encouraged in a taste for poetry
and the classics. Here she was introduced to Milton and Shakespeare,
and this relationship proved to be extremely beneficial. The Clares
encouraged Wollstonecraft in acquiring all the social skills necessary
for a young woman of the age. They also introduced her to someone
who was to prove influential in her emotional development. Fanny

Blood was another protégée of the Clares, two years older, and with a home life not dissimilar to that of Wollstonecraft, she had nevertheless acquired a certain cachet that dramatically impressed the younger girl. Indeed, she admitted feeling "quite a passion" for her mentor.[29] The lives of these two young women were intrinsically linked for a while as Wollstonecraft resided at the Blood family home.

In 1784, Wollstonecraft, along with two of her sisters, Eliza and Everina and her friend Fanny Blood, took a large house at Newington Green, and opened a school. This was common practice for women who needed an income and some independence. Wollstonecraft had early learned that if she was to succeed in life, then she must rely on her own resources. Her life up to this time had shown her the folly of relying on men: each masculine example, except perhaps for Mr. Clare, had been a disappointment.

The Dissenters of Newington Green
Some hundred years before Wollstonecraft moved to Newington Green, Daniel Defoe had been a resident. Since that time, the area had attracted dissident intellectuals bent on reforming society; one such was the famous dissenting minister Dr. Richard Price, whose chapel could be seen from the windows of Wollstonecraft's school. This radical political theorist was to wield enormous influence over Wollstonecraft. Dr. Price was at the center of a radical reforming group that crossed America and France as well as England. Men such as Franklin, Jefferson, Condorcet, and Priestley were among his correspondents. Here was a man Wollstonecraft could respect: not only was he an influential intellectual, he was also a man of humanitarian principles who cared for children, animals, and the vulnerable in society.

The time at Newington Green proved to be a critical period; for the first time, Wollstonecraft began mixing with radical intellectual thinkers, writers, and poets. She was welcomed into their midst, moved freely among the dissenting households and attended Dr. Price's chapel to hear him preach. The doctrine of these rational dissenters was based on the principles of John Locke. Locke was a Deist, expelled from Oxford in 1684, who determined to get rid of all the "unreasonable" elements in Christianity. Discarding the Trinity and the doctrine of predestination, which represented a key departure from traditional Christian teaching, Locke insisted "if one wanted to discourse reasonably and understandably, one really must discard any idea that could not be given a determinate shape and meaning."[30] The theological teachings embraced by Wollstonecraft during this period disputed much traditional doctrine: the Trinity, the concept of eternal punishment, and the notion of original sin.

As well as becoming a spiritually liberating period, it was also a time when Wollstonecraft began mixing with "liberated" literary women. Anna Barbauld was the daughter of dissenting Doctor Aikin, who became a successful poet and educational writer. Ann Jebb was the wife of Price's friend, and a dissenting writer who wrote political articles for the press. These women projected a powerful femininity that appealed to the equivocal nature of this woman of sentiment.

William Godwin's portrayal of Wollstonecraft's early years exhibits a woman who needed no male mediator between herself and her God. "Her mind," he suggests, "constitutionally attached itself to the sublime and amiable. She found an inexpressible delight in the beauties of nature, and in the splendid reveries of the imagination. But nature itself, she thought, would be no better than a vast blank, if the mind of the observer did not supply it with an animating soul. When she walked amidst the wonders of nature, she was accustomed to converse with her God."[31]

Wollstonecraft's early years had imbued her with an active social conscience: here was a young woman deeply concerned about those less fortunate in society and the plight of women was a particular concern. Claire Tomalin suggests, "Mary wanted to believe that individual will power and energy would better the state of the world, and that human nature was improving . . . It seemed to her far preferable to hope that men might grow less vicious as the circumstances of their lives grew gentler, rather than accept that women were given an appearance of virtue only by the crack of the whip."[32]

Four years after the opening of the school, Wollstonecraft wrote *Thoughts on the Education of Daughters* (1787). This first publication was inevitably prompted by the experiences she faced as an educator of young girls and was quickly followed by *Mary, A Fiction* (1788). *Original Stories from Real Life* (1788) was also published the same year, and the following year *The Female Reader* (1789). Didactic courtesy books had become a feature of eighteenth-century women's writing, acting as instruction manuals on good manners and breeding. Both Wollstonecraft and More wrote prolifically in this genre, attempting to educate and reform society as a whole, but women in particular.

Janet Todd identified the development of thought evident in Wollstonecraft's literary works over a decade. Her writings, she suggested, "show her mingling of rationalism and piety, her understanding of social as well as physical misery, and her firm belief in its divine purpose."[33]

Wollstonecraft was employed during the next five years as a reader and translator for Joseph Johnson, the radical bookseller of St. Paul's Churchyard.[34] During this time, she translated Lavater's *Physiognomy*, Jacques Necker's *Of The Importance of Religious Opinions* (1788) and C. G. Salzmann's *Elements of Morality* (1790). She also became reviewer and editorial assistant, contributing several articles to Johnson's *Analytical Review*. Johnson was to become an important influence in both her literary and personal life. He included her in his social circle, introducing her to men such as Tom Paine, supporter of the American Revolution; Henry Fuseli,[35] the German-Swiss painter and commentator on Rousseau; William Godwin,[36] the political and social theorist; William Blake, poet and radical thinker, and the novelist Thomas Holcroft. This group acted as intellectual stimulation to this budding reformer, and Wollstonecraft wrote to her sister in elation, "I am then going to be the first of a new genus . . . You know I am not born to tread in the beaten track, the peculiar bent of my nature pushes me on."[37]

The year 1789 witnessed an infinitely more confident Wollstonecraft; July of that year saw the beginning of the French Revolution, and her response to these events could be seen in tracts that were of a radical political nature. In 1790, she wrote *A Vindication of the Rights of Man* as a direct response to Edmund Burke's *Reflections on the Revolution in France* (1790). Wollstonecraft prized intellectual independence and this quality contributed to the burgeoning radicalism of her rhetorical style.

Her most famous work was undoubtedly *A Vindication of the Rights of Woman*, which had powerful implications for the role of women in society. *Vindication* was probably as important to Wollstonecraft as *Strictures* was to More. Both women negotiated a public space from which to promote their own particular brand of reforming literature. Their writing reflected a growing personal conviction of the moral and spiritual influence women could bring to bear on the political and public scene. Their didactic texts demanded that well educated, virtuous women take the helm and steer the nation toward a common humanitarian goal. They claimed a moral and spiritual imperative at the heart of the feminine, which could mediate on behalf of the weaker members of society, on the basis of the teachings of Christ Jesus. They did not see femininity as a restraining factor, sanctifying rather all the fine qualities inherent in motherhood and domesticity, giving women permission to take responsibility for reforming the manners and morals of society.

New England and Puritan Inheritance

Puritanism was the cultural and spiritual inheritance of nineteenth-century American society, and to understand American literature and culture, it is important to contextualize it against this background. Nineteenth-century America was engaging with similar debates to those of eighteenth-century Britain in that a duplicity had crept into its religious ideals. Doctrinal divisions had arisen between the "sensationalist" rhetoric of men such as Jonathan Edwards who argued for a God of fury holding his children perpetually over "the pit of hell," and the more reasonable Benjamin Franklin, an intellectual man, distinguished in literature and science. Boris Ford suggests "Franklin's Puritan background instilled into him a scepticism about human access to ultimate truths, and a sense of the innate frailty of fallen man. He accepted cheerfully that the mind is a bundle of impulses and desires controlled by reason at only the most superficial level."[38]

Into this doctrinal maelstrom was to step a female dissenting voice. On July 19, 1848, Stanton was to proclaim, "Let her live first for God, and she will not make imperfect man an object of reverence and awe . . . Thus she will learn the lesson of individual responsibility for time and eternity. That neither father, husband, brother, or son . . . can discharge her high duties of life or stand in her stead when called into the presence of the great Searcher of Hearts at the last day."[39]

To discover what prompted this religious radicalism, a brief look at Stanton's formative years will yield valuable insights.

Elizabeth Cady Stanton (1815–1902)

Stanton was born on November 12, 1815, to Daniel Cady and Margaret Livingston. Stanton wrote an autobiography that records her formative years and reveals the thoughts and experiences she was subject to. These early reminiscences reveal a powerful patriarchal influence at the heart of the family home. "My father," she writes, "was a man of firm character and unimpeachable integrity . . . Though gentle and tender, he had such a dignified repose and reserve of manner that, as children, we regarded him with fear rather than affection." She went on to reveal, "Our parents were as kind and considerate as the Puritan ideas of those days permitted, but fear, rather than love, of God and parents alike, predominated."[40]

Fear would seem to have been a predominant feature of Stanton's early years. Her father was a lawyer and her mother a woman of firm principles. A strong sense of morality and justice was early ingrained into her character. She records that her religious training invoked an overwhelming sense of fear, referring to this frequently: "Visions of the inferno were strongly impressed on my childish imagination. It was thought, at that time, that firm faith in hell and the devil was the greatest help to virtue." She recalls the clanging of the church bells, calling the inhabitants of Johnstown to prayer, "filled me with the utmost dread."[41]

Stanton clearly gave much thought to doctrinal issues from an early age. Her Scottish nurse, Mary Dunn, questioned her one day on discovering her pensively looking out of the nursery window: "Child, what are you thinking about?" She replied, "I was wondering why it was that everything we like to do is a sin, and that everything we dislike is commanded by God or some one on earth. I am so tired of that everlasting no! no! no!. At school, at home, everywhere it is 'no'! Even at church all the commandments begin 'Thou shalt not.' I suppose God will say 'no' to all we like in the next world, just as you do here."[42] Her nurse was shocked, considering such questioning of Calvinistic doctrine to be blasphemous.

A powerful influence on the spiritual education of the young Stanton came from the Rev. Simon Hosack. Born and educated in Scotland, he came to America to take charge of the Presbyterian Church in Johnstown. Speaking of him, she wrote, "The being I loved best on earth at that time was the gray-haired, heavy-browed, high-cheeked parson, and not a day passed without my seeing him. I loved as a child always loves one who is kind and tender, and who is never weary in answering satisfactorily endless questions."[43] Indeed, she credits him with the cultivation of her intellectual development, awakening "in my young and receptive brain a taste for rhetoric."[44] He regaled her with tales of life in his native Scotland, and she suggests that these early memories prepared her well for the visits she would make to Scotland in the course of her career.

A further major influence in the direction that Stanton's life was to take was caused by a tragedy in the family. When she was eleven years old, her beloved elder brother, who had just graduated from Union College, came home to die. He was the pride of his father's life, and had been a young man of great talent and promise, destined to join his father in the law firm. Believing that she could, in some way, make up for his death, she climbed upon her father's knee to comfort him. His response to this act was to set the seal on the future of his daughter: "Oh, my daughter, would that you were a boy!"[45]

This incident was to change the course of Stanton's life: "Then and there I resolved that I would not give so much time as heretofore to play, but would study and strive to be at the head of all my classes and thus delight my father's heart. All that day and far into the night I pondered the problem of boyhood. I thought that the chief thing to be done in order to equal boys was to be learned and courageous. So I decided to study Greek and learn to manage a horse."[46] The next day, she questioned her beloved Pastor, "Doctor, which do you like best, boys or girls?" His unequivocal response, "Why, girls, to be sure; I would not give you for all the boys in Christendom,"[47] gladdened the heart of his young protégée but did nothing to dampen her pursuit of masculine skills.

The pastor's library became her second home; she learned to drive; rode horses; and studied Latin, Greek, and mathematics with a class of boys much older than herself, taking the second prize for Greek at the village academy. She recalls how, as soon as school was dismissed, she ran to her father's office and laid the Greek Testament on his table, certain now of his endorsement; the ramifications of his resultant, "Ah, you should have been a boy!" turned her "joy to ashes" and inevitably hardened her resolve toward equalizing the sexes, even at this early stage. It was around this time that she was also to lose her close friend and confidant, her "noble and generous friend" as she referred to her pastor. In his will, he bequeathed to her his Greek lexicon, testament, and grammar, and four volumes of *Scott's Commentaries.* She acknowledges, "I never look at these books without a feeling of thankfulness that in childhood I was blessed with such a friend and teacher."[48]

The foregoing identifies the dominant familial and cultural influences that contributed toward the political and theological arguments of the mature Stanton. On the one hand, there is an image of a loving home life, but alongside this picture, there is the subtle, yet pernicious subordinating of the female. This clearly influenced Stanton's work as a leading campaigner for the Women's Rights Movement. At the same time, she started to become aware of other injustices in society. The prejudice displayed in the church against their black friend and helper disturbed her deeply, and the treatment of her own sex by their fathers, husbands, and brothers caused much consternation.

Her awareness of inequities in the law was stimulated by time spent in her father's office. Most of her time outside school, she began to spend among the lawyers. The tears and complaints of the women who came to her father for legal advice touched her heart. Her attention was drawn to the injustice and cruelty of the laws. In her neighborhood, many men still retained the old feudal ideas of women and property, and many of the women seeking advice had been made unhappy dependents of their sons, destitute and subject to the congeniality of their daughters-in-law.

Injustices meted out to women in the name of law had convinced Stanton of the need to take active oppositional measures. The budding reformer decided to take all her father's statute books and cut out the offending laws. Her plan was discovered but an idea was planted in her mind by her father. "When you are grown up, and able to prepare a speech, you must go down to Albany and talk to the legislators," he said, "tell them all you have seen in this office—the sufferings of these Scotchwomen, robbed of their inheritance and left dependent on their unworthy sons, and, if you can persuade them to pass new laws, the old ones will be a dead letter."[49] The seeds of discontent were sown, to bear fruit over the next half century.

The correlative to this "legal" training was a religious conversion experience that was to prove highly significant in her dissenting perspective. Stanton was still effectively a child, some fourteen years of age, but totally preoccupied with the old dogma of Calvinism. Sermons on predestination, justification by faith, and eternal damnation darkened her days. She wrote,

> I can truly say that all the cares and anxieties, the trials and disappointments of my whole life, are light, when balanced with my sufferings in childhood and youth from the theological dogmas which I sincerely believed, and the gloom connected with everything associated with the name of religion, the church, the graveyard, and the solemn, tolling bell. Everything connected with death was then rendered inexpressibly dolorous . . . At the grave came the sober warnings to the living, and sometimes frightful prophesies as to the state of the dead. All this pageantry of woe and visions of the unknown land beyond the tomb, often haunted my midnight dreams and shadowed the sunshine of my days.[50]

The next year saw her attendance at Mrs. Willard's Seminary at Troy, a fashionable school for girls, and while this period was influential in her scholastic and literary growth, it also witnessed the culmination of her harrowing religious experiences.

The Rev. Charles G. Finney became her tormentor. He was a terrifier of human souls, emphasizing God's hatred of sin, and His irreconcilable position toward the sinner. Even the most innocent girl believed herself a monster of iniquity! Doctor Finney preached the depravity and deceitfulness of the human heart, until Stanton could bear it no longer. So dismayed did she become that a fear of the judgment seized her soul: "Visions of the lost haunted my dreams. Mental anguish prostrated my health." She wrote, "Returning home, I often at night roused my father from his slumbers to pray for me lest I should be cast into the bottomless pit before morning."[51] Fearing for her health, her parents sent her away for a while, and she recollects, "My religious superstitions gave place to rational ideas based on scientific facts, and in proportion, as I looked at everything from a new standpoint, I grew more and more happy, day by day."[52]

Connections between the law, politics, and religion instilled into the mind of the young Stanton made a powerful contribution to the widely divergent literary genres she was to later employ. She became a regular contributor to the daily and weekly press,[53] and the first three volumes of the *History of Woman Suffrage* stand to her credit.

A public address given in 1848 and later used as a source for short published articles, exposes the beginnings of a religious sentiment clearly at odds with patriarchal theological exegesis: "There is a class of men," she argues, "who believe in the natural inborn, inbred superiority both in body and mind and their full complete Heaven descended right to lord it over the fish of the sea, the fowl of the air, the beast of the field-and last tho' not least the immortal being called woman." She urges this group toward an "attentive perusal of their Bibles—to historical research, to foreign travel," and with an audacious twist, she invites them to "closer observation of the manifestations of mind about them and to an humble comparison of themselves with such women as Catharine of Russia, Elizabeth of England distinguished for their statesmanlike qualities, Harriet Martineau and Madam de Stael for their literary attainments, or Caroline Herschel and Mary Summerville [*sic*] for their scientific researches, or for physical equality to that whole nation of famous women the Amazons."[54]

Stanton was intent on lifting contemporary conceptions of the feminine and was convinced, as were More and Wollstonecraft, that the improvement of the race was the prerogative of women. An article published on September 30, 1852, emphasizes, "We want the right sort of public sentiment and the most efficient means of obtaining it, is to place the right sort of reading in every family, that the women and children may be informed, and keep up such an incessant talking about voting for temperance men, that their husbands and fathers will be compelled for peace's sake, if no other, to cast their votes for honest, humane, total abstinence men."[55] She clearly gave to women and children a purity of sentiment capable of reforming louche and undesirable masculine behavior.

Didactic and reforming official suffrage documents and appeals poured from the pen of this avid promoter of liberty. It would be difficult to examine Stanton's writing and not acknowledge her tremendous influence on the suffrage movement. While acknowledging that achievement, my ultimate focus will be *The Woman's Bible*, to which she contributed and edited when she was aged eighty years. The preceding years had been spent lecturing widely as well as writing; the years from 1880, however, she devoted largely to literary endeavors. In fact, the age of the authors is worthy of note; the profound nature of the texts to be considered owes more to the intrepid tendencies of youth. These, however, were not the babblings of young radicals; More was in her late sixties when she wrote *Practical Piety*, and Eddy was well into middle age when she wrote *Science and Health*.

These important texts were the result of lives lived in societies and cultures that favored patriarchy, and written in an era in which religious leaders were expected to be men. The fact, then, that these women wrote and were published at all was remarkable, but their promotion of a "maternal" image of God and its consequent "election" of the female made a powerful contribution toward the spiritual authorization of womanhood.

The chapter will conclude by examining the formative years of Mary Baker Eddy for the purpose of contextualizing not only her early writing, but her ultimate argument, contained in *Key to the Scriptures*, for the spiritual equality of the sexes.

Mary Baker Eddy (1821–1910)

Mary Baker Eddy was born in New Hampshire in 1821, forty years after the close of the American Revolution. Her cultural and religious heritage had been formed by the early Puritans, the founding fathers of the United States of America. Having fled the religious oppression and corruption in the English Church, Puritans saw themselves as having been divinely chosen to reestablish Christian purity in a new land. Indeed, these early Puritans likened themselves to the children of Israel in their passage to the promised land.

The Bible was central to the life of Eddy's family. Each evening, along with her five siblings, she would listen while her father read from the Scriptures. Much of her early learning came from a close relationship with her grandmother who regaled her with tales of her Scottish ancestry. This grandmother, descended from the Scottish Covenanters, instilled a religious quest in the mind of her grandchild: "Your ancestors wrote their names on the covenant in blood," she told her. "Religion was more to our ancestors than their lives."[56] She talked at great length of that "pious" authoress, Hannah More,[57] and shared with her early literary manuscripts that her mother had written. These discussions of literary talents imbued Eddy with a burning ambition and a hunger and thirst after divine things.

The Baker family had been in New England for six generations and were respected as valuable contributors to their community. Mark Baker, Eddy's father, was a Justice of the Peace for his township, a deacon of the church, a school committeeman, and for many years, chaplain of the state militia. Her mother, Abigail Ambrose, was the daughter of Deacon Nathaniel Ambrose, a public-spirited and pious man. The Rev. Richard S. Rust's memories of her were of a woman who "possessed a strong intellect, a sympathizing heart, and a placid spirit, and as a mother was untiring in her efforts to secure the happiness of her family."[58] Eddy inherited her mother's intellect and sensibilities; as a small child she was deeply concerned about the plight of animals, singing to comfort them. Equally, and unusually for a child, she liked to listen to the weightier political and religious conversations taking place between her father and his business associates.

Albert Baker was destined to become a lawyer, but he and his young sister had a close bond. Desperate to become a scholar, she begged this brother to instruct her; when he questioned her as to the reason, her reply set the seal on her future: "Because when I grow up I shall write a book; and I must be wise to do it. I must be as great a scholar as you or Mr. Franklin Pierce. Already I have read Young's 'Night Thoughts,' and I understand it."[59] True to his word, this young man instructed his sister in moral science, natural philosophy, Latin, Greek, and Hebrew. At ten years of age, she was as familiar with Lindley Murray as with the Westminster Catechism that she had studied with her sisters every Sunday from babyhood. She was an apt pupil and learned quickly.[60]

Like Stanton, Eddy's religious experience suffered a grave crisis; her father's bitter doctrine of predestination and terrifying decree of endless punishment caused her deep consternation. She was far more comfortable with the God of love portrayed by her mother. At the age of twelve, however, she was expected to agree to the "unconditional election" necessary to unite with the church. A deep wrestling of souls resulted from this demand, with the daughter resolutely refusing to go along with this concept. With her pastor and all the eyes of the congregation upon her awaiting the necessary assurance that she had been "truly regenerated" she spoke unhesitatingly: "I can only say in the words of the psalmist, 'Search me, O God, and know my heart; try me, and know my thoughts; and see if there be any wicked way in me, and lead me in the way everlasting.'"[61]

The inner turmoil caused by this affair resulted in a fever, but the experience proved to be an important one. She records in her autobiography, "My mother, as she bathed my burning temples, bade me lean on God's love, which would give me rest if I went to Him in prayer, as I was wont to do, seeking His guidance. I prayed; and a soft glow of ineffable joy came over me. The fever was gone and I rose and dressed myself in a normal condition of health. Mother saw this and was glad. The physician marveled; and the 'horrible decree' of Predestination-as John Calvin rightly called his own tenet-forever lost its power over me."[62] Her mother, as had Stanton's, sent her daughter away for a time in an attempt to restore her peace of mind.

This period witnessed some of her first attempts at poetry. Her early writing witnessed a rapturous love of nature, and a confident affirmation that hope in God lifted the thought to higher regions where it was able to "soar above matter and fasten on God."[63] Her poems will be closely examined as one of the many genres she used to press her perspective.

By the age of fifteen years, Eddy had come into contact with a pastor who was to have an important influence on her spiritual growth. The Rev. Enoch Corser was a man of liberal culture, and according to his son, came to regard the young woman as the brightest pupil he had ever had. She must have made a strong impression on this old Calvinist preacher, as he told his son, "I never before had a pupil with such depth and independence of thought. She has some great future, mark that. She is an intellectual and spiritual genius."[64] To the young woman, he remarked, "Mary, your poetry goes beyond my theology, why should I preach to you!"

These formative years prepared Eddy well, the "independence of thought" allied to an education and a humanitarian spirit became the basis from which she embarked upon her career. Indeed, at the age of sixteen, as well as writing for newspapers and magazines, she was also becoming acknowledged as a fine young poet among her literary circle.

A letter written in that period between childhood and womanhood shows the state of mind with which she would meet some of the first dramatic challenges of her life. Written to her friend Augusta Holmes in 1841, it is a typical correspondence between two friends and though marked by an overt poetic sentiment, is important in that it discloses the issues uppermost in her mind at this time; friendship, illness, and a marked contrast between cold-hearted, insensitive man and the feminine, feeling heart:

Ever dear Augusta,

Can I *ever*, *ever* tell you my health will permit of my again enjoying one of the richest of heaven's earthly blessings, "the society of friends"?

No Augusta, I fear not; but pardon, pardon, my gloomy strain, for it is certainly some pleasure to have a sympathizing friend, to whom we can unbosome our very heart . . . To die, is almost *denied* me! but why complain? will not he that tempers the wind to the shorn Lamb, be mindful of me also? Yes Augusta, I know it; and I will try to rally my spirits and congratulate you on your heroism last evening, and I shall call you the *heroine* too, of that group of ladies that deserve a monument. How I should *enjoyed* [*sic*] being by your side, doing *good*; making *cold* hearted *man* raise his standard of female excelence, [*sic*] still higher.[65]

The rather oversentimentalized poetic tenor of this "heart directed" correspondence to her friend reveals a literary self-consciousness. Emerging through a rather adolescent style, it parodies a literary conceit made popular by the portrayal of "virtue in distress" in literature of sensibility. There is nevertheless a meaningful strain to be detected behind this extravagant posturing sentimentality: the value of friendship. Indeed, there are four references in this short letter. Equally, or possibly of more importance, however, is this early identification of the moral potential of the feminine, of that "group of ladies" on the reformation of male manners.

The year 1841 witnessed events that were to have a dramatic effect on Eddy; her beloved brother Albert died. His death was a calamity for the family, who had pinned such hopes on his future, but Eddy was inconsolable; her grief knew no bounds. The death of an older brother had a similar effect on the lives of both Eddy and Stanton, disrupting the hierarchical balance in each family.

It was the arrival of her future husband that brought a sense of stability back into the life of Eddy: she married George Washington Glover in 1843 and moved with him to South Carolina. This move to the South brought out another facet in the mind of the young woman—faced with the whole question of slavery, she became an outspoken abolitionist, writing prolifically for local publications. She endeavored to influence her husband to free the slaves on his property, arguing that it was a sin to own another human being.

Her life, however, was to take another unexpected turn: her devoted husband died within the first year of marriage. A business trip to North Carolina, on which her husband insisted she join him (her abolitionist demands had made her unpopular and he feared for her safety) witnessed the death of the young man from a raging epidemic of yellow fever. Eddy was left, a young and by now pregnant, widow.

The following five years were traumatic ones: her mother died, and her own health became so precarious that family members decided her child should be cared for by Mahala Sanborn, the woman who had been engaged to care for Eddy. In the space of a few years, she lost her brother, husband, mother, and son. The Sanborns moved away, taking George with them, and it was to be some forty years before mother and son were reunited.

Part of a poem *O For Thy Wings, Sweet Bird!* (published in August 1849) reflect her tenuous state:

> Blessed compared with me thou art—
> Unto thy greenwood home
> Bearing no bitter memory at heart;
> Wearing no earthly chain,
> Thou canst in azure bright soar far above;
> Nor pinest thou in vain
> O'er joys departed, unforgotten love.
> O take me to thy bower!
> Beguile the lagging hours of weariness
> With strain which hath strange power
> To make me love thee as I love life less!
> From mortal consciousness
> Which binds to earth—infirmity of woe!
> Or pining tenderness—
> Whose streams will never dry or cease to
> flow;
> An aching, voiceless void,
> Hushed in the heart whereunto none reply,
> And in the cringing crowd
> Companionless! Bird, bear me through
> the sky![66]

An overwhelming sadness pervades each stanza, that one word "companionless" portrays the agonizing desolation. Its tone mirrors that of Wollstonecraft in *Mary*: "In moments of solitary sadness, a gleam of joy would dart across her mind—She thought she was hastening to that world."[67] Both women had a vision of a higher and better world; a world that offered freedom from the bitter restrictions and earthly chains of this one. There is a notable lack of contrivance in this poem, distancing it from some of her earlier writing. A literary self-consciousness has been replaced: personal and life-changing experiences have led to an obvious literary maturing, in turn, igniting a responsive condolence in the heart of the reader.

That these harsh experiences contributed toward a spiritual awakening and ultimate transformation is clear when reading part of a later address to the Concord Church in February 1899: "Remember, thou canst be brought into no condition, be it ever so severe, where Love has not been before thee and where its tender lesson is not awaiting thee. Therefore despair not nor murmur, for that which seeketh to save, to heal, and to deliver, will guide thee, if you seekest this guidance."[68]

The inequalities, however, that were embedded in the secular notion of a civil society deeply concerned Eddy. The American Declaration of Independence had failed to include women in its demand for human equality and political freedom, as had the French Declaration of the Rights of Man. Wollstonecraft's *Vindication* had attempted to address the argument that full citizenship and individual rights should be extended to all. Eddy was equally determined to negotiate a position for women through an aggrandizement of the female virtues: "Woman," she writes, "should not be ordered to the rear, or laid on the rack, for joining the overture of angels. Theologians descant pleasantly upon free moral agency; but they should begin by admitting individual rights."[69] Eddy clearly empathizes with and reinforces More's earlier argument that the conduct of women was ultimately "one of the principal hinges on which the great machine of human society turns."[70]

CONCLUSION

The moral language of the literary and cultural contributions of these four writers indicates their early commitment to upholding the spiritual potential of womanhood.

Exploration of the formative years of Wollstonecraft, More, Stanton, and Eddy has thrown light on the familial and cultural influences they were subjected to. It has allowed identification of the social, political, and religious injustice they witnessed from an early age, which in turn led them to question the place of women in society. It has shown that religious conditioning caused deep unrest in that *their* understanding of Christ's message did not sit comfortably alongside patriarchal theological practice.

Their early writing, I would suggest, was a form of self-definition, reflecting a growing awareness of their subjugated place in a patriarchal society. Acknowledging that each woman possessed a high intellect and spirit of sensibility, I have identified religion as possibly the single most important influence in their reforming impulse and the basis on which their later political, moral, and spiritual arguments would be constructed.

The next chapter will investigate their forays into public morality.

CHAPTER 2

"THE RELIGIOUS IS PERSONAL IS POLITICAL"*

CORRUPT POLITICS, PERSONAL CONVERSION, AND THE REFORMING POTENTIAL OF SPIRITUALLY MINDED WOMEN

The well intentioned and well-principled author, who has uniformly thrown all his weight, though that weight be but small, into the right scale, may have contributed his fair proportion to that great work of reformation.

—Hannah More, *The Works of Hannah More*

Can we suppose that the omniscient God would have given these unqualified commands to powerless, incapable unimpressible beings?

—Hannah More, *Practical Piety*

Emancipation from the power of moral corruption was at the heart of these writers' works, and in this chapter I will demonstrate how each woman strove to promote in mankind a true and just sense of morality. Investing this higher moral code with a feminized perspective allowed women's sympathetic virtues to be more clearly identified and appreciated. The depravity that engulfed the black slave trade and the immorality that reduced women to simpering playthings[1] witnessed distinctive literary responses—satire and sensibility mingled with political discourse—and their strategies will be closely examined in this chapter.

---

* *The Woman's Bible*, vii.

The Grand Object: Emancipation from Moral Corruption

In the general preface to *The Works of Hannah More*, More suggests, "Between him who writes and him who reads, there must be a coalition of interests, something of a partnership, however unequal the capital, in mental property."[2] The "coalition of interests" in this period was the religious revivalism surfacing on both sides of the Atlantic. This reawakened blend of religious enthusiam was characterized by its strong emphasis toward moral and social reform. The distinguishing feature of this evangelical movement was the personal conversion its followers experienced. Along with this experience came the desire to convert and save souls on a grand scale.

The period from 1787 to 1792 witnessed an alliance between radical dissenters and conservative evangelists for the purpose of promoting the abolition campaign. The orientation of the culture of sensibility toward reform gave power to the female writers of the period. From the fusion of sensibility with evangelism there emerged a humanitarian reforming zeal that contributed to the abolition of the slave trade. Indeed, women were responsible for a quarter of all the antislavery poems written in the eighteenth century.

In 1788, More attempted to assist William Wilberforce[3] at the opening of his parliamentary campaign against the slave trade. At his request, she wrote her poem *The Black Slave Trade*, a powerful rendering of antislavery rhetoric. The literary style mirrored the popular verse style of the period: heroic couplets. The equipoise of the couplet form, however, is in distinct contrast to the "aggravated sin" being addressed and the cleverly ordered nature of her writing style serves to emphasize the grotesque *disorder* being addressed:

> If Heaven has into being deign'd to call
> Thy light, O LIBERTY! to shine on all;
> Bright intellectual Sun! why does thy ray
> To earth distribute only partial day?[4]

This stanza poses a question: acknowledging that the poem is addressed to the middle and upper class traditional Christian practitioner, it is an intriguing strategy, because while these lines pose a question, they obliquely answer it. Christian doctrine decrees the impartiality of God's light, and this basic Christian truth is supported by God and nature. Anything, then, that opposes this law of God, or anyone who does not stand against the perpetuation of this pernicious inhumanity is not exemplifying the teachings of Christ Jesus. Bearing in mind More's assertion that Christianity underlies sensibility, she adroitly establishes heavenly authority as the chief criterion in the overthrow of human slavery. More persists in the questioning vein:

> Why should fell darkness half the South invest?
> Was it decreed, fair Freedom! at thy birth,
> That thou shou'd'st ne'er irradiate *all* the earth?
> While Britain basks in thy full blaze of light,
> Why lies sad Afric quench'd in total night?[5]

The frequent references to light and dark emphasize the inequity between Britain and Africa. The liberal use of question marks impels her readers to examine their conscience, while use of figures of sound combined with her apostrophizing works to convey an immense strength of feeling:

> The cause I plead shall sanctify my song.
> The Muse awakes no artificial fire,
> For Truth rejects what Fancy wou'd inspire;
> Here Art wou'd weave her gayest flow'rs in vain,
> The bright invention Nature wou'd disdain.
> For no fictitious ills these numbers flow,
> But living anguish, and substantial woe;
> No individual griefs my bosom melt,
> For millions feel what Oronoko[6] felt;
> Fir'd by no single wrongs, the countless host
> I mourn, by rapine dragg'd from Afric's coast.[7]

The cause or purpose is sanctified, born of a holy and sacred intent to wash away the sins of the world, instigating a renewed religious fervor. Artifice, contrivance, and duplicity are anathema to More; her writing is from the heart and speaks to the heart of her reader. The intuitive Christian heart cannot be influenced by fictitious ills. More's use of rhetoric is factually persuasive. "Living anguish" and "substantial woe" imply large scale suffering. This image is reinforced by her juxtaposing of words such as "individual," "single," and "my bosom" alongside "substantial," "millions," and "countless." In the space of a few lines, she has syntactically engaged the thought of the reader with the vast scale of the inhumanity.

This was the period of "the Englishman's home is his castle." Home was fundamental in representing the core of family life, a protective shelter from the outside world. The female influence at the heart of the home nurtured and protected the emotional stability of the family. Socially and culturally, this space became the key locale from which to promote virtue and order. More's literary portrayal adeptly invades this cozy domestic scene in an attempt to disrupt its inherent complacency. This strategy is calculated to integrate and involve the reader in an attempt to stir the soul, the innermost feelings toward something better, higher, and holier.

More widens her approach:

> Perish th' illiberal thought which wou'd debase
> The native genius of the sable race!
> Perish the proud philosophy, which sought
> To rob them of the pow'rs of equal thought!
> What! does th' immortal principle within
> Change with the casual colour of a skin?
> Does matter govern spirit? or is MIND
> Degraded by the form to which 'tis join'd?
> No: they have heads to think, and hearts to feel,
> And souls to act . . . [8]

The intolerance of narrow-mindedness is attacked, along with that philosophical viewpoint that argued for the inherent inferiority of the black people. Exclamation marks represent strong, sudden cries that invite reader response and in effect encourage a mental jolt. Rhyming couplets, such as "Does then the immortal principle within / Change with the casual colour of a skin?" are used satirically to burlesque effect. More discredits the color of skin as of any relevance to the heart, soul, or mind of man with the use of that one word: "casual." Following the exclamations and questions, the abrupt "No" brings with it a powerful implication: "they have heads to think, and hearts to feel / And souls to act." The human responses of thinking, feeling and acting are precisely the senses More is appealing to. Her readers have been invited to think, she now moves them to "feel":

> Whene'er to Afric's shores I turn my eyes,
> Horrors of deepest, deadliest guilt arise;
> I see, by more than Fancy's mirror shewn,
> The burning village and the blazing town;
> See the dire victim torn from social life,
> See the scar'd infant, hear the shrieking wife!
> She, wretch forlorn! is dragg'd by hostile hands,
> To distant tyrants sold, in distant lands! [9]

Using a rhetoric of suffering, More endeavors to make the torment tangible. The clipped forceful phrases are rich in verbal texture, alliteration and syntax being used to emotional effect. More has a clear mental image that the words impart with precision. So clearly is she able to behold the images of barbarism, she writes as a witness to these events, giving her words the authority of a factual account. The frequent use of the letter "s" slows the reader, giving him more time to feel and see. More's juxtaposing of the familiar images of village, town, and social life with its implication of public civic community, is disturbing when set alongside the "hostile hands" of the tyrants perpetrating acts of terror to mothers and babies. Africa is presented as civilized and domestic, Britain as savage and tyrannical. Having commanded her readers to think and feel, More's instructions reach a climax:

> Barbarians, hold! th' opprobrious commerce spare,
> Respect HIS sacred image which they bear.
> Tho' dark and savage, ignorant and blind,
> They claim the common privilege of *kind*;
> Let Malice strip them of each other plea,
> They still are men, and men shou'd still be free.[10]

The order is specific, personal, and shocking in its implication: "Barbarians, hold!" The British middle and upper classes had been led to believe the primitive communities and tribes of black Africa to be barbarians: More, however, brings them face to face with their own barbarism. They were indeed as guilty, if not more so, than the slaves they sought to subjugate and control, whose only fault, she suggests, was ignorance and blindness.

The narrative of this poem served to alert, shock, and humiliate its readers, demanding that professing Christians practice their alleged faith. More's zealous advocacy for the cause of Christianity is apparent in the evangelistic tone of the final stanza, her demand for spiritual equality being rooted in the teachings of her faith: "There is neither Jew nor Greek, there is neither bond nor free, there is neither male nor female: for ye are all one in Christ Jesus."[11]

> And THOU! great source of Nature and of Grace,
> Who of one blood didst form the human race:
> Look down in mercy in thy chosen time,
> With equal eye on Afric's suff'ring clime:
> Disperse her shades of intellectual night,

Repeat thy high behest—LET THERE BE LIGHT! Bring each
benighted soul, great God, to Thee,
And with thy wide salvation make them free![12]

The epic nature of More's poem is apparent in its concluding stanza
where her poetic strategy draws together the three great causes that
infuse her abolition rhetoric: humanitarian, political, and religious
themes. Global Christianization resulting in salvation and liberty for
all is the proselytizing argument inherent in More's abolition discourse. This poem represents a powerful fusion of her belief system,
containing recurring themes and reflecting the ascending arguments
that culminate in her demand for the granting of spiritual liberty to
"each benighted soul."

Abolition sentiment served to assist in the construction of a grand
master discourse, a ceremonial literary style and epic spirit, the purity
of moral sentiment inherent in abolition discourse also emphasized
and empowered the sympathetic virtues inherent in womanhood.
Clare Midgley suggested that the sympathetic domestic femininity,
constructed in the arguments of abolitionists, furnished women with
a form of political agency.[13] The poetic perspectives of Hannah More,
imbricated as they were with hints of a "feminized" Christianity, made
a powerful contribution to the authorizing of women as reformers.

According to Robert Hole, this period was one of her most productive in terms of influence; More's writing during the 1780s, he
suggests, "applied her religious belief to society and social life." He
further suggests that women were her primary target: "She was convinced of their importance and influence. They had a vital role to play
in the preservation of the traditional order of things."[14]

Interclass Communication

"Women writers" suggests Krueger, "most notably Hannah More,
often dominated the creation of social narrative by adapting evangelical rhetorical strategies and conceptions of literary authority, drawing
the political conclusions implicit in women preachers' writings."[15]

Acutely aware of the power of religion and education in controlling and informing the lower classes, these rhetorical strategies are evidenced in More's *Cheap Repository Tracts*. These tracts, vested with a
dual purpose, specifically brought the plight of the black slaves to the
attention of the lower classes. The evils of the slave trade allowed More
to propagate her evangelical principles, and the abolition campaign

undoubtedly evinced an avenue through which the ethics of Christian benevolence could be transmitted.

The tracts also served to press a moral theme: the saving influence of Christianity. The portrayal of religious conviction as able to make human suffering bearable was a powerful proselytizing strategy. *The Evangelical Magazine* noted that "More was the first to try her hand at interclass communication between England's two nations."[16] Myers suggests, "Through female influence and moral power, this cultural myth's new woman would educate the young and illiterate, succor the unfortunate, amend the debased popular culture of the lower orders, reorient worldly men of every class, and set the national house in order."[17]

American Sensibilities:
Dissolution and Reconstruction

Notions of sentiment were permeating American political, religious, and literary culture around the early to mid-nineteenth century, a language of sympathy emerging as central to the developing ideas of citizenship and nationality. The language of patriotism and public virtue merged with domestic images, resulting in narrative that attempted to fuse the private sphere of women with the civic and public sphere of men. This was a period that led to an empowerment of the feminine: "Woman," suggested a Presbyterian minister in Newburyport, Massachusetts, in 1837, was "fitted by nature" for Christian benevolence, "religion seems almost to have been entrusted by its author to her particular custody."[18]

This period of American history is referred to by historians and literary critics as an emotionally disordered period, "traumatised" even and "anxious." Henry Seidel suggests that "thoughtful Americans . . . had come to believe that the American dream of a brotherhood of equality had been sold in the market place and was indeed only a dream."[19]

Keith Stavely believes that a secularization of the Protestant ethic was, in effect, leading to an "anarchy of individual consciences." He writes, "A society of that sort, one in which the Church was finally disestablished and social control maintained even more exclusively than before by 'invisible, refined, spiritual ties, bonds of the mind and heart' was exactly what nineteenth century New England was."[20] Literary women did not miss the opportunity this social atmosphere offered to them, and Eddy's writing of this period concentrated on the cause of women, as well as abolition.

In the November 1846 edition of *The Covenant*, she invites her readers to consider "woman's high and holy faith in the doctrines of divine inspiration, revealed in love." Reflecting on the *nature* of womanhood, she identifies their "sacred duties of a gifted destiny," suggesting that "with martyr strength and trust in Heaven" they may "exert this mysterious, potent influence over the minds of men—holding crime in awe, reclaiming vice and smiling it into virtue."[21] Arguing for the femininity of the "invisible, refined, spiritual ties, bonds of the mind and heart," Eddy proclaims, "Methinks if my pen was dipped in my heart, thus to transcribe from the tablets of feeling, it could not fail to waken oft the note responsive in other breasts—to thrill the electric chain of being, which binds the happy, or links the unfortunate in tenderness unutterable." The "invisible" links become identifiable as those spiritual qualities that bind the sisterhood of women with their families, individually and collectively:

> Behold with woman's nature, the ministering angel o'er the death couch, watch the scene till it darkens, when hope and love that so lately nestled warm in the bosom, is shrouded in the tomb! with life's most fairy day-dreams of bliss and daring schemes, all, all, hurried into its oblivious vortex . . . Vast as the amount of human suffering, is the bow of Omnipotence, and the realm for good deeds in unostentatious record; "If an hungered or athirst, sick, naked or a stranger, ye ministered unto me." Look again—we behold the mother . . . Art thou incredulous still, dear reader, heareth thine own heart no silent testimony to these sublime truths? . . . Nay, rather, if it is not a glorious superstructure whose frame-work is sure, founded in *friendship*, reared in *love*, supported by *truth*! and woman, last at the cross and first at the sepulchre, were befitting its fairy guardian; yea, it *were* sullying the chastity of her pure spirit, not to bid it God speed.[22]

The demise of the American dream left in its wake a nation in need of being ministered to; female credentials fitted them for this important task. The mother country needed, in effect, a gestation period in which to develop a reconstruction plan. Eddy's use of sentimental language and imagery contributed toward portrayal of the female as an embodiment of the Christly qualities and as such a sound framework on which to build a new order.[23] A society that valued justice and freedom was one in which subjugation and slavery could not be tolerated. Through aesthetic discourse, she underscored an ideology of separate spheres, appropriating meritorious qualities to the sphere inhabited by wives and mothers. These were very public proclamations of female excellence, and in a publication "Devoted to the Cause of Odd-fellowship," were clearly addressed to a male readership.

The Covenant of September, 1847, however, included a publication with a different tone; it registered a shift from her earlier advancement of social appreciation for the value of woman, toward a more overt political rhetoric. *Erin, the Smile and the Tear in Thine Eyes*, witnessed her criticism of social inequity:

> When Burke and Berkley are forgotton; [*sic*] when the name of Emmett shall cease to be spoken; when the last thunder-tones of O'Connell shall have died along the shore of the sweet isle of the ocean, then may Ireland be accused of want of intellect. The English philanthropist can view with telescopic eye, the *slave* writhing beneath the lash of the West India task-master, and his generous bosom heave with just indignation at the wrongs of suffering humanity . . . But a change must come . . . The civilized nations of the globe are beginning to take a more enlightened view of the relations they sustain to their fellow-men. Their religion is assuming a milder form, and a more liberal spirit is, becoming diffused through all the ramifications of their government.

Eddy seems to be suggesting that while there were clearly emerging signs, in some countries, of Enlightenment principles, England still retained a bigoted, narrow-mindedness: "When the English shall possess religion without bigotry, and their politicians legislate without parsimony, then shall Ireland 'strike the bold anthem' of the free."[24]

The sharp contrast between the nature and tone of these two publications reflects the author's deep concerns, as well as her ability to move easily between political and sentimental rhetoric. They show how she effectively crossed the boundaries between private and public, creating a dialogue that allowed her to transcend traditional gender stereotyping. Through a language of sentiment she effectively defined the relationship between privacy and nationality, and identification of the spiritual worth of women worked to promote their reforming potential. To the "pure spirit" of the female she urges "godspeed" an effective instruction to an initiator of reform.

Eddy was aware, however, of a need to tread carefully in literary terms; G. J. Barker-Benfield identifies problems associated with reforming women writers: "Women's self-assertion in writing was a declaration of war," he suggests, "threatening to disable men."[25] While conscious, therefore, of the shortcomings of those American theologians and politicians who failed to tackle effectively either the slavery problem or the woman question, Eddy's covert criticism came through a more surreptitious and thus less confrontational route.

On August 17, 1861, Eddy wrote to Major General Benjamin Butler, a prominent Civil War commander, in terms that appear to reflect her desire that women be seen to be morally active and politically informed:

> Dear Sir, Permit me individually, and as the representative of thousands of my sex in your native State, to tender the homage and gratitude due to one of her noblest sons, who so bravely vindicated the claims of humanity in your late letter to Sec. Cameron.
>
> You dared to assume in the dignity of defending with your latest breath our country's honor, the true position of justice and equity.
>
> The final solution of the great National query follows,—will it be rendered to black as well as white, men, women and children, whom you have the courage and honor to defend in this the hour of our Country's pain and purification?
>
> You [as well as we all] hold freedom to be the normal condition of those made in God's image. In this, the man, can only equal the soldier who lays down his life for his country, and by fairness of argument elucidates the justice which can save her, and transmit to posterity the success of a republican form of government in heritage perpetual, and undimned in its lustre.
>
> But I would not task your time or forbearance to persue [*sic*] farther comment on a letter which has thrilled with electric hope the homes and hearts of this section of our Country,—hope in God and the Right.
>
> The red strife between right and wrong can only be fierce, it cannot be long, and victory on the side of immutable justice will be well worth its cost.
>
> Give us in the field or forum a brave Ben Butler and our Country is saved. Respectfully.[26]

Eddy appears to have assumed, as did More, a mantle of spokesperson for her sex: and if, as suggested earlier, private letters were a rehearsal for public print, the language in this correspondence indicates her desire to connect the private character of women with the wider implications of citizenship.

While there may be an air of submissiveness in the opening paragraph, a patriotic tone soon emerges, mingling abolition and suffrage sentiment. Under the aegis of religious argument and in the name of honor, justice, and equity, she highlights the question of freedom being rendered to black as well as white, men, women, and children. Effectively reinforcing her argument, she draws on combat rhetoric: "In this, the man, can only equal the soldier who lays down his life." A patriotic sentiment is further augmented by references to "a republican form of government" alongside words such as "justice," "heritage," "luster," and "victory." Mingling with the language of patriotism and public virtue, is the familial imagery that Eddy is careful to include: "the hearts and homes" of the nation that are "thrilled with electric hope." It is interesting that she uses this "electric" imagery again. This language is visual, and gives credence to a suggestion that the "hearts and homes" are not a passive or subservient space, but rather, charged, vital, and awaiting stimulation.

Close analysis of this letter exposes a woman whose agenda was reform and who was intent on defining the female qualities as those on which a more virtuous society might be constructed. Butler's reply would have encouraged Eddy's pioneering spirit; his discharge of public duty he suggested was made easy by such commendations coming from the "noble and loyal of the land."[27]

The New Century

Poetry had long been a genre through which Eddy registered her ideals; nature and nurture are the notable features of *The New Century*. The style is simply structured around rhyming couplets and while the theme is a powerful argument for human rights, it draws on nature imagery and the ministering qualities of the maternal:

> Tis writ on earth, on leaf and flower:
> Love hath one race, one realm, one power.
> Dear God! how great, how good Thou art
> To heal humanity's sore heart;
> To probe the wound, then pour the balm—
> A life perfected, strong and calm.
> The dark domain of pain and sin
> Surrenders—Love doth enter in,
> And peace is won, and lost is vice:
> Right reigns, and blood was not its price.[28]

It is in its very simplicity that its authority lies, and the style, structure, and sentiment of Eddy's poem parallel More's in *The Black Slave Trade*:

> What page of human annals can record
> A deed so bright as human rights restor'd?
> O may that god-like deed, that shining page,
> Redeem OUR fame, and consecrate OUR age!
> And let this glory mark our favour'd shore,
> To curb FALSE FREEDOM, and the TRUE restore!

And see, the cherub MERCY from above,
Descending softly, quits the sphere of love!
On Britain's isle she sheds her heavenly dew;
. . . From soul to soul the spreading influence steals,
Till every breast the soft contagion feels . . .
She cheers the mourner, and with soothing hands
From bursting hearts unbinds th' Oppressor's bands;
Restores the lustre of the Christian name,
And clears the foulest blot that dimm'd its fame.[29]

Humanitarian reform is the focus of both these poems: Eddy's "Tis writ on earth, on leaf and flower: Love hath one race, one realm, one power" supports More's "A deed so bright as human rights restored." The essential ingredient in these poems is the figure of virtuous femininity. There is convincing evidence through feminized representations of the part women are to play in this restorative period. The invocation of Mother Nature reaffirms this basic postulate. The "soothing hands" that unbind the "oppressor's bands" (More) and the "healing" qualities required to "probe the wound, then pour the balm" (Eddy) represent an exaltation of maternal qualities. Indeed, More identifies the "cherub Mercy" as female. The tender compassion inherent within the feminine "breathes **her** spirit o'er the enlighten'd few," spreading her influence, "Till every breast the soft contagion feels." Solace, consolation, and comfort are pure expressions of maternal love: recognized by Richard Cadbury, the Quaker cocoa manufacturer: "Can Heaven bestow a warmer glow—Of sunshine from above—A purer, holier pledge below—Than in a mother's love."[30]

The combative and often aggressive characterization of the masculine, its need to dominate and subdue, often at the expense of shedding blood, has been eclipsed: "Right reigns, and blood was not its price." These poems speak to the hearts of their readers. Gendered emphasis works to powerful effect, portraying a sisterhood of linked souls, which, once roused and stimulated conjoin in galvanizing public opinion toward a more just and benevolent society.

I shall now take a closer look at the essentially "feminist" radicalism of Wollstonecraft and Stanton and their more extreme rhetorical strategies.

Moral Indignation and Millenarianism

The powerful impetus given to feminist reforming writers through the antislavery campaign was evident in the revivalist evangelical message central to the arguments of both British and American reformers in the eighteenth and early nineteenth centuries. Women were voluble as well as visible in the promotion of a reforming zeal. The New England Great Awakening witnessed converts at a ratio of three women to two men in the period 1798 to 1826, indicating the potential of proselytizing women.[31]

There is little doubt that Wollstonecraft had been a tremendous influence on her American "sisters." She was considered a powerful contributor to the feminist awakening in the United States: Cromwell notes that Lucretia Mott (one of the most important early feminists) kept a copy of *A Vindication of the Rights of Woman* at a center table in her home for forty years.[32]

At the World Anti-Slavery Convention in London in 1840, Stanton, who was a keen supporter of Wollstonecraft and her ideas, spent considerable time discussing them with Lucretia Mott. The argument in *Vindication* was unequivocal in its demand for equal rights for women. Employing the Enlightenment emphasis on natural law, reason, and equality, Wollstonecraft had suggested it was a patriarchal cultural and environmental influence on girls and women that contributed to their subjugation. Equal rights, therefore, extended to women, particularly educational rights, she argued, would do much to readjust this imbalance.

The arguments of feminists on both sides of the Atlantic drew heavily on religious ideals, and the Unitarians, Evangelicals, and, of course, the Quakers reflected a religious position that contributed to the movement for female suffrage.[33]

Stanton was married to an ardent young abolitionist and became a staunch campaigner for the cause. Under the aegis of abolitionism came the demand for freedom on a grand scale, with the rights of women becoming a key concern. The religious motivation for humanitarian reform gave women such as Anthony,[34] Mott,[35] and Stanton a powerful platform from which to demand equal rights for women. These two campaigns, abolition and women's rights, contributed to the burgeoning of a feminist agenda, in America as well as Great Britain.

It needs to be acknowledged, however, that there were primarily two strands within the promotion of the ideal of female equality. On one side was the evangelical tradition with its strong emphasis on promoting woman's mission as guardian of the nation's morals. This tradition promoted a doctrine of true womanhood. It represented an image of the "gentle sex" as able to offer succor and comfort from that metaphorical "womb" the refuge or sanctuary of the home. This sacred maternal mission was endowed with transcendental qualities that served to promote an ideal of female superiority. It was to this evangelical and primarily conservative tradition that More belonged and similarly Eddy.

The more militant, radical philosophical ideals advocated by Wollstonecraft and Stanton were the more revolutionary arguments that had inspired the French and American revolutions. They were concerned with breaking down traditional stereotypical images of the "weaker sex" that saw them confined and isolated from public life and decision making.

Scholars have largely identified the nature of Wollstonecraft's writing in political and revolutionary terms, and rightly so, but it was her intrinsic religious values that make her radical arguments so intriguing. At the time More was writing her important antislavery poem, Wollstonecraft was putting together a collection titled *Original Stories from Real Life* (1788) and a collection of texts for girls, *The Female Reader* (1789). From the year 1789 until 1798, she was employed as a reader and translator for Johnson's *Analytical Review*, translating such works as *Of the Importance of Religious Opinions* (1788) by Jacques Necker, and *Elements of Morality* (1790) by C. G. Salzmann.

These were powerful texts, intended to rouse the minds of her female readers to their reforming potential. The intent of *The Female Reader* was, in her own words, "to fix devotional habits in a young mind," and she made "no apology for introducing the book which contains devotional pieces." "Religion," she argued, is the only solace for women when "oppressed by sorrow, or harassed by wordly cares," and "piety is not to be acquired in the hour of trouble; it must have been a cherished inmate of the soul, or it will not afford consolation when every other source fails."[36]

Through carefully chosen devotional pieces and reflections on topical concerns, the reader becomes aware of an author well acquainted with her maker. She has clearly chosen descriptive pieces carefully with a specific purpose.[37] The antislavery movement, as I have already suggested, was argued in religious and moral terms and Wollstonecraft used these texts to promote her arguments on the woman question and the evil nature of the slave trade, but underpinning the structure of her arguments are cogent religious perspectives.

Civic Virtue and Domestic Economy

The implications of female superiority were powerfully enhanced through the authors' association with abolition sentiment. Distinctive gender divisions actually worked to reinforce an ideology of female authority. Leonore Davidoff and Catherine Hall suggest that middle-class men "who sought to be someone, to count as individuals because of their wealth, their power to command or their capacity to influence people were, in fact, embedded in networks of familial and female support which underpinned their rise to public prominence."[38] Humanitarian reform, building on this ideal, sought to lift humanity into a feminized spiritual realm replacing brutality with the milk of human kindness.

The years 1788 to 1797 were active literary ones for Wollstonecraft. The preface to *Original Stories* sets out her strategic intentions: "to make religion an active, invigorating director of the affections, and not a mere attention to forms."[39] Her contributions to the *Analytical Review* reflected this purpose. "Aimed at a general educated public of liberal persuasion interested in literature, politics, philosophy, religion and science,"[40] it gave her a wide and varied readership; by June 1789 she was contributing well over thirty reviews to an issue. The character and nature of her ideological perspectives inevitably emerge in these contributions, and a review of *The interesting Narrative of the Life of Olaudah Equiano, or Gustavus Varsa, the African* registers her deconstruction of contemporary values:

> The life of an African, written by himself, is certainly a curiosity, as it has been a favourite philosophic whim to degrade the numerous nations, on whom the sun-beams more directly dart, below the common level of humanity, and hastily to conclude that nature, by making them inferior to the rest of the human race, designed to stamp them with a mark of slavery. How they are shaded down, from the fresh colour of northern rustics, to the sable hue seen on the African sands, is not our task to inquire, nor do we intend to draw a parallel between the abilities of a negro and European mechanic; we shall only observe, that if these volumes do not exhibit extraordinary intellectual powers, sufficient to wipe off the stigma, yet the activity and ingenuity, which conspicuously appear in the character of Gustavus, place him on a par with the general mass of men, who fill the subordinate stations in a more civilized society than that which he was thrown into at his birth.[41]

This review, marked by its ironic trope, witnesses Wollstonecraft's disputation of the theorists' arguments for black subservience as "fanciful."

The reason for their skin difference "is not our task to enquire," though she suggests it may quite simply be protection for those "on whom the sun-beams more directly dart." I believe she effectively cuts the whole argument down to size in the review by identifying the utter sameness of character of Gustavus with men in general.

Strategically it is not unlike More's *The Black Slave Trade*: "Does then the immortal principle within / Change with the casual colour of a skin?" Through mockery of this serious issue, Wollstonecraft succeeds in emphasizing its gravity. Calling attention to the small-mindedness of the arguments, she underlined their insubstantiality.

Black Slaves, White Women, and the Promotion of "Human" Rights

Barker-Benfield suggests that "Wollstonecraft illustrated the capacity of antislavery writers to put themselves 'in the Negro's place.'"[42] Confirming Wollstonecraft's habit of merging the interests of subjugated women with black slaves, he writes, "In a brilliant simile, she compared woman's automatic subjection to man, her pleasingness—that is, 'blind propriety'—to sugar, and asked: 'Is sugar always to be produced by vital blood? Is one half of the human species, like the poor African slaves, to be subject to prejudices that brutalize them, when principles would be a surer method to sweeten the cup of man?'"[43]

This sentiment was powerful in its implications: sugar production was a contentious issue in the 1790's suffused with its implicit betrayal of civilized morality. To ally this with her cause for the 'vindication' of women was certainly an effective proselytizing stratagem. Denial of freedom, in the case of black slave or white woman, was acceptable only to those who were blind or greedy, blind to the cause of common humanity and greedy for material gain. "A desperate disease," as Wollstonecraft referred to this barbarism, "required a powerful remedy," and she challenged the double standards at work in both politics and religion:

> Injustice had no right to rest on prescription; nor has the character of the present clergy any weight in the argument. You find it very difficult to separate policy from justice: in the political world they have frequently been separated with shameful dexterity. To mention a recent instance. According to the limited views of timid, or interested politicians, an abolition of the infernal slave trade would not only be unsound policy, but a flagrant infringement of the laws (which are allowed to have been infamous) that induced the planters to purchase their estates. But is it

not consonant with justice, with the common principles of humanity, not to mention Christianity, to abolish this abominable mischief? There is not one argument, one invective, levelled by you at the confiscators of the church revenue, which could not, with the strictest propriety, be applied by the planters and negro drivers to our Parliament, if it gloriously dared to shew the world that British senators were men: if the natural feelings of humanity silenced the cold cautions of timidity, till this stigma on our nature was wiped off, and all men were allowed to enjoy their birth-right—liberty, till by their crimes they had authorized society to deprive them of the blessing they had abused.[44]

Through powerful abolition sentiment, Wollstonecraft targets the British establishment. She uncovers with deft literary precision the hypocrisy at the heart of officialdom, portraying their support of an "abominable mischief" carried out in the name and nature of a Christian nation. Now was the time to highlight the spiritual poverty at the heart of the public sphere; demanding that the "natural feelings of humanity" be allowed to take precedence over the "cold cautions of timidity," she called for a society in which all were "allowed to enjoy their birth-right—liberty."

The ideological potency with which Wollstonecraft's abolition discourse is infused was a powerful reproof to the "specious errors" inherent in unjust legislature. Any semblance of credibility in the unjust arguments of priest or parliament needed exposing and Wollstonecraft clearly casts herself in the mold of truth teller: "Plausibility, I know, can only be unmasked by shewing the absurdities it glosses over, and the simple truths it involves with specious errors. Eloquence has often confounded triumphant villany; but it is probably that it has more frequently rendered the boundary that separates virtue and vice doubtful."[45]

Wollstonecraft strikes at the heart of the masculine world of politics; its detachment of justice from policy, she argues, inverts constitutional laws and institutes barbarous codes and practices. She pours scorn on the timidity of "British senators," arguing the need for the sensitivity and benevolence that marked the feminine. The warmth of feeling and tenderness associated with the maternal human nature, silences—melts even—the cold conventionality of Machiavellian politics. Bearing in mind the masculine and political genre of *A Vindication of the Rights of Man*, Wollstonecraft's agenda appears to be a "feminization" of masculinity. This is not without irony when considering her persuasive efforts to "masculinize" femininity in *A Vindication of the Rights of Woman*.

Vindication aimed to instill in women nobler ambitions. Critical of historical gender assumptions, Wollstonecraft argued that the acquirement of knowledge, scholarship, and learning be made available to woman. Exaggerated sensibility was neither useful nor appropriate and she was clearly intent on showing its destructive tendencies: "their minds are not in a healthy state," she wrote. "Strength and usefulness are sacrificed to beauty, and the flaunting leaves, after having pleased a fastidious eye, fade, disregarded on the stalk, long before the season they ought to have arrived at maturity . . . one cause of this barren blooming, I attribute to a false system of education."[46]

Nature narrative is a common trope in Wollstonecraft's writing, and "flaunting" leaves had connotations of sexual provocativeness. The chief purpose of these beautiful 'flowers' is visual delight. Women's physical beauty, and therefore their appeal, as that of the flower, Wollstonecraft argues, is transitory and temporal. She is critical of male writers who have argued that female education be directed toward rendering them pleasing: "formed to please and to be subject to him . . . it is her duty to render herself *agreeable* to her master."[47] She argues that through cultivation of strength of character and morals, this "barren blooming" would be replaced with fertile productivity.

Wollstonecraft uses strong rhetoric to counteract the ritualistic language of gallantry that she considered served to incarcerate women in a perpetual state of slavish dependency. The condescending use of feminine phrases, seductive forms of patriarchal language and the flattering of their "fascinating graces" she argued, kept women in an abiding state of infancy.

BIRDS OF A FEATHER?

Confined then in cages like the feathered race, they have nothing to do but to plume themselves, and stalk with mock majesty from perch to perch.

—Mary Wollstonecraft, *A Vindication of the Rights of Woman*

Antislavery rhetoric worked on a number of levels and its rehabilitating potential was not overlooked by reforming women. The destruction of "slavish dependency" was a common goal, and this is apparent when examining More's satirical style in *The White Slave Trade*.[48]

Wollstonecraft's arguments, it has been noted, were the opposite of More's more measured language and perspectives, though similarities appear when we look closely at More's "Hints towards forming a Bill for the Abolition of the White Female Slave Trade, in the Cities of London and Westminster." The style and tone suggest it could have been written by either writer: in spite of More's apparent aversion to her contemporary, its political and sexual innuendo hints at a rebelliousness not usually associated with More. Its power lies in its "tongue in cheek" ability to highlight inequity between the sexes through connection with "master" and "slavery" issues, raging at this time. It usefully exhibits the "covert" feminist at her most satirical, at the same time allowing for the connecting of characteristics peculiar to each woman:

> Whereas many members of both Houses of Parliament have been long and indefatigably labouring to bring into effecta bill for the amelioration of slaves in our foreign plantations, as well as for the intire abolition of the Slave trade itself; and whereas it is presumed that the profound attention of these sage legislators to this great foreign evil prevents their attending to domestic grievances of the same nature; it is therefore humbly requested, that whilst these benevolent senators are thus meritoriously exerting themselves for the deliverance of our black brethren, that the present writer be permitted to suggest the following loose hints of a bill for the abolition of slavery at *home*—a slavery the more interesting, as it is to be feared that it may in some instances be found to involve the wives, daughters, nieces, aunts, cousins, mothers, and grandmothers even of those very zealous abolitionists themselves.[49]

More was a clever and experienced rhetorician and it could be said that the pace of this passage mimics and in effect reinforces the protracted nature of abolition attempts. Terms such as:"long been," "by which," "whereas," and "whilst these" highlight the politicians' tactics of "playing for time" or "hedgeing of bets." The final sentence works as a literary representation of the delaying and teasing tactics of those politicians who talk too much and do too little, with the length to final closure reinforcing the endless postponement of antislavery legislators. More continues by linking this "great foreign evil" with its homegrown variety:

> In our West India plantations, the lot of slaves is of all descriptions; here it is uniform. In our islands there are diversities of masters; if some are cruel, others are kind; and the worst are mortal. Here there is one, arbitrary, universal tyrant, and like the Lama of Thibet he never dies. His name is FASHION. Here, indeed, the original subjection is voluntary, but once engaged, the subsequent servility of the slaves keeps pace with the tyranny of the despot. They hug their chains, and because they are gilt and shining, this prevents them, not from feeling, but from acknowledging that they are heavy. With astonishing fortitude

they carry them about, not only without repining, but as their glory and distinction. A few females indeed are every where to be found who have manfully resisted the tyrant, but they are people *whom nobody knows.* As the free people are the minority, and as, in this one instance, the minority are peaceable persons, no one envies them an exemption from chains, and their freedom is considered only as a proof of their insignificance.[50]

Fashionable society had a code of social conduct, a unique style or way of doing things. This code could be defined in the word "consummation" or its derivative "consumed." *The Lawes Resolution of Women's Rights*[51] argues, "It is true, that man and wife are one person, but understand in what manner. When a small brook or little river incorporateth with Rhodanus (Rhone) Humber or Thames, the poor rivulet loseth her name: it is carried and recarried with the new associate; it beareth no sway."

The inequalities inherent within the marriage contract inevitably created a fertile breeding ground for servility, and while More was keen to uphold orthodoxy and traditionalism in her vision of a utopian society, this essay is sharply critical of the state of marriage. As a self-styled guardian of the nation's morals, More believed the holy state of matrimony to be the ideal, (though this was obviously not the case for *every* woman, as neither More nor her sisters married). The arguments More and Wollstonecraft were intent on pressing, however, were that educated, virtuous women had a tremendous potential for influence, on their husbands, their children, and indeed all those within their home sphere. More was keen to emphasize the extent to which the female sex had become blinded to the means wherewith they were kept in subjection:

A multitude of fine fresh young, slaves are annually imported at the age of seventeen or eighteen; or, according to the phrase of the despot, *they come out.* This despot so completely takes them in as to make these lovely young creatures believe that the assigned period at which they lose the gaiety and independence of their former free life is, in fact, the day of the emancipation.

I come now to the question of *impolicy.* This white slavery, like the black, is evidently an injury to fair and lawful commerce, for the time spent in training and overworking these fair slaves might be better employed in promoting the more profitable articles of health, beauty, simplicity, modesty, and industry, articles which many think would fetch a higher price, and by which traffic, both the slave and the slave-owner would be mutually benefited.

Many of these elderly female slaves excuse their constant attendance in the public markets, (for it is thought that, at a certain age, they might be emancipated if they wished it,) by asserting the necessity of their attendance, till their daughters are disposed of . . .[52]

The younger slaves are condemned to violent bodily labour, from midnight to sunrise. For this public service they are many years preparing by means of a severe drill under a great variety and succession of posture-masters.[53]

Hole points to "her profound distaste for young men who had become accustomed to 'the voluptuous ease, refined luxuries, soft accommodations, obsequious attendance, and all the unrestrained indulgences' of the world of fashion . . . For such a man, marriage may be 'little more than a selfish stratagem to reconcile health with pleasure.' . . . A wife cannot hope, and should not seek, to gratify within marriage the passions which such men had been used to indulging." More argues that modern marriage and its emphasis on indulgent pleasure, while outwardly offering women a semblance of security, quickly degenerated into an unequal relationship with one side holding the reins of power. Where there was not a mutual intellectual attraction, the relationships often became prosaic and unrewarding.

While it is possible to read these passages "without inferring in them a sexual connotation,"[54] it has to be noted that More's overt sexual innuendo is at extreme odds with her usual writing style of rectitude and decorum. Reference to "the violent bodily labour, from midnight to sunrise" demanded of the younger slaves may well have raised a few eyebrows among her contemporaries.

The argument, however, was unequivocal: if women were to rise above the role of sexual plaything, which inevitably led to a subjective state, the need was to rise somewhat in the scale of existence, seize the high moral ground, reinstate a sound sense of propriety and Christian morality, and effectively lead the nation from within that powerbase of "home." More sets out clearly in this essay the byzantine manner by which the freedom of half the nation's population had been destroyed. Disenfranchising women of their sacred duty, as caretakers of the nation's morals, was a profound injustice, and one that she intends to redress.

More concludes her powerful expose:

From all the above causes it is evident, that the White Slave Trade has increased, is increasing, and ought to be diminished.

'Till, therefore, there be some hope that a complete abolition may be effected, the following regulations are humbly proposed.

Regulation I That no slave be allowed to spend more than three hours in preparing her chains, beads, feathers, and other implements for the nightly labour.

II That no slave be allowed to paint her person of more than two colours for any market whatever.

III That each slave be allowed at least sufficient covering for the purposes of delicacy, if not for those of health and comfort.

IV That *no little* slave be compelled to destroy her shape, and ruin her health, by being fastened to different instruments of torture, for the sake of extracting sweet sounds, till some time after she can walk alone; and that in her subsequent progress she be not obliged to sit or stand at it more than half her waking hours.

V That no slave be put under more than four posture masters, in order to teach her such attitudes and exercises as shall enable her to fetch more money in the markets.

VI That no slave be carried to more than three markets on the same night.

VII That no trader be allowed to press more slaves into one *hold* than three times as many as it will contain.

VIII That the same regard to comfort which has led the black factor to allow the African Slaves a ton to a man, be extended to the white slaves, who shall not be allowed less than one chair to five slaves.

IX That no white slave *driver*, or horses, be allowed to stand in the street more than five hours in a dry night, or four in a rainy one.

X That every elderly female slave as soon as her youngest grand-child is fairly disposed of, be permitted to retire from her more public labours without any fine or loss of character, or any other punishment from the despot.

To conclude, the BLACK SLAVE TRADE has been taken up by its opposers, not only on the ground of *inhumanity* and *impolicy*, but that of *RELIGION* also. On the two first points alone have we ventured to examine the question of the WHITE SLAVE TRADE. It would be a folly to enquire into it on this last principle, it *can* admit of no such discussion, as in this view it could not stand its ground for a single moment; for if that principle were allowed to operate, mitigations, nearly approaching to abolition, must inevitably and immediately take place. THE END.[55]

Provocative satire would be the most likely term to describe the tenor of this final onslaught; but the seriousness of its intent is marked by its "religious" intimation. In the conclusion, she identifies the tri-une nature of the attack on black slavery: inhumanity, impolicy, and religion (a trinity of sorts). When it comes to the question of female slavery, its utter anathamization to Christ's Christianity, she believes, is expiatory.

The tenth regulation followed by its concluding postulate leads me to suggest that although More asserts "it would be a folly to enquire into it on this last principle," (religion), she has probably preempted the need to do that by linking it closely with religious edict. Following a suggested "trinity" association, might More now be covertly linking *her* decree with those divine commands, the Ten Commandments?

More's conclusion reflects the all-encompassing nature of her opposition to the grotesque practice of one human being effectively owning another, be it black slave or white wife. Inhumanity and impolicy mark this trafficking in human lives, but when viewed through the principle of religion, these acts are anathema and could not be tolerated "for a single moment." The primary and fundamental source, which makes her argument unassailable is religion. If a true spirit of religion were active and functioning within the collective heart of the nation, the mitigating circumstances surrounding white female slavery, as well as black serfdom, would be obliterated. This work may, as Hole suggests, be lighter than some of her other works, but its strategic delivery makes it a powerful text.

The White Slave Trade was published in a rather insignificant, provincial journal in 1805, *The Weekly Entertainer; or agreeable and instructive repository*, and while one may wonder at its readership, More possibly hoped it would not be those of her own circle. This journal, aimed at the male rather than the female reader, would have been an ideal vehicle through which to highlight the woman question on the back of the antislavery movement. It also witnesses a shift from More's earlier social and cultural reforming initiatives toward her application of religious principles to political reform.

The effectiveness of these women authors' reforming initiatives will be judged as the argument progresses; what is already becoming apparent is their literary agility in pressing humanitarian arguments that connected female servitude with black slavery issues. Through an agency of moral reform, they attacked irreligious attitudes that they associated with the masculine and public world, contrasting these with the sympathy and benevolence at the heart of that private home space.

Langford's argument that "sensibility's galvanizing of public opinion was fundamental to the remarkable legislative initiatives aimed at humanitarian reform during the last third of the eighteenth-century"[56] highlights the potential for women reformers who identified a heightened state of consciousness as the chief conduit of moral reform. The spiritual and cultural implications for women resulting from this perspective will be closely examined.

Bury the Woman in the Citizen

Stanton's arguments witness the merging of abolition and suffrage debate. Summing up the years from 1840 to 1866, she described herself and Anthony as "students 'in the school of anti-slavery,' who learned there the lessons of human rights."[57] Ann Gordon, in the introduction to *Selected Papers of Elizabeth Cady Stanton and Susan B. Anthony* identifies that through their interest in reform they effectively "built a new woman's rights movement on the ideas, skills, and personnel of the older antislavery movement, and established themselves as valuable contributors to their own cause and to the crusade against slavery."[58]

The year 1866 witnessed the launching of what Frederick Douglass[59] called "the good ship Equal Rights Association,"[60] and this proved to be a pivotal moment in the lives of Stanton, Anthony, and indeed, the movement as a whole. Merging the interests of subjugated women with black slaves, activists agreed, at the Eleventh National Woman's Rights Convention, in New York City in May to "bury the woman in the citizen, and our organization in that of the American Equal Rights Association"; further, they resolved to "secure Equal Rights to all American citizens, especially the right of suffrage, irrespective of race, color or sex."[61] Effectively, this move was to grant women the right to vote, along with white and black men, in addition to granting the right to set the radical political agenda.

The pursuance of justice and common humanity extended to all mankind was quintessential to the cause Stanton embraced. Part of a letter she wrote to Elizabeth J. Neall from Johnstown on November 26, 1841, evidences this: "If the true sentiments of an author appear in his works then will my work ever breathe love & justice equality for woman."[62]

Antebellum American consciousness, already sensitive to the political configuration of abolitionism, was to receive a rude awakening at the hands of its female reformers. Enjoined by the Bible to be silent, their emergence onto the public and political platform as campaigners for human rights brought them into conflict with political leaders of the day. Stanton was effectively involved in legal reform; Gordon suggests that "by 1848 she had transformed the antislavery conflict about individual responsibility and moral equality into a legal claim that women were endowed with the same natural rights as men, deserved equal protection of their individual liberty, and should organize themselves to secure their rights in the laws and institutions of the land."[63]

A letter written from York, on August 3, 1840, to Stanton's cousin, Gerrit Smith, usefully introduces her perspective:

We hear that in America you abolitionists are sad & depressed, there are so many clouds darkening your horizon & I wonder not. The thought that three millions of our fellow beings and country men groan in bondage & the day of their freedom yet uncertain (though it will surely come) is enough to sadden any heart. Would that you were here you would find much to cheer you. Mr Birney, Mr Scoble, Henry & myself are going through all the principal towns in the Kingdom. These three gentlemen lecture almost every evening—horrifying the British public with the enormities of our slavery system. Loud cries of shame! shame! fill the House whenever the negro pew is mentioned, & the bursts of indignation that follow some of Henry's graphic descriptions are music to an antislavery ear. We are kindly & warmly received everywhere, we find it is no disgrace to be an abolitionist in England, but requires some moral courage not to be one, as many of our eloquent clergy have proved . . . Night after night we hear many of the British clergy of all sects, declare most solemnly that no American clergyman who is not an abolitionist in America both in theory & practice, shall ever enter their pulpits again.[64]

That the letter was written on her honeymoon, and while visiting York contributes to its local interest. The depth and scale of the slavery problem are apparent, but Stanton clearly feels a certain euphoria at their welcome in England, noting even that it required "moral courage" *not* to be an abolitionist in this climate. She points to the racial segregation in American churches as a key issue in the mind of British people, but the overall impression of the letter is that her cousin should take courage, both from the abolition progress made in Britain, and the warm support of its people.

Six months later, Stanton was writing to Elizabeth J. Neall, whose Quaker family were distinguished for their contributions to abolition. Neall was a delegate of Philadelphia's Female Anti-Slavery Society, and on the point of marriage to John Gay; Stanton's letter gives further evidence of the concerns uppermost in her mind. She explains that her visit to England has been of much benefit to the women there, who are now forming societies to aid the American suffrage movement: "I found many many women fully & painfully convinced of our present degradation as women," she writes. "They assemble once a week to get & impart what information they can on the subject of slavery." She continued, "I read an article of John G's in the 'friend of man' about the convention. I am sorry he is not right on the woman question. You must never say yea Lizzy until he renounces all divine right to govern you or decide in all cases where you differ, dear me! what a mighty shadow some of Paul's private opinions have afforded, under which all the 'Lords of Creation' may shelter their cruelties & wrongs towards woman & make injustice a divine command."[65]

This letter, sharply critical of marriage laws as they related to women, also exposes her dissenting religious arguments on the subject. At the time of writing, Stanton had been married for six months, but she took what must in that period have seemed a radical stance, insisting the word "obey" be removed from her own marriage ceremony. She explained, "I obstinately refused to obey one with whom I supposed I was entering into an equal relation."[66]

Liberation Theology

Stanton's letters are a powerful indicator of her political and religious perspectives, her right to be a free and independent thinker: a letter to Elizabeth Pease, in February 1842, reinforces her contempt for the hierarchical "divine right" of a husband. Stanton is clearly a woman intent on making her own decisions without interference or deference. Though the theme of the letter is undoubtedly antislavery, its keynote is her admiration for the man, William Lloyd Garrison: "He is a great reformer an honest, upright man, ever ready to sacrifice present interest to stern principle, & having no fear of man. I have full confidence in him, he would be Garrison & no one else the world over."

Bearing in mind this is a man at severe odds with her husband, and her overt praise could be considered somewhat impolitic. She continues the letter in equally glowing terms:

> Most men will compromise a little sometimes, for policy, as they miscall dishonesty, but Garrison not a hairs breadth where principle is involved. What a noble exhibition of his character, we had at the London Convention . . . Being the champion of antislavery in this country he would have undoubtedly received more attention & had more influence in the Convention than any other delegate—he knew that, & yet single & alone he dared (by refusing to take his seat) to say to that august assembly, you have made a false decision, & I shall take no lot nor part with you so long as you withold justice from my friends.[67] He is an advocate of "Human Rights" not black man's merely. His religious opinions are summed up in Christ's sermon on the mount & I believe he tries to obey those plain commands in all his dealings with the world . . . Would that people were as willing to take Christ's commands literally, as they are the figurative language of Paul. By telling you what I love in Garrison you may see wherein I sympathize with his party.[68]

Stanton clearly held Garrison in high regard, and perhaps writing of him in such glowing terms in a private letter may not have seemed too provocative, until that is, it has been contextualized. The letter is included because it clearly evidences that her own opinions supersede any sense of deference to her husband. William Lloyd Garrison was a man totally at odds with Henry B. Stanton. Their unresolved dispute was a longstanding one, based on irreconcilable differences with regard to political involvement in the antislavery movement.

Henry Stanton believed that only by forcing political parties to make an issue of slavery could it be addressed and abolished. Garrison totally opposed this proposition, believing that abolitionists should refuse to take any part in a political system corrupted by slavery. In 1840, while Henry Stanton was in the midst of founding the Liberty party, Garrison went so far as to publicly denounce him. This was no friendly dispute, and for Elizabeth Cady Stanton to heap such praise upon a man who had publicly condemned her husband was unusual to the extreme.

The key to understanding her outspoken appreciation and support of Garrison's views I believe, however, to be in those two words "Human Rights." This issue, wider than abolition alone, was a critical one to Stanton. Christ's message of justice and mercy for humanity was inherent in the practical Christianity proposed by Stanton, and in Garrison she recognized a kindred spirit.

The feeling must have been mutual, as at the invitation of Garrison, Stanton addressed the American Anti-slavery Society. The text was printed in the *National Anti-Slavery Standard* ensuring a wide readership:

This is generally known as the platform of one idea-that is negro slavery. In a certain sense this may be true, but the most casual observation of this whole anti-slavery movement, of your lives, conventions, public speeches and journals, shows this one idea to be a great humanitarian one. The motto of your leading organ, "The world is my country and all mankind my countrymen," proclaims the magnitude and universality of this one idea, which takes in the whole human family, irrespective of nation, color, caste or sex, with all their interests, temporal and spiritual—a question of religion, philanthropy, political economy, commerce, education and social life, on which depends the very existence of this republic, of the state, of the family, the sacredness of the lives and property of Northern freemen, the holiness of the marriage relation, and the perpetuity of the Christian religion. Such are the various phases of the question you are wont to debate in your conventions. They all grow out of and legitimately belong to that *so-called* petty, insignificant, annoying subject, which thrusts up its head everywhere in Church and State—the "eternal nigger." But in settling the question of the negro's rights, we find out the exact limits of our own . . . The health of the body politic depends on the sound condition of every member. Let but the finest nerve or weakest muscle be diseased, and the whole man suffers; just so the humblest and most ignorant citizen cannot be denied his rights without deranging the whole system of government.[69]

No temerity here, then; this powerful proclamation that proposes the overthrow of "negro slavery" reads like an amended American Declaration of Independence. This was an argument no *thinking* person could have failed to grasp, its political and religious opinion supported by sound logic: "Where no individual in a community is denied his rights, the mass are the more perfectly protected in theirs." She carefully connects the rights of women with black slaves in a rhetorical battle plan aimed at decimating a corrupt economy. Highlighting the pernicious nature and inhumanity at the heart of this despotism, she concludes, "This one act has, in its consequences, convulsed this Union. It has corrupted our churches, our politics, our press . . . yes, beneath the flag of freedom, Liberty has crouched in fear."[70]

This abolition discourse has an ethos of authority, reflecting the urgency of a progressive thinker. The American dream, heretofore imbricated with the belief system of the Pilgrim fathers, men who strove to establish a nation in true freedom, had been forfeited through greed and materialism: liberty, the emblem of their once great nation now "crouched in fear." The degradation resulting from the immorality and inhumanity of slavery, she suggests, has purged their land of its cultural, social, and spiritual heritage. All the manifestations of a sovereign state, the church, government, and press, repressed and corrupted, and Stanton brings sharply into focus the painful dismantling of its Puritan ethics. "In spite of noble words, deeds of thirty years of protest, prayers and preaching," she argues, "slavery still lives, the negro toils on in his weary bondage; his chains have not yet melted in the intense heat of the sun of righteousness."[71]

Stanton widens her attack on what she terms this "dangerous miasma of slavery"[72] with a resolute precision: "The mission of this Radical Anti-Slavery Movement is not to the African slave alone, but to the slaves of custom, creed and sex, as well." With this in mind, she brings the reader face-to-face with the consequences of subjection and servitude:

It was thought a small matter to kidnap a black man in Africa, and set him to work in the rice swamps of Georgia; but when we look at the panorama of horrors that followed that event, at all the statute laws that were enacted to make that act legal, at the perversion of man's moral sense and innate love of justice in being compelled to defend such laws; when we consider the long, hard tussle we have witnessed here for near a century between the spirit of Liberty and Slavery, we may in some measure, appreciate the magnitude of the wrong done to that one lone, friendless negro, who, under the cover of darkness and star-spangled banner, was stolen from his African hut and lodged in the hold of the American slaver.[73]

This carefully worded persuasive passage identifies the scale of immorality resulting from this "small matter" of a "lone" abduction; and Stanton is keen to portray how, just like the diseased state earlier referred to, it spread, leading to an extensive perversion of the puritan sentiment. It displays with a poignant potency, the consequences for the perpetrators of the crime, as well as the disenfranchised.

Stanton then notably links female servitude and black slavery with a condemnatory: "To you, white man, the world throws wide her gates; the way is clear to wealth, to fame, to glory, to renown; the high places of independence and honor and trust are yours; all your efforts are praised and encouraged, all your successes are welcomed with loud hurrahs and cheers; but the black man and woman are born to shame."[74] She goes on to argue that while "noble men" may have "eloquently and earnestly . . . denounced slavery," this "privileged class can never conceive the feelings of those who are born to contempt, to inferiority, to degradation. Herein," she says, "is woman more fully identified with the slave than man can possibly be . . . She early learns the misfortune of being born an heir to the crown of thorns, to martyrdom, to womanhood."[75]

Stanton's enthusiasm for her cause is palpable; not only does she identify her sex with martyrdom, but there is clear affiliation with the sufferings of Christ Jesus. Indeed, religious argument now supersedes the political as the suffragist proceeds to attack contemporary patriarchal religious argument. To a clergyman who suggests "in no country in the world does woman hold so high a position as here!" she replies, "Why, sir, you must be very ignorant, or very false." She continues:

Are not nearly two millions of native-born American women, at this very hour, doomed to the foulest slavery that angels ever wept to witness? Are they not doubly damned as immortal beasts of burden in the field, and sad mothers of a most accursed race? Are they not raised for the express purposes of lust? Are they not chained and driven in the slave-coffle at the crack of the whip of an unfeeling driver? Are they not sold on the auction-block? Are they not exposed naked to the coarse jests and voluptuous gaze of brutal men? Are they not trained up in ignorance of all laws, both human and divine, and denied the right to read the Bible? . . . And these are the daughters and sisters of the first men in the Southern States? Think of fathers and brothers selling their own flesh on the auction-block, exposing beautiful women of refinement and education in a New Orleans market, and selling them, body and soul, to the absolute will of the highest bidder. And this is the condition of woman in republican, Christian America, and priests dare look me in the face and tell me that for blessings such as these my heart should go out in thankfulness![76]

Stanton is an able rhetorician and this public diatribe registers an unbridled passion. It is reminiscent of More's "White Slave Trade" without the satire, and because of that, I imagine it would have attracted an angry response from the pulpit. This is more than an argument for women's rights; it hints at the religious position Stanton will adopt as her career progresses. Seizing the high moral and spiritual ground, she continues, "No, proud priest, you may encase your soul in holy robes, and hide your manhood in a pulpit, and, like the Pharisee of old, turn your face away from the sufferings of your race; but I am a Christian—a follower of Jesus—and 'whatsoever is done unto one of the least of these my sisters is done also unto me.'"

Stanton displays a powerful religious authority in the tone of her argument, and her combative language is rather masculine in style, but there is an unmistakable feminine sensibility, which contributes to the argument that woman's heightened state of consciousness allows communion with her God. She writes, "Though . . . the whole English language, [be] as dead to me as Egyptian hieroglyphics, yet can I still talk with God."[77] Disputing further the need of priestly intercession she continues, "I sometimes feel the pulsations of the great heart of God. He comes to me in all his works; I have worshipped him in the glorious sun, and moon, and stars, and laved [*sic*] my soul in their silent majesty and beauty. I have asked the everlasting hills, that in their upward yearnings seem to touch the heavens, if I, an immortal being, though clothed in womanhood, was made for the vile purposes to which proud Saxon man has doomed me, and in solemn chorus they all chanted NO!"[78]

Literary landscape imagery more usually associates the feminine with valleys and green pastures indicating a regulated and more lowly position; mountains and high peaks are portrayed as majestic, imposing masculine representations.[79] It is interesting, therefore, to witness

Stanton identifying female authority through lofty landscape imagery, and indeed this will become more obvious as her edict draws to a close. Stanton has an amazing ability to shift writing style quickly and apparently effortlessly, without losing her footing; this work reads like a literary collage, so adept is she at juxtaposing key issues.

The eight pages that make up this address register a diverse linguistic approach; political debate sits beside a language of feeling and sympathy, rational criticism mingles with romantic idealism, and theological argument is juxtaposed with suffrage rhetoric.

"I have asked," said Stanton—and the reader can now feel the depth of her entreaty—"this bleeding heart, so full of love to God and man, so generous and self-sacrificing, ever longing for the pure, the holy, the divine, if this graceful form, this soft and tender flesh was made but to crawl and shiver in the cold, foul embrace of Southern tyrants, and, in stifled sobs, it answered, No!" In a tone of spurious indebtedness she continues, "Thank you, oh Christian priests, meekly I will take your insults, taunts and sneers. To you my gratitude is due for all the *peculiar blessings* of slavery, for you have had the morals of this nation in your keeping. Behold the depths into which you have plunged me—the bottomless pit of human misery! But perchance your head grows dizzy to look down so far, and your heart faints to see what torture I can bear! It is enough!"

The peaks and troughs now register a gender divide more in keeping with Stanton's argument, the "bottomless pit" is replaced by the "holy mounts": "I rejoice," she writes, "that it has been given to woman to drink the very dregs of human wretchedness and woe. For now, by an eternal law of matter and of mind, when the reaction comes, upward and upward, and still upward, she shall rise. Behold how far above your priestly robes, your bloody altars, your foul incense, your steepled synagogues, she shall stand secure on holy mounts, mid clouds of dazzling radiance, to which in your gross vision, you shall not dare even to lift your eyes."[80]

This elaborate and provocative syntax concludes with a gleeful derision. The editor's footnote points out, "An additional paragraph in the manuscript reveals that behind 'our fans & banjo's,' the woman and the black man 'laugh at least' at how poorly the white man uses his freedom, 'at his awkward somersets in church & state,' and his failure 'in all the acts of war & government & social life.'"[81]

The foregoing gives the merest glimpse of the vigorous efforts on behalf of human rights that were waged by Stanton in the mid-nineteenth century. Her outspoken antislavery rhetoric inevitably contributed toward the American abolition movement. The propagating of social, civil, and religious codes that restored freedom to the black slave and equality to women would leave in its wake a more ethical and refined civilization. What also becomes apparent, however, is the burgeoning of attempts at spiritual reform allied to her demand for women's equality.

CONCLUSION

Legally to abolish unpaid servitude in the United States was hard, but the abolition of mental slavery is a more difficult task . . . The rights of man were vindicated in a single section and on the lowest plane of human life, when African slavery was abolished in our land. That was only prophetic of further steps towards the banishment of a world-wide slavery, found on higher planes of existence and under more subtle and depraving forms.

—Mary Baker Eddy, *Science and Health with Key to the Scriptures*

William Wilberforce identified women as "the medium of our intercourse with the heavenly world the faithful repositories of the religious principle,"[82] and in this chapter, I have been keen to identify how this perception of the feminine was promoted.

Across a diversity of literary genres, these writers emphasized the value and superiority of the virtuous feminine nature and the power of the home as a reformatory space. Historians suggest that this period witnessed a feminization of religion resulting in the maternal achieving an almost sanctified status.[83] The cult of sensibility, identified by Barker-Benfield as "a distinct world view infused with religious values and claiming to reform a fallen population by conversion,"[84] was in part responsible for this phenomenon.

The key to understanding how these women were able to impress their abolition views on a grand scale is to understand the nature of the religious revival taking place on both sides of the Atlantic, and I have been keen to identify how this atmosphere was responsible for the considerable opportunities for women to transcend rigid gender divisions of earlier periods.

Harnessing this developing trend of social consciousness and communal responsibility, the ethics of benevolence gained momentum. Antislavery rhetoric had become a trope permeated by several campaigns, not least of these being "the woman question." Parliamentary reform, civil rights, and liberties were all implicated within this language of moral indignation. The range of the authors literary exertions ensured a wide readership that was instrumental in creating an environment in which the message of reform could flourish, and, as I have identified, contributed toward a moral transformation of society

In the next chapter, I will explore how More, Wollstonecraft, Stanton, and Eddy sought to build upon their growing public fame *and* notoriety. I will focus on how they sought to lift the heavy hand of oppression from women, asking, along with Mary Astell, "*If all Men are born free,* how is it that all Women are born slaves?"[85]

Chapter 3

Education, Sensibility, and Religion

Intelligent Intuitivism, Fixed Principles, and a First Cause

O fairest of creation, last and best of all God's works.

—John Milton, *Paradise Lost*

Woman! by Heav'ns the very Name's a Crime,
Enough to blast, and to debauch my Rhime.
Sure Heav'n it self (intranc't) like Adam lay,
Or else some banish'd Fiend usurp't the sway
When Eve was form'd; and with her, usher'd in
Plagues, Woes, and Death, and a new World of Sin.
The fatal Rib was crooked and unev'n,
from whence they have their Crab-like Nature giv'n;
Averse to all the Laws of Man, and Heav'n.
O Lucifer, thy Regions had been thin,
Were't not for Womans propagating Sin.

—Robert Gould, "Love Given O're"

When Church and State combine, no protest under chains can set
the captive free. To my mind, the matter calls not only for discussion,
but for outspoken rebellion.

—E. C. Stanton, *The Selected Papers of Elizabeth Cady Stanton*
and Susan B. Anthony

The historical religious ranking of women will be visibly readjusted in this chapter.

Stimulating and enhancing the reforming initiative set in motion through abolition and suffrage discourse, our authors now seek to devolve a spiritual and sanctified status upon the feminine. At the heart of the argument is a demand for a spiritual sensibility, a religious perspective that valued and empowered women as important contributors to the reformation of male manners. This chapter holds the key to what went before and what is to follow, in that it seeks to identify the literary means of empowering those quintessentially religious sentiments that form the essence of true femininity.

Commonly held perceptions of womanhood swung between representations of the spiritual Mary and the sinning Eve.[1] The cult of sensibility could be said to mirror this perception, and for the purpose of exalting pure femininity, the sharp distinction made between sensibility and its counterfeit representation will be examined. The "fixed principle" or fundamental truth upon which More's poem *Sensibility* (1782) was structured acts as a touchstone to the reformatory arguments of this chapter.

FIXED PRINCIPLES

The image of God implanted in our nature is now more rapidly expanding; and, as it opens, liberty with maternal wing seems to be soaring to regions far above vulgar annoyance, promising to shelter all mankind.

—Mary Wollstonecraft, *A View*

Wollstonecraft persistently located her arguments within a religious framework. Literary criticism of her works through the years has tended toward analysis of her radical political and feminist ideals, overlooking the fundamental religious fervor that permeates her writing.

The first chapter of *Vindication* argues succinctly for a need to get back to "first principles." Exposing her radical religious perspectives she argues that the idea of woman being created *for* man "must be allowed to fall to the ground . . . Supposing woman to have been formed only to please, and be subject to man, the conclusion is just, she ought to sacrifice every other consideration to render herself agreeable to him." Wollstonecraft expresses doubts that a Supreme Being could have allowed so debasing a design: "But, if, as I think, may be demonstrated, the purposes, of even this life, viewing the whole, [be] subverted by practical rules built upon this ignoble base, I may be allowed to doubt whether woman were created for man: and, though the cry of irreligion, or even atheism, be raised against me, I will simply declare, that were an angel from heaven to tell me that Moses's beautiful, poetical cosmogony, and the account of the fall of man, were literally true, I could not believe what my reason told me was derogatory to the character of the Supreme Being."[2]

Wollstonecraft is clearly not an atheist; she is a woman intent on exposing what she considers to be religious subversion, blind and bigoted beliefs that she sees as responsible for the subjugation of women. The "blind submission" imposed upon the clergy, she argues, cramps their opportunities of improvement, declaring boldly, "I build my belief on the perfection of God."[3] Wollstonecraft's dissenting doctrinal arguments are fundamental to her exposition of the corruptions of femininity. Her texts, while identifying the potential for spiritually minded women, nevertheless sharply criticize contemporary female behavior and the way woman is publicly portrayed.

INTELLIGENT INTUITIVISM

Wollstonecraft argued for the advantages of equal educational opportunities, the cultivation of the arts *and* sciences: "It is obviously the cultivation of these alone, emphatically termed the arts of peace, that can turn the sword into a ploughshare . . . Ignorant people, when they appear to reflect, exercise their imagination more than their understanding: indulging reveries, instead of pursuing a train of thinking; and thus grow romantic, like the croisaders; or like women, who are commonly idle and restless."[4]

Already, Wollstonecraft has characterized female nature in markedly oppositional terms: the sheltering wing of maternalism, that wing that promises to shelter *all* mankind, has powerful connotations in terms of female protective powers. "Wings," metaphorically speaking, have sheltering properties and also symbolize a state of soaring ascendancy. It is important to note, however, that it is "the image of God implanted in our nature" that accredits this portrayal. The second model of womanhood represents a highly materialistic version: ignorant revelers, idle and restless.

Clearly, Wollstonecraft is as critical of women as she is of the oppressive and restrictive system of subjugation: education she considers to be the route that will effectively lead women out of their submissive and dependent states toward a dignified equal social status. In *Thoughts on the Education of Daughters*, a chapter titled "Unfortunate Situation of Females, Fashionably Educated, and Left Without a

Fortune" paints a vivid picture of life's opportunities for women like herself:

> Few are the modes of earning a subsistence, and those very humiliating. Perhaps to be an humble companion to some rich old cousin, or what is still worse, to live with strangers, who are so intolerably tyrannical, that none of their own relations can bear to live with them, though they should even expect a fortune in reversion. It is impossible to enumerate the many hours of anguish such a person must spend . . . Painfully sensible of unkindness, she is alive to every thing, and many sarcasms reach her, which were perhaps directed another way. She is alone, shut out from equality and confidence, and the concealed anxiety impairs her constitution; for she must wear a cheerful face, or be dismissed. The being dependant [*sic*] on the caprice of a fellow-creature, though certainly very necessary in this state of discipline, is yet a very bitter corrective, which we would fain shrink from.[5]

This is a sharp denunciation of the life open to women who were not under the protection of either father or husband. "Humble" and "humiliating" were the states to which they were reduced; "tyrannical" was the regime they were forced to reside under, and "anguish" marked their subordinate state. This clearly autobiographical impression highlights the consternation of having to "live with strangers": a letter written to Jane Arden on December 20, 1778, reiterates, "There is no prospect of my quitting this place in a hurry, necessity not choice ties me to it, (not but that I ~~feel~~ receive the greatest civility from this family)—yet, I am detained here only by prudential motives, if I was to follow the best of my inclination I shod [*sic*] haste away.—You will not wonder at this,—when you consider I am among Strangers, far from all my former connexions."[6]

The anguish caused through dependency on "the caprice of a fellow-creature" clearly wears away at the sensibilities, as a further letter notes: "I have a heart too susceptible for my own peace . . . my health is ruined, my spirits broken, and I have a constant pain in my side that is daily gaining ground on me:—My head aches with holding it down . . . I am tired so good night."[7] These letters, while drawing attention to an extreme sensitivity also hint at the later tensions, reflected in her different literary tones.

TOWARD A CIVILIZATION FOUNDED ON REASON AND MORALITY

It is time to effect a revolution in female manners—time to restore to them their lost dignity—and make them, as a part of the human species, labour by reforming themselves to reform the world.

—Mary Wollstonecraft, *A Vindication of the Rights of Woman*

"It is very absurd to see a woman, whose brow time has marked with wrinkles, aping the manners of a girl in her teens," writes Wollstonecraft in *Thoughts on the Education of Daughters*. "If the understanding is not exercised, the memory will be employed to little purpose." She goes on:

> Girls learn something of music, drawing, and geography; but they do not know enough to engage their attention, and render it an employment of the mind. If they can play over a few tunes to their acquaintance, and have a drawing or two (half done by the master) to hang up in their rooms, they imagine themselves artists for the rest of their lives. It is not the being able to execute a trifling landscape, or any thing of the kind, that is of consequence-These are at best but trifles, and the foolish, indiscriminate praises which are bestowed on them only produce vanity . . . Whatever tends to make a person in some measure independent of the senses, is a prop to virtue . . . attention to moral duties leads to piety.[8]

Wollstonecraft endeavored to distinguish with clarity in her writing the difference between trifling and flimsy materialism and its substantial, significant opposite. Keenly aware of the potential damage to women as the result of an exaggerated "sensibility," she was quick to condemn the practice of bestowing "indiscriminate" and unearned praise.

Men had for centuries portrayed woman as weak and ineffectual and the production and praise of inferior work did not result in the exercising of their faculties, but simply assisted in keeping them in a subservient and dependent state. This counterfeit expression of sensibility led to vice and disadvantage: it was only through a pursuit of excellence, Wollstonecraft considered, that a woman could seize some measure of independence, both in her life and from the senses. The pursuit of an intelligent intuitivism would release them from enslavement to the senses.

A reasoned understanding resulting from a sound education was essential if women were to demonstrate moral excellence and regain their lost dignity. "Dancing and elegance of manners are very pleasing," she writes, "if too great a stress is not laid on them. These acquirements catch the senses, and open the way to the heart; but unsupported by solid good qualities, their reign is short."[9]

Train Up a Child

The Biblical admonition to "train up a child in the way he should go: and when he is old, he will not depart from it"[10] appears to underlie the method of reform pressed by each author.

Wollstonecraft transcribed *Elements of Morality* (1790) from German into English and through "this little work" written by C. G. Salzmann, was able to promote her own opinions regarding the education of children:

> This little Work [fell accidentally] into my hands, when I began to learn German, and, merely as an exercise in that language, I attempted to translate it; but, as I proceeded, I was pleased to find that chance had thrown in my way a very rational book, and that the writer coincided with me in opinion respecting the method which ought to be pursued to form the heart and temper, or, in other words, to inculcate the first principles of morality . . . I term it a translation, though I do not pretend to assert that it is a literal one; on the contrary, beside making it an English story, I have made [some additions, and] altered many parts of it, not only to give it the spirit of an original, but to avoid introducing any German customs or local opinions . . . I wished to insinuate a taste for domestic pleasures into the hearts of both parents and children.[11]

That social reform could only be effected through the equal educational opportunities of its children Wollstonecraft understood, as she proceeded to "inculcate the first principles of morality" through texts that drew pictures from real life. Addressing parents, she claims, "The design of this Book is to give birth to what we call a GOOD DISPOSITION in children . . . A good disposition is, in my opinion, a superior degree of knowledge: knowledge consists in being acquainted with the characteristics of things; but a good disposition is not confined to a bare acquaintance with their distinguishing characters, it extends to their intrinsic value, and the effects produced by them, to which affection or aversion is, at all times, necessarily attached."[12]

The text, through didactic argument, inculcates a desire for holiness: it exemplifies the family as the birthplace of a good disposition, emphasizing the supreme importance of family life in the reordering of society. The first principles of morality are secured on a bedrock of Christianity, and it is to the mother that the task of forming the heart and temper of her offspring is given:

> But where shall I find, asks the affectionate mother, a person who possesses sufficient abilities to instruct my children in this manner?— Respectable woman, since thou hast sufficient tenderness and sense to be anxious about the person to whom thou wishest to instruct the weighty charge of educating thy children, I approach thee with respect, and with pleasure offer thee my advice. The properest person to form the character of thy children, is thyself.
>
> Your sex has undeniably more tenderness than ours; the female voice is, in general, more persuasive and soft, and more easily insinuates itself into the hearts of children. They have a greater affection for [their mother, if she do not resign the office,] than for any other person in the world, and your vivacity and tenderness will enable you to give a degree of interest and familiarity to the tales, which a man who enters into the busy scenes of life will seldom be able to equal.
>
> To you does the pleasing task belong of forming their tempers, and giving them habits of virtue; for as the sight of your breast is a hint to you that you were destined to suckle your children, so is the consciousness of your abilities, and the domestic ties, which so firmly attach your children to you, hints from God, that the first formation of their character [belongs to] you.[13]

Salzmann and Wollstonecraft are adamant that the teaching of the finer principles was the mother's God-given responsibility. The onus for the acquisition of a virtuous soul was upon them. This heavenly assignment was their life mission, and the reader can feel the covert censure applied to those women who "resigned" their office. The gendered perspectives in this narrative are worthy of comment; as Wollstonecraft has made it clear that she took the liberty of altering parts of the original text, it is interesting that she chose to maintain the masculine persona. References to "your sex" could have been replaced by "our sex," or more anonymously "the female sex." She was in a unique position, however, translating the text to suit her perspectives, but hiding behind a masculine persona.

The translation of *Elements of Morality* set the stage for the reforming zeal of *Vindication*. This work was published two years later and though a didactic work, its genre was decidedly more political:

Vindication, while incorporating the characteristics of her previous publications, did not include moral tales or fictional narrative as a means of imparting its reforming message. This politically motivated polemic was precise, unequivocal and explicit in its unambiguous argument for women's rights, and while counseling the mother in *Vindication*, Wollstonecraft is careful to identify reciprocal benefits:

> fulfilling the duties of a mother, a woman with a sound constitution, may still keep her person scrupulously neat, and assist to maintain her family, if necessary, or by reading and conversations with both sexes, indiscriminately, improve her mind. For nature has so wisely ordered things, that did women suckle their children, they would preserve their own health, and there would be such an interval between the birth of each child, that we should seldom see a houseful of babes. And did they pursue a plan of conduct, and not waste their time in following the fashionable vagaries of dress, the management of their household and children need not shut them out from literature, [or] prevent their attaching themselves to a science, with that steady eye which strengthens the mind, or practising one of the fine arts that cultivate the taste.[14]

Her "plan of conduct" necessitated fulfilling the "natural" order of things. This order, however, was not at the *expense* of the woman, but rather contributed toward an enlarged understanding. It was "the idle bustle of morning trifling" that "drew women from their duty to render them insignificant" that attracted Wollstonecraft's most censorious criticism. The demand for accomplished womanhood is clearly outlined: "We shall not see women affectionate till more equality be established in society, till ranks are [confounded and women freed, neither shall we] see that dignified domestic happiness, the simple grandeur of which cannot be relished by ignorant or vitiated minds; nor will the important task of education ever be properly begun till the person of a woman is no longer preferred to her mind. For it would be as wise to expect corn from tares, or figs from thistles, as that a foolish ignorant woman should be a good mother."[15]

Wollstonecraft links her argument for productive womanhood with scriptural imagery; to expect corn or figs from tares and thistles is just as unlikely as that uneducated, uncultivated mothers should successfully nurture and sustain their offspring. The book of Proverbs cites a powerful portrayal of ideal womanhood: "Who can find a virtuous woman? for her price is far above rubies. The heart of her husband doth safely trust in her. She openeth her mouth with wisdom; She looketh well to the ways of her household; She considereth a field and buyeth it; She layeth her hands to the spindle; She stretcheth out her hand to the poor; Her children arise up, and call her blessed; her husband also, and he praiseth her."[16]

Here is introduced a vision of woman as vindicated from subjugation *through* her feminine attributes. Her virtue and wisdom[17] equip her as a domestic economist. Indeed, her benevolent nature renders her worth inestimable: while caring for the needs of her husband, children, and the poor, she is also portrayed as contributing to the household economy, buying and selling fields. Her status as an equal falls naturally to her as a consequence of her virtuous nature.

Subverted Femininity

Male critics were quick to condemn apparently liberal-minded women set on disrupting what they considered to be the *natural* order of things. Disputing suggestions of woman as of equal status to themselves they wrote to discredit a "subversive" female element. Richard Polwhele's[18] repressive quelling of "liberated" women usefully contextualizes contemporary opinion.

Polwhele contributed to traditional conservative publications of the day and was sharply critical of outspoken female authors. His esteem for Hannah More as an ideal feminine representative was notable and contrasted sharply with his opinion of Mary Wollstonecraft: "Miss Hannah More may justly be esteemed, as a character, in all points, diametrically opposite to Miss Wollstonecraft."[19]

His satirical poem *The Unsex'd Females* was aimed at readers of the *Anti-Jacobin Review* and the *Gentleman's Magazine*. The language used in this work appears patriarchal and imperialistic, representing the cultural perspective of a dominant masculine ideology. Its assumptions and conceptions constituted the required code of conduct for female behavior. Its tone privileges and champions the "softer charms" of the female. Applauding this "natural" perspective, Polwhele uses overtly aggressive and personally offensive rhetoric to portray the more liberal woman. Use of words such as "despising," "defiance," "vengeance," and "imperious" in the opening lines of the poem lends a bellicose and belligerent tone:

> Survey with me, what ne'er our fathers saw,
> A female band despising NATURE'S law,
> As 'proud defiance' flashes from their arms,
> And vengeance smothers all their softer charms,
> I shudder at the new unpictur'd scene,

> Where unsex'd woman vaunts her imperious mien;
> See Wollstonecraft, whom no decorum checks,
> Arise, the intrepid champion of her sex;
> O'er humbled man assert the sovereign claim

The second line invokes the fundamental principle upon which Polwhele's argument is to be structured: "Nature" is the grand basis of all laws human and divine; the woman who has no regard to nature, either in the decoration of her person, or the culture of her mind, will soon "walk after the flesh, in the lust of uncleanness, and despise government." The misogynistic stereotyping of the female character is breathtaking, but close reading of the narrative suggests a latent fear on the part of the writer. The supreme rule of a sovereign certainly suggests the necessary subservient humility of her subordinates. A powerful female milieu was therefore to be avoided at all costs. The intrepid championing of the rights of woman by Wollstonecraft was anathema to Polwhele and his contemporaries. His inclusion of other eminent female writers by name indicates his fear of the burgeoning effect the "call to the cause" might have on the female population:

> To the bold heights where glory beams, aspire,
> Blend mental energy with Passion's fire,
> Surpass their rivals in the powers of mind
> And vindicate the Rights of womankind.
> She spoke; and veteran BARBAULD caught the strain

This stanza highlights what I would suggest was the covert, but nevertheless very real fear in the mind of men like Polwhele; female aspirations would lead them to "heights" and "powers of mind" that could rival, surpass even, those of men. This attitude exposes the fears and weaknesses in a hierarchical belief system where superiority and subservience sit so uncomfortably alongside each other. It is clear from the foregoing that the cultural milieu of masculine monopoly needed to be penetrated if women were to seize any sense of authority.

A Culture of Sensibility: The Behavioral Pattern of the Protestant Ethic

While the cult of sensibility was a movement of influence largely associated with women, it is important to note that this did not prohibit masculine assimilation of its finer qualities; indeed, its refining and reforming potential was not lost on the male authors of the period who pressed its civilizing influence.[20]

The fundamental nature of this cult led to the enfranchisement of a religion of the heart. This "Protestant ethic," as it became known, was not confined to one creed, but rather embraced all faiths, its nucleus being the Christian belief of revealed religion. A personal, spiritual relationship between God, man, and nature was the focus of its ideological perspective. It defined itself against the practice of Deism, which relied on truths allied to human reasoning; indeed, *this* practice was antipathetical to sensibility's emphasis on the spiritual or transcendental qualities that promoted an ideology of feminized culture. The cult of sensibility argued against the coldly reasonable religion of the day as it sought to effect reform in society.[21]

The continuous struggle over the meanings and values of this cult is emphasized by Grant who contends, "Sensibility may be founded on the rock of moral sense, but the sentimental frequently becomes perilously close to foundering on the rocks of sensuality."[22] This argument, in effect, mirrored that which tried to portray woman as sensual and disruptive, and it was therefore of major importance to proponents of a spiritual sensibility to elucidate and validate its fixed principles. The metaphysical perspectives are sharply contrasted with its materialistic and sensual opposite in More's poem *Sensibility*, written in 1782, and described by Anne Stott as "an advocacy of the religion of the heart."[23]

> Sweet SENSIBILITY! Thou secret pow'r
> Who shed'st thy gifts upon the natal hour,
> Like fairy favours; art can never seize,
> Nor affectation catch thy pow'r to please:
> Thy subtle essence still eludes the chains
> Of definition, and defeats her pains.[24]

This stanza is a plenary exposition of the true nature of sensibility: this omniscient power, bequeathed only to the chosen, hidden from the world and defeating any attempts at explanation or circumscription, is a birth blessing and cannot be acquired by art or affectation. The tone of the narrative emulates the refined, cultured, and tender atmosphere that, More suggests, is at its heart. The promotion of woman as blest, as the receiver and presenter of blessings is implicit in More's discourse, as it enshrines the nature of the feminine as a divine benefactress. It holds within its discourse a secret promise that portends female equality on spiritual terms.

The thought is allowed to run on through the use of open couplets, and the pattern of the verse does not dominate the reading of the poem, giving the reader a flexible and inspirational modus operandi. Spiritual reflection, rather than human logic is appealed to, and these spiritual and moral qualities, invested by More in sensibility, could not be successfully "affected" by those proponents of a materialistic persuasion.

The aggrandizement of a quality so associated with the feminine held out tremendous potential for women to capitalize on its "secret pow'r" and reforming influence: power as a faculty so generally associated with the male. More's poem sanctions sensibility with an authority that supersedes the standards codified by gender, effectively inaugurating a *spiritual* hierarchy, and she identifies its intangibility through linking this "gift" with "fairy favours." These mythical creatures, portrayed as supernatural beings in possession of magical powers, were useful representations of this mystical quality. They also hint at those higher *spiritual* beings, those authentic divine messengers, also depicted in human form with wings: angels.

The importance of this stanza to the clarification of not only the meaning of sensibility, but also its redemptive significance to women, cannot be overstated. References to "secret pow'r," "natal hour," and "pains" clearly connect this "gift" closely with the maternal and motherhood, so the suggestion that this "subtle essence . . . defeats her pains" is a rather intriguing one; is More referring to the "pains" of childbirth? In light of the reference to "natal hour" this would seem a credible explanation. Genesis 3:16 confirms that God said to the woman (after she was beguiled by the serpent), "I will greatly multiply your pain in childbearing; in pain you shall bring forth children." Could More be suggesting then that this "secret pow'r" offers woman some sort of spiritual compensation? If so, she clearly sees sensibility as a powerful spiritual attribute, with tremendous redemptive potential:

> SWEET SENSIBILITY! Thou keen delight!
> Unprompted moral! sudden sense of right!
> Perception exquisite! fair virtue's seed!
> Thou quick precursor of the lib'ral deed!
> Thou hasty conscience! reason's blushing morn!
> Instinctive kindness e'er reflexion's born![25]

Sophisticated literary devices contribute to the rich assonantal effect; the alliteration and structural style add to an elaborate and

intricate linguistic strategy. The reader is struck by the prolific use
of exclamation marks in this stanza. Exclamation marks are used to
indicate words that represent strong, sudden cries and were used frequently and especially by women writers of the period. Could this
suggest an excess, or loss of control? I would suggest not; these typo-
graphical insignia reinforce More's use of ellipses, eliminating the
need for all but a few carefully chosen words.

More expounds the virtues that characterize sensibility: "Moral,"
"right," "exquisite," and its "instinctive" responsiveness toward
human suffering. The "reason" so commonly associated with the masculine is covertly criticized here: "Instinctive kindness" has responded
"e'er reflexion's born," the "lib'ral deed" being accomplished before
the "reasoned" thought has had time for ratiocination. Having already
emphasized the *power* inherent within this female phenomenon, the
subtext to this stanza includes a political emphasis. The binary nature
of words such as "right," "lib'ral," "conscience," and of course "blush-
ing morn" suggests an incorporation of political values and reflects a
politicizing of sensibility. The assumption, therefore, could be made
that sensibility is to become a springboard for political didacticism as
well as the restructuring of cultural and religious attitudes.

More continues by condemning the artifice so prevalent among
women in the higher echelons of eighteenth-century society, and
she does this in the manner of fashionable contemporary literary discourse. The next stanza parodies sensibility:

> To those who know thee not no words can paint,
> And those who know thee, know all words are faint!
> *She* does not feel thy pow'r who boasts thy flame,
> And rounds her every period with thy name,
> Nor she who vents her disproportion'd sighs
> With pining *Lesbia* when her sparrow dies.[26]

The duplicitous worldliness evidenced by women who were able to
operate their nerves by acts of will is roundly condemned by More.
The skillful engagement of affectation evidenced by a callous disregard
for humanity, while expressing an obsessive preoccupation with animals
was a key element of this feigned sensibility.[27] Phonemes are used to
good effect, as segments of stream of speech sounds, the final word
on each line indicating a more ponderous reflection, which, as already
noted, is the opposite of "instinctiveness." Having slowed her readers
through this syntactical strategy, she now gives them time to reflect
on the negative connotations inherent in these multifunctional words:

"paint," "faint," "flame," "name," "sighs," and "dies." The reader cannot fail to note their negative associations.

The artifice inherent in the "painted" face was cruelly addressed by Alexander Pope in *Epistle to a Lady* ("Chameleons who can paint in white or black"), and in *The Rape of the Lock* he refers to woman as a "painted vessel."[28] Fainting was a tactic frequently used to emphasize the delicacy of the female constitution, while the word flame could be linked with overt passion. Sighing was a wile to draw attention to the person, or as a result of boredom, and the damage to the cause of sensibility that this inappropriate female behavior caused, More is intent on addressing.

The next stanza reinforces an image of "constructed" femininity. With an idiosyncratic perceptiveness and hyperbolic sentiment, More deconstructs the feminine counterfeit:

> So exclamations, tender tones, fond tears,
> And all the graceful drapery FEELING wears;
> These are her garb, not her, they but express
> Her form, her semblance, her appropriate dress;
> And these fair marks, reluctant, I relate,
> These lovely symbols may be counterfeit.[29]

As in the previous stanza, the final word on each line is chosen with precision, so that the natural conclusion is "counterfeit." "Tears," "wears," "express," and "dress" all relate, or could be linked to affectation. The simulation of authenticity is obviously of deep concern to More. This stanza warns of the need to look beneath the surface. "Garb" is a covering; Elizabeth I, concerned that fashion could be used by the poor to emulate the style of the rich, warned of "the confusion of all places being great where the meanest are as richly apparelled as their betters."[30] The most avid consumers of fashion were the wives and daughters of men in the lower social orders, so impersonation or artifice, on both a physical as well as mental level, was clearly a point at issue. More argued for the recognition of sensibility as a spiritual phenomenon, warning against its material or counterfeit opposite. This representation was quintessential to the platform of reform purported by More.

More's analysis of social conditioning was shrewd, and her literary attempts to redress the balance witnessed her application of Christianity to social theory. Fiercely critical of immorality and insincerity in either sex, she threw contempt on the male who, "scorning life's low duties to attend / Writes odes on friendship / while he cheats his friend." Honesty and integrity were at the heart of her reforming ideal, but it was to women that she ultimately threw down the gauntlet. Addressing those women who "unreluctantly yielded themselves to be carried down the tide of popular practices," she wrote in the most stringent of terms. Vigilance against the wiles of evil and a life devoted to the glory of God was their whole duty, and their "noblest style and title" she exclaimed was "that of a Christian."[31]

The importance of More's poem to this chapter cannot be overstated; adroitly encapsulating the "sensibility" argument, its empowerment of woman emerges through a fundamental locating of her spiritual status as a birthright. The appropriation of an intuitive and inspirational consciousness to woman was an important step in the reforming initiative of these authors. The next stage was twofold: the dismantling of a patriarchally constructed femininity and the publication of didactic manuals aimed at the cultivation of female understanding.

Exoneration, Justification, and the Curbing of Female Imagination

Probably the most important and well known texts of Wollstonecraft and More were *A Vindication of the Rights of Woman* and *Strictures*, respectively. While suggesting that *Strictures* had perhaps more in common with *Thoughts on the Education of Daughters*, I will now examine the parallels and divergences between the two polemics. Mitzi Myers suggests that Wollstonecraft and More are united, despite their political differences, in "perceiving a society infected with fashionable corruption, [to which] both preach a militantly moral middle-class reform grounded in women's potentiality."[32]

Vindication, as well as being a didactic manual for women, argued for a change in the public perception of their role in society; it worked to penetrate a masculine cultural milieu, targeting texts that attempted to denigrate or vilify women and with clinical precision deconstructed their mischievous literary campaigns. Challenging a misuse of sensibility and promotion of passive collusion, Chapter V suggests, "The opinions speciously supported, in some modern publications on the female character and education, which have given the tone to most of the observations made, in a more cursory manner, on the sex, remain to be examined." She is dismissive of prejudiced male authors who have "artificially structured" and falsely characterized the nature of women. Rousseau's behavioral prescriptives for women are specifically targeted and challenged: "I shall begin with Rousseau," she suggests, "and give a sketch of his character of woman":

> Sophia, says Rousseau, should be as perfect a woman as Emilius is a man, and to render her so, it is necessary to examine the character which nature has given to the sex. He then proceeds to prove that woman ought to be weak and passive, because she has less bodily strength than man; and hence infers, that she was formed to please and to be subject to him; and that it is her duty to render herself *agreeable* to her master-this being the grand end of her existence. Still, however, to give a little mock dignity to lust, he insists that man should not exert his strength, but depend on the will of the woman, when he seeks for pleasure with her.[33]

Using a masculine and combative style, Wollstonecraft is scathing in her attack on Rousseau's depiction of the character of woman. Weakness and passivity are anathema to her perception of responsible womanhood. The origin of the argument for women's inferiority is covertly referred to in this paragraph: "formed to please and to be subject to him." Here we have the grounds for what seemed to be the positing of woman as secondary and thus inferior—"formed to please." The covert reference here is to that *second* record of creation in Genesis 2, that account in which woman was formed from the rib of man. This account, so fundamental to an argument for female subservience, disregards the simultaneous creation of male and female, in God's image, already recorded in Genesis 1. Woman seen in this secondary light, it could be argued, was indeed merely an appendage to man.

The two opposing creation accounts, and their important relevance to women, will be examined in later chapters. Suffice to say at this point that the argument of men such as Rousseau, Gould, and Polwhele for the "natural" and "religious" grounds upon which to base masculine superiority was firmly established in this doctrinal perspective.

Wollstonecraft argued that the "artificial structure" of passivity and subjugated femininity had so infused society that women were as much to blame as men for their blind acquiescence in masculine superiority. To *Vindication* therefore she gave the multifarious task of arguing not only for the rights of women to social equality and a sound education, but of awakening women themselves to their responsibility as equal citizens. Her aims were clear: to discredit the perception of women as overemotional, artificial, and weak; to combat the encouraged manipulative behavioral patterns that in turn led to degeneracy of manners and morals, and to encourage nobler ambitions, a strength of mind and body with which to govern themselves with sobriety. The pursuit of intelligence, compassion, virtue, and a cultivated mind would serve to render women inspiring influences in the construction of a more just and moral society.

This treatise on female rights and manners impressed upon women the strategies used by men to construct feminine characteristics and thereby circumscribe their agency. Wollstonecraft presented a rigorously logical and philosophical argument for the equality of women:

> It is vain to expect virtue from women till they are, in some degree, independent of men; nay, it is vain to expect that strength of natural affection, which would make them good wives and mothers. Whilst they are absolutely dependent on their husbands they will be cunning, mean, and selfish, and the men who can be gratified by the fawning fondness of spaniel-like affection, have not much delicacy, for love is not to be bought, in any sense of the words, its silken wings are instantly shrivelled up when any thing beside a return in kind is sought.[34]

This paragraph makes clear that Wollstonecraft, like More, seeks to enhance the role of motherhood to society. Humiliation, she argues, breeds cunning; only through a proper sense of respect and equality, indeed a coming-together of the mental as well as the physical, can a true and loving relationship be realized. Unequal relationships where one partner holds the balance of power inevitably lead to the "cunning" and "meanness" she refers to. The symbolically expressive nature of her narrative, the use of words that are instantly transcribed into a visionary experience, bring a cogency to her argument.

The depiction of "love" with "silken wings" is beautifully poetic and paints a vivid picture of its fragile and ephemeral nature. Applied in a practical sense, however, Wollstonecraft is using the language of sensibility against itself. The covert message is: beware the oversentimentalization of love, beware the affectation referred to by More, and strive rather for a natural affection built upon mutual approbation.

Admonishing husbands and fathers, she continues,

> Men are not aware of the misery they cause, and the vicious weakness they cherish, by only inciting women to render themselves pleasing; they do not consider that they thus make natural and artificial duties clash, by sacrificing the comfort and respectability of a woman's life to voluptuous notions of beauty, when in nature they all harmonize.
>
> Cold would be the heart of a husband, were he not rendered unnatural by early debauchery, who did not feel more delight at seeing his child suckled by its mother, than the most artful wanton tricks

could ever raise; yet this natural way of cementing the matrimonial tie, and twisting esteem with fonder recollections, wealth leads women to spurn. To preserve their beauty, and wear the flowery crown of the day, [which] gives them a kind of right to reign for a short time over the sex, they neglect to stamp impressions on their husbands' hearts, that would be remembered with more tenderness when the snow on the head began to chill the bosom, than even their virgin charms.[35]

Nature and philosophy mingle in the rhetoric of this reasoned treatise. Use of the word "respectability" anchors this portrayal of true "womanhood," emphasized by the use of this word twice within the space of a few lines: to be respectable is to attract respect. It is an outright attack on artifice, debauchery, trickery all characterized as inherently "unnatural" and incongruous, while the cementing of the "natural" qualities—comfort, care, consideration and charitable kindness—prompts the prevalence of harmony within the state of holy matrimony.

When mutual attraction is based on more than physicality, then neither age nor time will diminish the respect and dignity of one partner for the other. I would suggest that Wollstonecraft is endorsing here, despite her calls for "independence," the value of separate spheres. The idyll of an intelligent, caring maternal influence at the heart of the home, welcoming her thoughtful, earnest and sober mate is to her a "beautiful sight." This utopian vision of marriage, however, has a price:

> Moralists have unanimously agreed, that unless virtue be nursed by liberty, it will never attain due strength—and what they say of man I extend to mankind . . . To render women truly useful members of society, I argue that they should be led, by having their understandings cultivated on a large scale, to acquire a rational affection for their country, founded on knowledge, because it is obvious that we are little interested about what we do not understand . . . That women at present are by ignorance rendered foolish or vicious, is. I think, not to be disputed; and, that the most salutary effects tending to improve mankind might be expected from a REVOLUTION in female manners.[36]

Traditional gender definitions were in need of radical change, according to Wollstonecraft's arguments; liberty extended to the female sex would reap societal reform from which all would benefit. Appealing to the higher minds of each sex, she suggests,

> In treating, therefore, of the manners of women, let us, disregarding sensual arguments, trace what we should endeavour to make them in order to co-operate, if the expression be not too bold, with the supreme

Being. By individual education, I mean, for the sense of the word is not precisely defined, such an attention to a child as will slowly sharpen the senses, form the temper, regulate the passions as they begin to ferment, and set the understanding to work before the body arrives at maturity; so that the man may only have to proceed, not to begin, the important task of learning to think and reason. Consequently, the most perfect education, in my opinion, is such an exercise of the understanding as is best calculated to strengthen the body and form the heart. Or, in other words, to enable the individual to attain such habits of virtue it will render it independent.[37]

On the one hand, Wollstonecraft is suggesting a "revolution" in female manners, but juxtaposed alongside this she contends for female cooperation. What is the reader to understand from these apparently antithetical positions? I would suggest that these two perspectives encapsulate what is at the heart of Wollstonecraft's vision for female emancipation: a revolutionary demand for female education, a cultivation of knowledge, which as well as instilling a sense of their own worth will render women more valuable contributors to society.

Conversely, cultivation of the heart as well as the understanding was a necessary component of cooperation with the supreme Being. This "co-operation" proposal is interesting. At first reading, it may simply suggest that woman needs to acquire the attributes that will allow her to fulfill her maternal mission, but use of the word "bold" hints at another meaning. Cooperation, or a working together with the Supreme Being, was traditionally a male prerogative; he had already claimed this office, and to suggest a personal collaboration or working relationship between *woman* and her maker, without the traditional masculine mediation, would have been considered provocative.

In a text noted for its rational arguments, her recognition of the "important task of learning to think and reason" surprisingly comes secondary to the need for "sharpening the senses," "forming the temper," and "regulating the passions," vis-à-vis the assimilation of sensibility. The subjection of sensibility to reason is clearly not as sharply defined as might be expected in a treatise of this nature.

Wollstonecraft argues for that type of education that strengthens the very fibers of the being, that constructs and supports the character, giving constancy and resolution to the female mind:

for the little knowledge which women of strong minds attain, is, from various circumstances, of a more desultory kind than the knowledge of men, and it is acquired more by sheer observations on real life, than from comparing what has been individually observed with the results of experience generalized by speculation. Led by their dependent situation and domestic employments more into society, what they learn is rather by snatches; and as learning is with them, in general, only a secondary thing, they do not pursue any one branch with that persevering ardour necessary to give vigour to the faculties, and clearness to the judgement.[38]

She argues for the acquirement of accomplished femininity through persistent methodological study. She demands this type of education for women with the express purpose of making them independent. It is only through an enlarged understanding and emancipated liberty that women will be in a position to improve the whole sex. Taking an adroit literary swipe at patriarchal doctrinal theology, she proclaims, "Let men take their choice, man and woman were made for each other, though not to become one being; and if they will not improve women, they will deprave them!"[39] The subsuming and oppression of the married woman within the state of marriage is an injustice Wollstonecraft is intent on reversing.

TREATISE VERSUS ENTREATY

I have been much pestered to read the 'Rights of Women,' but am invincibly resolved not to do it. Of all jargon, I hate metaphysical jargon.

—Hannah More, *Memoirs of the Life and Correspondence of Mrs. Hannah More*

Strictures will now be examined in the light of More's significant oppositional stand against Wollstonecraft. Were the implications for female reform undermined by More's sharp censure of Wollstonecraft's polemic? Certainly the fundamental divisions between the opposing camps were overtly portrayed; More's deep hostility toward speculative revolutionary theories, and the French Revolution in particular, mark her conservative political arguments. Historical contextualization helps to clarify the schism that existed between the political affiliations of the two writers.

The French Revolution traumatized the political scene in Britain, dividing politicians and intellectuals into two camps: radical Jacobins saw the revolution across the channel as an opportunity for political and humanitarian reform in Britain, while the counterrevolutionary anti-Jacobins attempted to maintain the old order. In spite of their conflicting political opinions, the juxtaposing of these two texts reveals the fluctuating struggles that ultimately converged in the common language of the cult of sensibility. Gender definition was central to the arguments of both sides, and the subversive potential within the cult of sensibility became a key political issue: thus, while the radical republicanism of *Vindication* contrasts sharply with the Whiggish discourse of *Strictures*, the identification of a common language becomes clearly evident.

The argument in this chapter is constructed upon the writers' promotion of female influence toward the betterment of society, and it is important to note the blatant parallels in the literary negotiations of these works. Indeed, their arguments for the reforming potential of *educated* women are so similar that the uneducated eye would be hard pressed to distinguish between them. Whether the demand be for "revolution" or "influence," the implicit representation of virtuous femininity is at the heart of the argument in both these texts.

The introduction to *Strictures* exhibits the tone that is to be reflected throughout, an unmistakable solicitation or entreaty: "Some reflections on the present erroneous system are here *with great deference* submitted to public consideration."[40] More's humility is almost tangible. While Wollstonecraft's introduction, though not quite as deferential, still struggles not to sound too dictatorial: "I would not lead my readers to suppose that I mean violently to agitate the contested question respecting the equality or inferiority of the sex; but as the subject lies in my way, and I cannot pass it by . . . I shall stop a moment to deliver, in a few words, my opinion."[41]

The author-reader relationship was an uneasy one for women writers, and a female audience was perhaps harder to placate; so while needing to appear firm in their convictions, an overconfidence or swaggering approach was to be avoided. This perhaps goes some way to explaining the different literary tones of the two writers. More was concerned that her influential friends would regard her criticism of their manners and morals as deeply offensive, with the result that her works were of a more modest, placatory nature.[42] Wollstonecraft undoubtedly had a more disruptive agenda that she pursued with a rather imperious masculinity.

The *attitude* of each to her reader is distinctive, and while their political persuasions might appear irreconcilable, their multidimensional arguments inevitably coincide in their demand for the cultivation of the "understandings" of women: "The chief end to be proposed in cultivating the understandings of women," suggests More, "is to qualify them for the practical purposes of life."[43] The word "practical" More uses prolifically, and in this context she is clearly promoting a down-to-earth, sensible education in preference to prestigious academic qualifications.

The impression gleaned from close study of More's discourse is that education will fit them to become effectual reformers from the "heart" of the nation. She expects women to develop their own talents, and through mental improvement, influence those in their own sphere:

> To woman, therefore, whatever be her rank, I would recommend a predominance of those more sober studies, which, not having display for their object, may make her wife without vanity, happy without witnesses, and content without panegyrists; the exercise of which will not bring celebrity, but improve usefulness. She should pursue every kind of study which will teach her to elicit truth; which will lead her to be intent upon realities; will give precision to her ideas; will make an exact mind; every study which, instead of stimulating her sensibility, will chastise it; which will give her definite notions; will bring the imagination under dominion.[44]

Why should More propose the "chastisement" of female sensibility, having written at such length on its powerful potential for women? I would suggest that More is concerned with identifying the benefits to society of the more discerning reader. This was the age of the novel, and as women became more literate and leisured, the opportunities for frivolous pastimes became more prevalent. More was keen to counter the negative connotations of sensibility, the highly imaginative and overemotional, and to promote in women rather a desire for honest investigation, a search for truths with which to govern their domain with sobriety.

The diversity of qualities that More recommends should be incorporated into female study exhibits the importance she attached to the societal role of women. That these attributes should "make her wife without vanity" emphasizes the value of the more spiritual qualities in preference to those physical ones. Discernment of the truth confers upon women a power with which they can regulate the manners and morals of society. Rejecting all that is "dazzling" they can exert an elevating moral influence. The orientation toward a determinate intelligence and moral sensibility echoes the tone of her arch rival. More's plan of conduct for women mirrors Wollstonecraft's: "fulfilling the duties of a mother," pursuing a "plan of conduct," and disregarding "the fashionable vagaries of dress," women can assist in maintaining the family. This duty, however, need not preclude their learning: "With that steady eye which strengthens the mind the fine arts, literature and even the sciences are all within their capabilities."[45]

More takes the argument further, insisting that it is indeed only through study that an undue sensitivity to emotion will be chastised rather than stimulated. Sharply rebuking bodily or mental excitement of the passions she calls instead for a *depth* to female understanding. Superficial knowledge leads to a "low standard of intellectual excellence," resulting in women making themselves look ridiculous: "the superficial nature of their education furnishes them with a false and low standard of intellectual excellence, so that women have sometimes become ridiculous by the unfounded pretentions of literary vanity: for it is not the really learned, but the smatterers, who have generally brought their sex into discredit, by an absurd affectation, which has set them on depicting the duties of ordinary life."[46]

A "smattering" of superficial knowledge (More), learned by necessity in fits and starts or "snatches" (Wollstonecraft), is clearly a contributory factor to the deficiency of female education and the cause of their absurd affectation infecting other areas of their behavior. An assumed intelligence is clearly as problematic to More as a simulated sensibility, and she is keen to emphasize that: "Considerable advantages are reaped from a select society of both sexes. The rough angles and asperities of male manners are imperceptibly filed, and gradually worn smooth, by the polishing of female conversations, and the refining of female taste."[47]

Wollstonecraft identifies the physical effects resulting from moral beauty: "I know that libertines will also exclaim, that woman would be unsexed by acquiring strength of body and mind . . . I am of a very different opinion, for I think that, on the contrary, we should then see dignified beauty, and true grace . . . only insipid lifeless beauty is produced by a servile copy of even beautiful nature."

> To render the person perfect, physical and moral beauty ought to be attained at the same time; each lending and receiving force by the combination. Judgment must reside on the brow, affection and fancy beam in the eye, and humanity curve the cheek, or vain is the sparkling of the finest eye or the elegantly turned finish of the fairest features: whilst in every motion that displays the active limbs and well-knit joints, grace and modesty should appear. But this fair assemblage is not to be brought together by chance; it is the reward of exertions [calculated] to support each other; for judgment can only be acquired by reflection.[48]

This discourse reflects Wollstonecraft's vision of the ideal woman. Her reference to "lifeless beauty" and "servile copies" evokes images of doll-like creatures devoid of any real purpose in life other than physical attraction. Weak constitutions reflect even weaker natures, and integrity is sacrificed at the altar of personal gratification. Physical beauty on these terms becomes a curse to woman and Wollstonecraft identifies the lackluster effects of this restricted existence. True beauty, according to Wollstonecraft, is not just a gift of nature, it is the result of firm resolve and reasoned sensibility. The cultivated, disciplined mind utilizing its powers of reasoning is evidenced in a vivacity of person, a spiritedness of character; it is the attainment of moral as well as physical beauty adding dignity and grace to the female form. More identifies that "where there is more beauty and more weakness, there should be greater circumspection and superior prudence."[49]

The discriminating reader will draw the conclusion that, while More pursues a *bête noire* approach toward the *feminist* argument for women's rights and their "contentions for equality," she is quietly advocating that principled, intellectual, virtuous women are *already* equal—"those higher minds in each sex." These higher minds must make effective use of a particular talent, and that is their proclivity for influence: "Among the talents for the application of which women of the higher class will be peculiarly accountable, there is one, the importance of which they can scarcely rate too highly. This talent is INFLUENCE. We read of the greatest orator of antiquity that the wisest plans which it had cost him years to frame, a woman could overturn in a single day . . . We are led to reflect with the most sanguine hope on the beneficial effects to be expected from the same powerful force when exerted in this true direction."[50] This most fundamental of female talents, More is keen to see used to positive effect. The power of female influence when exerted in "this true direction" she regards as a powerful instrument of reform. The battle between good and evil was to be fought on the home front in the hearts and the minds of middle England, and More called to the women of England to bring into action "powers of which the effects may be commensurate with eternity":

> I would call on them to come forward, and contribute their full and fair proportion towards the saving of their country. But I would call on them to come forward, without departing from the refinement of their character, without derogating from the dignity of their rank, without blemishing the delicacy of their sex: I would call them to the best and most appropriate exertion of their power, to raise the depressed tone of public morals, and to awaken the drowsy spirit of religious principle . . . At this period, when our country can only hope to stand by opposing a bold and noble unanimity to the most tremendous confederacies

against religion, and order, and governments, which the world ever saw . . . to come forward with a patriotism at once firm and feminine for the general good![51]

Mingling the language of patriotism and public virtue with filial and domestic duty, More's rhetoric served to stimulate and inspire what she viewed as the natural endowments of the female disposition; their piety and consolation that, she suggests, are concealed and lying dormant. Her linguistic vivacity attempted to revive and mobilize these qualities to the cause of the nation, though never must the nation's women lose sight of the refinement of their character. Dignity needs to be maintained, delicacy sustained: indeed beauty, rank, talents and virtue need to blend, instigating a patriotism "at once firm and feminine." This is a wake-up call, and the juxtaposing of rousing, nationalistic language alongside images of sloth and torpidity—"slumbering energy" and "drowsy spirit"—serves to reinforce the ardor, zeal, and spirit necessary to turn the tide of inertia.

"Where the spirit of the Lord is, there is liberty."

The chapter of *Strictures* "On the Effects of Influence" concludes in a menacing tone: "If you neglect this your bounden duty, you will have effectually contributed to expel Christianity from her last citadel. And, remember, that the dignity of the work to which you are called, is no less than that of preserving the ark of the Lord."[52]

The authorial presence of More pervades the moral sensibility of this discourse, and her narrative is richly threaded with Christian symbolism. The "ark of the Lord" refers to the chest that contained the tables of the law,[53] and the task of preserving this "ark" was given only to those worthy followers of God. To equate, therefore, the role of women with this vital mission was a powerful proselytizing strategy. More was convinced that only through the practice and promotion of the principles of piety could women be instrumental in defending their nation against the threat of revolutionary egalitarianism.

The preservation of social order would result, she argued, from the lives of dedicated women at the heart and helm of the nation, steering confidently toward a world imbued with charity and benevolence. This in turn could not fail to contribute toward women's importance: "Christianity [being] the great and leading circumstance which raises women's importance,"[54] and More's agency was instrumental in advancing the cause of a revised and feminized Christian evangelicalism.

More and Wollstonecraft had close links with American reformers, and their influence undoubtedly crossed continents. A letter I discovered at the Bristol Record Office from a private collection reinforces this suggestion. From Barley Wood and dated simply March 21, More writes to Bart Huber:

> I really have so many letters from persons I do not know, that my friends are often set aside for strangers. My transalpine friends and correspondents are all come home, and are succeeded by less amusing, tho [*sic*] not less pious Translatlantic ones. For instance, I received last night no less than eight books or pamphlets from the respective authors in New York, Boston and Connecticut. Most of these I suppose will require acknowledgment . . . But they forget that I am old and have left off reading, and that I have a sickly body, and a sinful soul of my own to take care of. To speak more seriously it is very gratifying to see that religion with all the spirit and energy of a new principle is rising and flourishing in several Provinces of North America, in waiting for and which I am only beginning to think with clarity; so low they appeared to have sunk in the scale of religion and morals, and manners.[55]

The letter reflects More's lively interest in a variety of topics; serious comment sits comfortably alongside friendly banter, it equally identifies the close philosophical and literary links between English and American authors, confirming that suggested potential for influence. That influence is evident when examining the literary contributions of Stanton and Eddy. Drawing on letters, published and prescriptive works, and other documents, I will trace their establishment of a public dialogue. As editorial and publication opportunities became available, they stepped outside conventional literary parameters becoming contributors to journals and magazines more commonly associated with a male readership; this allowed their influence to be extended.

Motherhood: The Key to Female Emancipation?

The following pronouncement by William Lyman in the early part of the nineteenth century emphasized the power of wives and mothers to influence, not only those within their home sphere, but on a wider scale, their powers were to be used to "drive discord, infidelity and licentiousness from our land." According to Lyman, "Mothers do, in a sense, hold the reins of government and sway the ensigns of national prosperity and glory. Yea, they give direction to the moral sentiments of our rising hopes and contribute to form their moral state. To them therefore our eyes are turned in this demoralizing age, and of them we ask, that they would appreciate their real worth and dignity, and exert all their influence to drive discord, infidelity and licentiousness from our land."[56]

Lyman was not alone in his call to the women of the land; other New England ministers were echoing his sentiment. The representation of woman as "holding the reins of government" and swaying "the ensigns of national prosperity and glory," however, was irreconcilable with the powerless creature who had no legal existence apart from her husband's.

Stanton, recognizing the incongruities surrounding the representation of women and intent on promoting their "real worth and dignity" aspired to the reconstruction of a femininity that was spiritually and morally authorized. Her literary style is bold, political and overtly feminist. An address given in September 1848 shows her admiration for More, giving further credence to the effectiveness of influence.[57]

> It has happened more than once that in a great crisis of national affairs, woman has been appealed to for her aid. Hannah More one of the great minds of her day, at a time when French revolutionary and atheistical opinions were spreading—was earnestly besought by many eminent men to write something to counteract these destructive influences—Her style was so popular and she had shown so intimate a knowledge of human nature that they hoped much from her influence. Her village politics by Will Chip, written in a few hours showed that she merited the opinion entertained of her power upon all classes of mind. It had as was expected great effect. The tact and intelligence of this woman completely turned the tide of opinion and many say prevented a revolution, whether she did old Englands [sic] poor any essential service by thus warding off what must surely come is a question—however she did it and the wise ones of her day gloried in her success. Strange that surrounded by such a galaxy of great minds, that [sic] so great a work should have been given with one accord to a woman to do.[58]

This passage shows the impact More's writing had in America. She is recognized as a pioneer in the field of intellectual reformers, her achievements highly prized as contributing toward the empowerment of women. Stanton builds on this framework: admonishing those in political and religious circles who sought to subjugate women, she demands equal opportunities for that half of the population that was oppressed and enslaved:

I should feel exceedingly diffident to appear before you wholly unused as I am to public speaking, were I not nerved by a sense of right and duty—did I not feel that the time had fully come for the question of woman's wrongs to be laid before the public—did I not believe that woman herself must do this work—for woman alone can understand the height and the depth, the length and the breadth of her own degradation and woe. Man cannot speak for us—because he has been educated to believe that we differ from him so materially, that he cannot judge of our thoughts, feelings and opinions by his own.[59]

Her powerful opening sets out the basis of the argument and why it falls to woman to speak out on these emotive issues: "Rights," "duty," "woman's wrongs," "degradation," and "woe." These words encapsulate the very heart of her proposition. The opening lines see the overt challenging of woman as "silent, obedient, chaste." "Man cannot speak for us," she declares, "*because* he has been educated to view woman as quite distinct from himself."[60] The renegotiation of gendered values is of key importance if the years of subordination and disadvantage are to be overturned and woman to be given a voice:

Among the many important questions which have been brought before the public, there is none that more vitally affects the whole human family than that which is technically termed Woman's Rights. Every allusion to the degraded and inferior position occupied by woman all over the world, has ever been met by scorn and abuse. From the man of highest mental cultivation, to the most degraded wretch who staggers in the streets do we hear ridicule and coarse jests, freely bestowed upon those who dare assert that woman stands by the side of man—his equal, placed here by her God to enjoy with him the beautiful earth, which is her home as it is his—having the same sense of right and wrong and looking to the same Being for guidance and support. So long has man exercised a tyranny over her injurious to himself and benumbing to *her* faculties, that but few can nerve themselves against the storm, and so long has the chain been about her that however galling it may be she knows not there is a remedy.[61]

Identifying the restrictive practices imposed upon women by their menfolk, Stanton highlights the scorn and abuse with which female reformers are faced, not only from the lower class male, but also the "man of highest cultivation." She draws attention to the fact that even eloquent and dignified women are powerless and subservient to "the most degraded wretch" if he happens to be a male wretch.

FIRST CAUSE

An important point to note in Stanton's argument is her proprietorial right to God. Patriarchal divine intercession is set aside by the elemental rights given to woman by her God. Identification of woman as accountable to her God without the need of male mediation inevitably introduces a challenge to that accepted doctrinal hierarchical system. The establishment of gender equality as a law of God is a powerful means of authorizing the feminine, though Stanton is clearly aware of the "storm" of protest that may result. She suggests that so "benumbed" have become the faculties of the female mind due to their state of subservience that they "know not there is a remedy." This suggestion echoes that of More in *The White Slave Trade*, where she points to the willing acquiescence of female "slaves": "They hug their chains, and because they are gilt and shining, this prevents them, not from feeling, but from acknowledging that they are heavy."[62]

Stanton's narrative resonates with implications of what she sees as the social, civil, and religious injustice toward women. Linguistically she attempted to rouse them and make them aware of the nature of their subjugation to men, thereby lifting impositions that for centuries had been used to oppress them. She concedes that woman's sphere may have become enlarged: "As the nations of the earth emerge from a state of barbarism, the sphere of woman gradually becomes wider," but she argues, "not even under what is thought to be the full blaze of the sun of civilization is it what God designed it to be."[63]

These are not the conventional arguments of a woman trying to raise the collective feminine consciousness. She does not identify woman as appealing to her male superior in order to glean some semblance of equality. Stanton emerges almost as a spokesperson for her God, identifying the inalienable rights of woman, already granted to her by God. It needs to be acknowledged that while Stanton's views did attract criticism, and from both sexes, in her argument for the refining influence of women "might not her presence do much towards softening down this violence-refining this vulgarity?"[64] She was not a lone voice.

A sermon delivered by Joseph Buckminster to a women's group in Boston identified not only the reforming potential of spiritual women, but significantly, referred to Christianity in the feminine. He further suggested that while men, "the self-styled lords of Creation," were actively pursuing a life in the public, political sphere, "the dependent, solitary female" sought God. "I believe," he said, "that if Christianity should be compelled to flee from the mansions of the great, the academies of the philosphers, the halls of legislators, or the throng of busy men, we should find her last and purest retreat with woman at the fireside; her last altar would be the female heart; her last audience would be the children gathered around the knees of a mother; her last sacrifice, the secret prayer, escaping in silence from her lips, and heard perhaps only at the throne of God."[65]

While there is clearly an authorizing of the feminine here, and the churches indeed became a space that women occupied, with masculine ministerial consent, patriarchal New Englanders nevertheless subscribed to a discriminatory hierarchical system. The exercising of a moral influence from within the private domestic sphere was the height to which woman might aspire. The lack of a legal and political voice reinforced her position as an inferior and Stanton, like More and Wollstonecraft before her, argued that only education could provide the key to access the wider world.

At the same time, therefore, as seizing the emerging opportunities that a feminizing of religious culture offered, Stanton provocatively challenged the assumed intellectual, moral, and physical superiority of the male:

> Let us consider his intellectual superiority. Man's superiority cannot be a question until we have had a fair trial. When we shall have had our colleges, our professions, our trades, for a century a comparison may then be justly instituted. When woman instead of being taxed to endow colleges where she is forbidden to enter, instead of forming societies to educate young men shall first educate herself, when she shall be just to herself before she is generous to others—improving the talents God has given her and leaving her neighbour to do the same for himself we shall not then hear so much of this boasted greatness. How often now we see young men carelessly throwing away the intellectual food their sisters crave. A little music that she may while an hour away pleasantly, a little French, a smattering of the sciences and in rare instances some slight classical knowledge and a woman is considered highly educated. She leaves her books and studies just at the time a young man is entering thoroughly into his—then comes [*sic*] the cares and perplexities of married life. Her sphere being confined to her house and children, the burden generally being very unequally divided, she knows nothing beside and whatever yearning her spirit may have felt for a higher existence, whatever may have been the capacity she well knew she possessed for more elevated enjoyments—enjoyments which would not conflict with these but add new lustre to them—it is all buried beneath the weight that presses upon her.[66]

The foregoing contrasts the servility of woman with the presumption of man: Stanton argues that talents are given by God to woman as well as to man, but because custom has decreed it is man who is educated, woman finds herself derogated because of her impoverished opportunities.

Drawing on her judicial legacy, Stanton demands a "fair trial"; female capacity for intellectual achievement can be assessed only when educational opportunities are equal. Stanton is quick to counter a boasted intellectual superiority resulting from prejudicial circumstances. She challenges male privilege at the expense of woman, pointing to the ability of the female to combine maternal duties with a developing intellect. She does not see one conflicting with the other; she considers that an enlarged understanding "adds luster" to her management of the household. Again, this emulates Wollstonecraft, who suggested that "fulfilling the duties of a mother . . . the management of their household and children need not shut them out from literature, [or] prevent their attaching themselves to a science."[67]

Whatever the opinions of their detractors, these women are promoting the reorganization, not the overthrow of social order; feminist or antifeminist, their aims are not to disrupt the natural order of things. Indeed quite the contrary, their objectives are the unifying and enriching of humanity, and as More acknowledged, through an enlargement of the female understanding, "men themselves will be sure to be gainers." Combine this with Stanton's suggestion that "so long has man exercised a tyranny over her injurious to himself" and the mutual benefits to mankind resulting from a more tolerant and democratic approach to the woman question become evident. Stanton insists, "The individuality of woman must be asserted and upheld, and she must ever hold in her own hands the means of self-support and protection. What we now demand is, the reorganization of our social institutions."[68]

Tyrannical Treatment Targeted

Stanton challenged restrictions placed upon women using every available genre, and when a damning review of a female author's work appeared in the *National Anti-Slavery Standard* of January 13, 1855, Stanton seized the opportunity to press her cause.

Ruth Hall: A Domestic Tale of the Present Time written by Fanny Fern was not unlike Wollstonecraft's *Mary*; it was a fictionalized "autobiography" in which she had the temerity to "unveil" the domestic tyranny suffered by so many women. The reviewer was "indignant" that she (the author) could "so far forget a Christian law and a natural instinct" as to hold her own father and brother up to public "ridicule and contempt." "The Mohammedans," he continued, "pronounce their most dreadful anathema upon him who is guilty of filial irreverence."[69]

Stanton's appraisal of the review, published in February 1855, was a caustic satirical response that would have given wider publicity, not only to the novel, but to her own attempts at highlighting the miserable degradations women were forced to endure, often at the hands of their benefactors: "If by any unfortunate blunder in society," she began, "she awakes to the consciousness that her legal protectors are her tyrants, in spite of all the beautiful things that have been written and said on conjugal, filial and fraternal devotion, her honest indignation will ever and anon boil up and burst forth in defiance of all ties of blood and kindred."[70]

> In the name of womanhood, I thank Fanny Fern for this deeply interesting life experience. To me the tale of sorrow is beautifully and truthfully told. It matters not whether the selfish male monsters so graphically sketched in "Miss Hall," that compound of ignorance, formality and cant, are all of her own family,—enough that plenty of just such people live. This is some woman's experience. If it is her own life, so much the better. Heaven has witnessed these petty tyrannies in the isolated household long enough. When woman does at length divest herself of all false notions of justice and delicacy, and gives to the world a full revelation of her sufferings and miseries,—the histories of all other kinds of injustice and oppression will sink into utter insignificance, before the living pictures she shall hold up to the unwilling vision of domestic tyrants.[71]

That women were excluded from public life and political debate was of major concern to Stanton, but the indolence that surrounded the cruel servility many were forced to endure, in isolation, and often at the hands of their "protectors" was anathema to this suffragist. This review furnished the opportunity to publicly deride and dispute the cozy familial scene as, in some cases, a sham, which by the very nature of its "privacy" provided protection to the perpetrators. Hinting again at martyrdom she suggests that "hardship and struggle always crush the weak and insignificant, but call forth and develop the true and noble soul," and fanning the flame of religious rebellion, she continues, "the great lesson taught in Ruth Hall is that God has given to woman sufficient brain and muscle to work out her own destiny unaided and alone." The notion that God made woman to "depend on man" is, she says, simply "a romance and not a fact of every-day life."

> Fanny Fern has been severely criticized for drawing her sketches from familiar scenes and faces. If her pictures are not pleasing ones, it seems to me the censure more justly belongs to the living subjects, than the artist who has too faithfully drawn the sketch. That she is truthful, is seen from the fact that the public readily pronounced her work an autobiography. Authors generally claim the privilege of writing about what they have seen and felt. Men have given us all their experience, from Moses down to the last village newspaper; and how much that is palatable have they said of woman? And now that woman has seized the brush, and brought forth on the canvas a few specimens of dwarfed and meagre manhood, lo! what a furor of love and reverence has seized our world of editors and critics! You who have ridiculed your mothers, wives and sisters since you first began to put pen to paper, talk not of "filial irreverence." This is but a beginning, gentlemen. If you do not wish us to paint you wolves, get you into lambs' clothing as quickly as possible. It is our right, our duty, to condemn what is false and cruel wherever we find it.[72]

The "indignant" male reviewer of Fern's text handed to Stanton a public platform from which to justify her religious and suffrage sentiment. It was an opportunity to reach those who might otherwise not have read her didactic tracts and she clearly did not waste the opportunity. With literary precision she deconstructed a religious perspective that, in the name of Christianity, had supported the systematic degradation of women. Her impassioned eloquence invoked Heaven as a witness to the tyrannical treatment of the female sex even within their own private space.

A strategy common to Stanton, More, Eddy, and Wollstonecraft, was taking it upon themselves to speak on behalf of their sex and "in the name of womanhood," hinting at a common cause that they no doubt hoped would strengthen their case. They were aware, however, that if they were to awaken women to the traditions of injustice, they needed a reasoned argument that exposed woman as compliant in her own subservience: "When woman does at length divest herself" indicates that woman had a part to play in her own liberation.

Stanton's text works to expose the bias at the heart of nineteenth-century New England religious thought. Her vocabulary attaches to the notion of womanhood the very qualities embodied in the life of a Christian disciple: "Hardship," "struggle," "suffering and poverty," which she emphasizes are just the qualities that in turn "call forth and develop the true and noble soul." Juxtaposed alongside this representation are the "ignorance," "cant," and "tyranny" of "selfish male monsters," and it is evident to which sex she attributes true heavenly aspirations. Narrative that evidently emerges from the "heart" as well as the "head" of its author seeks to lay its message at the altar of Christianity ennobling the meek and merciful. It reflects on the Christian qualities of truth, justice, mercy, and a proper sense of love. It routs hypocrisy and seeks to restructure society on a foundation of unprejudiced and honorable behavior. If the message is characterized by meekness, it works to emphasize the *might* of meekness.

The literary style is elaborate and of a rather grandiose nature; it manifests a somewhat epic spirit, its message being of profound human importance. "Christian law" and "natural instinct" are enshrined in its vocabulary; science and sensibility ground its arguments. Her provocative "This is but a beginning, gentlemen" indicates the resolve at the heart of her plea. She turns to that fountainhead of bigotry:

> If all tyrannical parents, husbands and brothers knew that the fantastic tricks they play at the hearthstone, would in time be judged by a discerning public, no one can estimate the restraining influence of such a fear. Woman owes it to herself, to her sex, to the race, no longer to consent to and defend the refinements of degradation to which Christian woman is subject in the nineteenth century . . . If woman had done her duty to her sires and sons, think you it would have taken them nearly one hundred years, after giving to the world a declaration of rights that made every king in Europe tremble beneath his crown, to see that a woman has a right to the property she inherits, and to the wages she earns with her own hands?[73]

Stanton identifies that collective collusion at the "hearthstone." Consensual defense of what she describes "the refinements of degradation," accommodated and advanced through stealth and chicanery required public disclosure. Dishonesty and deception promulgated female subservience, and like a festering wound, was a perpetual source of bitter, rancorous irritation. Stanton inveighed against the hypocrisy inherent in an antislavery paper that could allow such a hostile review of one who wrote on the subject of female subjection, while purporting the support of liberation and human rights. She condemned the duplicity of writers who preached compassion, but practiced inhumanity in the name of Christianity: "The next *mulatto slave* that comes North, and gets upon a platform . . . read him the laws of the Mohammedans and Christians . . . tell him his speech has no literary merit,"[74] she angrily proclaims.

The next sentence strikes at the heart of specious superficiality: "Because a villain for his own pleasure, has conferred on me the boon of existence, by what law, other than the Christian one—'Love your enemies'—am I bound to love and reverence him who has made my life a curse and a weariness, and who possesses in himself none of the Godlike qualities which command my veneration?"[75] Honor and respect she identifies as reciprocal qualities that by their very nature need to be practiced to be procured.

Arguing against the trivialization of woman, and the tyrannical behavior of man, she pleads for the moral and intellectual cultivation of women: for mothers who, with propriety and noble ambition, govern their family with judgment; who lead by example, inspiring their young charges and their husbands, giving "direction to the moral sentiments" and assistance in forming their moral states. Educated mothers will then indeed, as pronounced by William Lyman, "hold the reins of government and sway the ensigns of national prosperity and glory."

These arguments would appear to build upon those earlier ones pressed by More and Wollstonecraft, hinting at a universal influence. More's imperative—"God has delegated to you . . . the awfully important trust of infusing the first principles of piety into the tender minds"[76]—is clearly recognizable in Stanton's argument.

While attempting to shame the *Anti-Slavery Standard* for its hypocritical position, Stanton used the opportunity to benefit her cause. The shameful review allowed her to publicly identify and attack tyranny in all its forms and her arguments sit very comfortably alongside Wollstonecraft's: "Parental affection, indeed, in many minds, is but a pretext to tyrannize where it can be done with impunity, for only good and wise men are content with the respect that will bear discussion . . . Woman, however, a slave in every situation to prejudice, seldom exerts enlightened maternal affection; for she either neglects her children, or spoils them by improper indulgence . . . The formation of the mind must be begun very early, and the temper, in particular, requires the most judicious attention."[77]

Arguing for the enlightenment of woman as a check to tyrannical male behavior, "maternal affection" is identified as the determining factor in the formation of cultivated minds. Each writer pressed for reform on this platform, and using genres that encompassed the private and public spheres, they moved easily, changing tone and style to suit their readership. Their arguments are linked by the promotion of home as a primary reformatory site and woman as a major force in behavioral reform.

SACRED DUTIES AND GIFTED DESTINY

Appropriate roles for women were being contentiously debated in nineteenth-century New England and Eddy's writing of this midperiod of her life reflected this turbulent atmosphere. Her earlier writing was not as controversial as it became later, but displayed those sentimental tendencies observed in Wollstonecraft's texts.

A poem published in 1848 titled *The Wife* exhibits woman apparently glorying in marital subservience; and while Stanton was adamantly arguing for independence within the marriage state, Eddy extolled the virtues of submission: "She stood beside him, in the spring-tide hour / Of joy and hope, when Hymen fanned the flame. / Of wedded love, and with devotion's power / Knelt in submission to the new born name; / And life so bright, so beautiful did seem, No cheating fantasy or pleasing dream."[78] Eddy wrote in terms that reflected appropriate societal gender divisions, building her claims for female excellence upon women's traditional roles, and as that letter to her friend Augusta explained, to "make cold hearted man raise his standard of female excelence [*sic*]."[79]

Eddy made useful inroads into the public consciousness through her contributions to *The Covenant*. Writing for this largely male audience allowed her to challenge prejudice and promote rather an appreciation of woman's finer nature: "Let us reflect on a wise necessity of her nature which constitutes her . . . a practical *secret* of which even poets have sung with sublime pathos, chanting its spell in praises eloquent; while philosophy's most powerful or dangerous dogmas have yielded, when to resist, was to strive unmanfully, to the timid tear and silent persuadings."[80]

The feminine idiolect contrasts with Stanton's use of words and style of expression; while reference to a "timid tear" and "silent persuadings" might suggest weakness and passivity, Eddy was actually complying with that literary code that accredited these emotional responses with superior powers: *feminine* powers that as well as having a responsiveness to another's distress, had the innate authority to overthrow "dangerous dogma." To suggest the "unmanliness" of resistance was a clever ploy and might have appealed to an "Oddfellow's"[81] code of conduct.

Eddy portrays the female nature in somewhat transcendental terms; she appropriates qualities that as well as being secret and mysterious are omniscient. In common with the arguments of the other writers, Eddy makes clear this gift accords a powerful influence to women. Fulfilling sacred duties, adhering to a religious code and regulating their own sensibilities allowed women to fulfill their "gifted destiny."

August 1846 saw the publication of a short story by Eddy: the style of *Emma Clinton, or a tale of the Frontiers* was entirely in keeping with the genre of sentimental novel. It was a didactic tale that registered a sensitivity to beauty and sublimity and worked to expose inequalities in societies and families, emphasizing the value of a female influence at the heart of each. Its romantic genre and egalitarian principle belies its politically incorporated values:

"Twas near the close of the eighteenth century, that period which 'tried men's souls' in the struggle for liberty, to throw off the galling yoke of Britain's tyranny and establish a firm foundation for a happy republic." These opening lines echo the virtuous republican sentiment used by Wollstonecraft in her *Letters.* This utopian state, this sweet equality could not be found where oppression and tyranny reigned: the fiction goes on to introduce a British aristocratic family who fled their homeland to "seek asylum at the home of the brave, where poverty was not deemed a crime, and where [his] heavy losses in wealth, (and consequently rank in England) would not deny a just claim on society."[82]

Through distinctly gendered narrative, the heavy hand of oppression and inequity is identified as a bigoted Britain; this contrasts sharply with the sheltering sanctuary imagery through which America is typified. This portrayal serves to link America with its Puritan history, that sheltering wing of maternalism as cited by Wollstonecraft, under which New England settlers sought a new spiritual beginning. This imagery usefully sets the stage for the connecting of national character with private citizen and a proselytizing strategy continues in gendered terms, as Eddy seeks to celebrate the meritorious qualities of the female mind.

The story is centered around Emma, the daughter of the family, who is represented in terms that link her with the motherland, or America, while the father appropriates the more British patriarchal standard. The mother, "accustomed to the conventional polish of society, possessing a rarely gifted and well-stored mind, was a fit guardian for the youth and inexperience of her daughter; and from the rich store-house and garniture of her own thoughts, she found a useful deposite [*sic*] for all their hid treasure, in her ardent and developing mind."[83]

Portrayal of the female mind as a "rich store-house" or depository of precious gifts cooperates well with the "sweet sensibility," as identified by More. The valuable nature of this unseen power is emphasized by "hid treasure"; its maternal purpose was exalting: "Seeking to engrave on its spotless tablets, delicacy of feeling, purity, and elevation of purpose, with decision of character, which would prepare her for the mutations of life, and make up the sum total of real wealth."[84]

There is an extraordinary compatibility here between this portrayal of private development, and that of revised national formation. The daughter was in every way a just repository for her mother's fine sensibilities: "A high marble forehead wore the tracery of thought; a slight delicate form, rounded in every outline, completely developed the spirit it enshrined in beautiful contrast with the voluptuous cast of oriental beauty." This conventional language of sensibility, with its covert censure of eastern sexuality, again mirrors Wollstonecraft's: "Judgment must reside on the brow, affection and fancy beam in the eye, and humanity curve the cheek."[85] Eddy's juxtaposing of human nature and national character serves to qualify those qualities identified as feminine, as central to the construction of a more just and benevolent society.

As the story progresses, autobiography apparently mingles with fiction: the "decision of character" that Emma's mother has instilled into her daughter, results in her choosing a suitor whom her father deems unsuitable. With the words "I am half-frantic rendered already by your woman's nature," the father disinherits his daughter; in some ways this deprivation of heritage mirrors the family's ousting from their homeland.

Emma's husband, like Eddy's, dies of yellow fever and Emma, like Eddy, is left a young and pregnant widow; Eddy even includes at this stage in the tale, her eulogic poem *The Wife*. Emma, like Eddy, bears a beloved son, but the premature death of the mother, again in both cases, leads to the slow dismantling of female influence. An earlier suitor of Emma's reappears, only to desert her again, marrying another and fathering a son. Unprotected and alone, Emma dies of a broken heart. The wife of the errant suitor also dies early. Two sons, whom Eddy describes as bereft of a "mother's deep and holy love," that love capable of "restraining and governing by a hidden empire in the heart of her child," are thus left to a patriarchally influenced future. Barbaric tendencies surface, Emma's son, seeking to wreak revenge on his mother's errant suitor, lures the young man "from the path of rectitude" toward a life of crime and wretchedness. This is a warning tale.

Abrams identifies this genre, described by Edgar Allan Poe as "'the prose tale,' as a narrative which can be read at one sitting of from half an hour to two hours, it is limited to 'a certain unique or single effect' to which every detail is subordinate."[86] The "unique effect" of this prose tale, I would suggest, is the power of maternal influence "A mother," wrote Eddy, "is the strongest educator, either for or against crime."[87]

The conclusion confirms the religious didacticism that underlies each writer's reformatory attempts: "Bitterly did he [the errant suitor] reproach himself for the ruin he had wrought! but repentance came too late as he remembered those words of the inspired oracle, 'Whatsoever a man soweth that shall he also reap.'"[88]

Having identified Eddy's literary means of empowering womanhood through the annals of a male publication, it is interesting to note the shift in style as she writes material for the "drawing-room" or private sphere. "Woman's Rights—What are they?" represents the diversity of Eddy's style and tone, and this poem, first published under that title in *Gleason's Pictorial Drawing-Room Companion* in February 19, 1853, provides a platform from which her tenets on reclamation of female rights may be identified.

This poem, like More's *Sensibility*, is significant in that it emphasizes key aspects of the argument for female ascendancy. Interestingly, in further editions the title became simply "Woman's Rights." Having lost its questioning vein, the poem becomes a powerful proselytizing argument on behalf of woman and her spirituality.

The simple structure of this sixteen-line poem, written in couplets, belies its potent message. Women's leadership qualities are enshrined in its narrative. In the space of a few lines, public and private spheres have merged, effecting an aggrandizement of the female virtues, sanctioning and qualifying woman "to lead the way."

> Grave on her monumental pile;
> She won from vice, by virtue's smile,
> Her dazzling crown, her sceptered throne,
> Affection's wreath, a happy home;
>
> The right to worship deep and pure,
> To bless the orphan, feed the poor;
> Last at the cross to mourn her Lord,
> First at the tomb to hear his word
>
> To fold an angel's wings below;
> And hover o'er the couch of woe;
> To nurse the Bethlehem babe so sweet,
> The right to sit at Jesus' feet;

To form the bud for bursting bloom,
The hoary head with joy to crown;
In short, the right to work and pray,
"To point to heaven and lead the way."[89]

The poem opens in dignified fashion implying woman's majestic and epoch-making characteristics. Targeting those wrongs, which for centuries had resulted in female subjugation, this work clearly distinguishes between the portrayal of woman as beguiling temptress and spiritual intermediary. The tone of the first stanza is pensive yet confident as it seeks to make that separation between vice and virtue. Within the first four lines it successfully makes the transition; virtue and all the qualities associated with this pure state sanction and validate the sovereignty of this "new" woman. The structure of this short but powerful piece of poetry reflects that "last and best" rising scale of creation argument.

Eddy bases her narrative on biblical hermeneutics and is succinct in pressing for woman's worth. The elaborate vocabulary—"monumental," "dazzling," "crown," "sceptered," "throne"—signifies eminence, dignity, and exaltation. When juxtaposed with the final line of the first stanza, "a happy home," it might appear incongruous. This last line confirms the seat of female authority to be the home. The home is portrayed as a monument to woman. Fulfilling this office, woman's vocation is clear. Her maternal qualities exalt her to divine status. Eve, as the precursor to the multitude of ills associated with woman, has been overshadowed by Mary, the holy mother. Purity, as exemplified by this mother, has eclipsed the suggestion of woman as fallen. Woman's virtue has instigated her "rights." These "rights" Eddy lists in each stanza. Clearly these "rights" are enshrined in her maternal instincts.

It is interesting to note that the very qualities that would subordinate woman on earth, actually work to authorize her in this poem. The final stanza climaxes her portrayal: woman has indeed earned the right not only "to work and pray," but even "to point to heaven and lead the way." Eddy's use of punctuation reinforces her suggestion that while a "happy home" is the nucleus, her influence knows no bounds: to emphasize this the period is not used until the last line.

Maternal influence

Placing woman at the heart of her reformatory plea, Eddy lays out her ideal:

A mother is the strongest educator, either for or against crime. Her thoughts form the embryo of another mortal mind, and unconsciously mould it, either after a model odious to herself or through divine influence, "according to the pattern showed to thee in the mount." . . . Children should obey their parents; insubordination is an evil, blighting the buddings of self-government. Parents should teach their children at the earliest possible period the truths of health and holiness. Children are more tractable than adults, and learn more readily to love the simple verities that will make them happy and good.[90]

The notion of "self-government" is important in the context of female emancipation. Having been taught to govern themselves from an early age, women will not readily yield to an authority that is patently unjust and immoral. Study of the scriptures "according to the pattern showed to thee in the mount" indicates Christ's sermon on the mount,[91] which prescribes a disciplined rule for life.

The key to a more just and equal society, Eddy argues, is the early assimilation of truth. In this, she mirrors Wollstonecraft: "It is the irregular exercise of parental authority that first injures the mind, and to these irregularities girls are more subject than boys. The will of those who never allow their will to be disputed, unless they happen to be in a good humour, when they relax proportionally, is almost always unreasonable. To elude this arbitrary authority girls very early learn the lessons which they afterwards practise on their husbands."[92]

Eddy points to the inherent goodness in children, arguing it is the example that is set in the home that blights the early budding: "If some fortuitous circumstance places promising children in the arms of gross parents, often these beautiful children early droop and die, like tropical flowers born amid Alpine snows. If perchance they live to become parents in their turn, they may reproduce in their own helpless little ones the grosser traits of their ancestors . . . Nothing unworthy of perpetuity should be transmitted to children."[93]

Again, there are similarities to Wollstonecraft's argument that the weakness of women is largely the result of tyrannical treatment: "If the mind be curbed and humbled too much in children; if their spirits be abased and broken much by too strict an hand over them; they lose all their vigour and industry."[94] Eddy identifies "the offspring of heavenly-minded parents" as more likely to "inherit more intellect, better balanced minds, and sounder constitutions," suggesting that teachers of schools be selected "with as direct reference to their morals as to their learning or their correct reading. Nurseries of character should be strongly garrisoned with virtue."[95]

Eddy's arguments effectively contribute, through their linking of education, sensibility, and religion, toward the identification of a mind-set with a powerful reforming potential. Allied to that potential is the reciprocal autonomy it bestows. Through appropriate language she sought to liberate debased womanhood and sanction the "new woman." A person who is the legal property of another may become a helpless victim of a dominant influence, and she sought to free women from a subservient state: "The rights of man were vindicated in a single section and on the lowest plane of human life," she argued, "when African slavery was abolished in our land. That was only prophetic of further steps towards the banishment of a worldwide slavery, found on higher planes of existence and under more subtle and depraving forms . . . God has built a higher platform of human rights, and He has built it on diviner claims. These claims are not made through code or creed, but in demonstration of 'on earth peace, good-will toward men.'"[96]

Eddy, like Stanton, based her arguments for the abolition of worldwide slavery on a law of God. Condemning those male hypocrites who preached Christianity while practicing a tyrannical rule over their household, each woman used scriptural discourse to confirm and credit her opinions. Eddy used the power of the word, not only to draw attention to women's spiritual potential, but to make her male readers aware of the misconception *they* had labored under, believing woman to be their inferior.

True liberty, she argues, makes all men free: "Discerning the rights of man, we cannot fail to foresee the doom of all oppression. Slavery is not the legitimate state of man, God made man free . . . Citizens of the world, accept the 'glorious liberty of the children of God,' and be free! This is your divine right."[97]

CONCLUSION

Sensibility is the most exquisite feeling of which the human soul is susceptible: when it pervades us, we feel happy; and could it last unmixed, we might form some conjecture of the bliss of those paradisiacal days, when the obedient passions were under the dominion of reason, and the impulses of the heart did not need correction . . . Sensibility is indeed the foundation of all our happiness.

—Mary Wollstonecraft, *Mary*

The baptism of the Holy Ghost is the spirit of Truth cleansing from all sin; giving mortals new motives, new purposes, new affections, all pointing upward. This mental condition settles into strength and freedom, deep-toned faith in God; and a marked loss of faith in evil, in human wisdom, human policy, ways and means. It develops individual capacity, increases the intellectual activities, and so quickens moral sensibility that the great demands of spiritual sense are recognized.

—Mary Baker Eddy, *Prose Works* "Miscellaneous Writings"

In this chapter, I have identified the means by which the authors were able to project moral and spiritual values upon the cult of sensibility. Having distinguished clearly between the two versions of the cult, they proceeded to empower women through an identification of their natural proclivity toward an innate spirituality.

Drawing on maternal images, these writers went on to associate the feminine with the highest representation of womanhood: the holy Mother. This in turn allowed them to portray the essentially feminine qualities at the heart of the cult of sensibility, investing women with a special propensity and responsibility for individual and collective moral reform. Having set up a hierarchy of mental qualities, our authors argued that women draw on intellect as well as intuition in order to achieve their potential, and as Wollstonecraft suggested, they "labour by reforming themselves to reform the world."[98]

The next chapter will seek to identify how personal experience sourced a renewed religious sentiment through which they effectively built upon the earlier arguments, how they sought to contribute toward representation of the spiritual equality of the sexes through revised scriptural interpretation.

CHAPTER 4

WOMAN'S RIGHT TO REVELATION

SPIRITUAL SUFFRAGE AND THE WORD OF GOD

The heart is therefore an active center where the ideas and impressions received are transformed into deeds; Not only is the heart the center of moral life, but finally the center of religious life as well . . . The heart is the secret place of their inspiration . . . The heart thus becomes the place of divine vision.

—The Encyclopedia of Religion

The subject of "divine vision" is central to the promotion of sensibility as a mental state that allows receptivity to divine signals, and will form the core argument of this chapter.

Having differentiated between the material and spiritual representations of this cult, I want to examine a burgeoning controversy regarding the opposing definitions of the Deity. Was the nature of the Supreme Being, as had been identified by centuries of theological doctrine, that of a harsh patriarchal dictator, or was it rather the more benevolent and sympathetic matriarchal one being portrayed by these female reformers? If indeed God could be invoked as Mother as well as Father, this feminine representation inevitably sanctioned a spiritual status for women. Barker-Benfield highlights the dissenting opportunities that this portrayal offered, suggesting that "feeling was at the heart of the debate over the face of God" and concluding that "the reconceptualizing of human nature corresponded to a reconceptualizing of God."[1]

PUBLIC HUMILIATION

Attempts by the authors to "reconceptualize" God through empha-sizing feminine aspects of the divine nature resulted in their public anathematization.

More and Eddy were the subject of public caricaturing: the one by Augustine Birrell the other by Mark Twain, respectively. More suf-fered at the hands of her tormentors during her lifetime, but Birrell attempted to besmirch her memory: "To libel the dead is, I know, not actionable indeed it is impossible; but evil-speaking, lying, and slandering are canonical offences from which the obligation to refrain knows no limits of time or place."[2] These were serious accusations, and no doubt had they been made in her lifetime, would have elicited some response.

A common form of attack and derogation of women intellectuals was in the form of satire, evidenced by Walpole's reference to Woll-stonecraft as that "hyena in petticoats." Birrell ultimately resorted to this cruel satirical style:

> I freely admit that the celebrated Mrs. Hannah More is one of the most detestable writers that ever held a pen. She flounders like a huge conger-eel in an ocean of dingy morality. She may have been a wit in her youth, though I am not aware of any evidence of it . . . she was an encyclopaedia of all literary vices. You may search her nineteen volumes through without lighting upon one original thought, one happy phrase. Her religion lacks reality. Not a single expression of genuine piety, or heart-felt emotion, ever escapes her lips. She is never pathetic, never terrible. Her creed is powerless either to attract the well-disposed or make the guilty tremble . . . Mrs. Hannah More was a pompous failure.

His pedantic attacking of her literary ability and religious persua-sion was offensive, but to suggest she lacked genuine piety and heart-felt emotion was to strike at the very heart of More's lifework and showed a crass misunderstanding of her mission. In summary fashion, Birrell resorted to attacks on her demeanor: "Hannah More was the first, and I trust the worst, of a large class—'the ugliest of her daugh-ters Hannah,' if I may parody a poet she affected to admire."[3] Birrell evidently believed that any woman who stepped outside her sphere forfeited the right to honor or good manners.

Eddy was similarly attacked by Mark Twain whose literary diatribe was likened by Vic Doyno in his foreword to Twain's text, *Christian Science*, to "being operated upon—without anaesthesia—by a hostile, precise brain surgeon while a bulldog tears at your writing arm." His arguments, according to Doyno, are "the verbal equivalent of the scalpel, the broad-ax, the rapier, and the hammer."[4] Using his formidable debating skills, Twain attacked Eddy's literary ability by endeavoring to ridicule her. Her writing he described as "desert vacancy, as regards thought," "puerility," "sentimentality," "confused and wandering statement," and "metaphor gone insane." He went on to say "she has never been able to write anything above third-rate English, that she is weak in the matter of grammar, that she has but a rude and dull sense of the values of words, that she so lacks in the matter of literary precision that she can seldom put a thought into words that expresses it lucidly to the reader and leave no doubts in his mind as to whether he has rightly understood or not."[5]

Twain's vacillating tendencies are in evidence as he also suggests the following:

> In several ways, she is the most interesting woman that ever lived, and the most extraordinary. When we do not know a person—and also when we do—we have to judge his size by the size and nature of his achievements, as compared with the achievements of others in his line of business—there is no other way. Measured by this standard, it is thirteen hundred years since the world has produced anyone who could reach up to Mrs. Eddy's waistbelt. Figuratively speaking, Mrs. Eddy is already as tall as the Eiffell tower. She is adding surprisingly to her stature every day. It is quite within the probabilities that a century hence she will be the most imposing figure that has cast its shadow across the globe since the inauguration of our era.[6]

There can be little doubt that Eddy's achievements, "as compared with the achievements of others in his line of business," have been quite remarkable, but whether a century hence she can be described as "the most imposing figure that has cast its shadow across the globe" is not as quantifiable.

Christine Trevett, in her paper "Woman, God and Mary Baker Eddy," explains, "Mary Baker Eddy figures scarcely at all in the writings of feminism. Nor is she given consideration by many Christian writers who are regarding afresh, and forging anew, the language of their tradition . . . Unorthodox, provocative and not always consistent Mrs Eddy's teachings might be, but it seems remarkable that they are for the most part disregarded completely by those writers who have been seeking to understand women's views of the Biblical tradition and themselves to forge a new language of theology and of prayer."[7]

Her writings, for whatever reason, appear to have lacked the scholarly investigation I expect to bring to her works.

PRIVATE LIVES, PUBLIC VOICES

The virulent personal attacks each author was subject to served to focus and intensify their arguments for the rights of women. The shift in theological direction and change of literary tone appear to result from personal trauma. Each woman became more confident and outspoken with age. The style of the later works I believe tended toward a culmination of romanticism and protestantism.[8] This reflects the "association of ideas" referred to by Burke in *Sublime and Beautiful*, and identified by writers of sentimental literature as a cumulative ascending perception.[9]

This later writing emphasizes the connections between sensibility and a religion of the heart. *The Encyclopedia of Religion* explains that "the spirit liberated from the passions and the affections is to be replaced with the understanding of divine things and the love of God."[10] The problems associated with the somewhat flexible interpretations of the cult of sensibility were overcome by spiritual certainties. The Bible was central to their arguments. Opposition served to ignite an intensity of sentiment, which in turn inspired an originality of thought. The fresh and innovative argument that appeared to emerge from the very core of their being was quintessential to their zealous reforming initiative.

A clearly identifiable reformist religious register is what marks Wollstonecraft's discourse; it underlies her radical social and political theory, effectively supporting and sustaining her arguments. The marked change of tone represents a distinctive transcendental nature resulting from a renewed spiritual awakening. Disappointed with the public world of masculine politics and religion and its inability to produce the promised reform, Wollstonecraft submitted to the sublimity of nature.

Her *Letters from Sweden* reflect this spiritual awakening; aesthetic and gendered values, identifiable in the landscape and beauty of nature, are expressed in a distinctive literary mode. This renegotiation contrasts sharply with the political tenor of *Vindication* and the "cool eye of observation" with which she viewed the terrors in France. These letters reflect a reengagement with the sublime and evidence a shift in outlook and tergiversation of thought: "The majesty of nature elicits an overflow of emotion," she writes, "in these respects my very reason obliges me to permit my feelings to be my criterion. Whatever excites emotion has charms for me."[11] Letter LX reflects an optimistic note: "Yes; I shall be happy—This heart is worthy of the bliss its feelings anticipate—and I cannot even persuade myself, wretched as they have made me, that my principles and sentiments are not founded in nature and truth . . . the tightened cord of life or reason will at last snap, and set me free."[12]

More's *Strictures* were published at the height of her career, but her writing of the early nineteenth century reflected a woman chastened. This was due to a severe crisis that spanned almost three years and threatened to undermine her life's work and personal integrity. The Blagdon controversy will be examined in more detail as the chapter progresses. More's *Practical Piety* reflects this period of rehabilitation and theological transformation and the change of tone is clearly apparent in her later works.

Stanton's "reminiscences" track a life dedicated to the empowerment of women. An address in June 1882 presented to the Emma Willard Seminary at Troy, New York, evidences a woman who at the age of sixty-seven was emphasizing the value of the older woman. With "the pressing cares of family life ended," Stanton suggests, "the woman may awake to some slumbering genius in herself for art, science, or literature, with which to gild the sunset of her days." This results in "new inspiration for the work that still remains for us to do."[13]

As Eddy approached her eighth decade, she was still encompassed by the disputes that had surrounded her foray into the public and masculine world of the Bostonian theological academy. Attempts to publicly humiliate and destroy her lifework emerged not only from patriarchal insecurities but also from jealous associates.[14]

A law suit[15] was brought against Eddy by a former student through a certain Frederick Peabody. Peabody was a lawyer who, on behalf of his client, attempted to "flay Mrs. Eddy in the eyes of the world," according to Gillian Gill. Gill maintains that the twin aims of revenge and financial reward were at the root of this litigation and she suggests that "he [Peabody] aimed to bring Mrs. Eddy down and fatally sabotage her movement."[16] "Peabody," suggests Gill "was the chief conduit of information, or misinformation, about Mrs. Eddy," and his failure to secure success on behalf of his client left him "howling in impotent rage and protest."[17] Attempting to wreak revenge for his public humiliation he supplied damaging and ill-founded documentation to Samuel Clemens, alias Mark Twain, and this alliance resulted in "the most famous collection of essays on Mary Baker Eddy and her religion that has ever been written."[18]

Despite the successful outcome for Eddy, the debacle left her facing charges of "feminine instability" from certain followers who insisted that a masculine 'head' of her sect was the only sensible path to follow. Eddy's response to this personal attack was in the form of an essay, which, after writing, she chose not to publish. It will be thoroughly examined later in this chapter.

"THE GRAND CAUSES WHICH COMBINE TO CARRY MANKIND FORWARD"[19]

The coalition of conviction and purpose so evident in Wollstonecraft's writing had a prodigious and progressive effect in advancing the cause of human rights. Her writings have faced intense critical investigation through the years; her politicosocial ideological perspectives have been at the forefront of feminist criticism. I would argue, however, that it was Wollstonecraft's religious ideals that formed the nucleus of her arguments for social justice. This religious thread is the animating spirit that can be traced from her first novel, right through to her *Letters*.

Wollstonecraft's *Vindication* and *View* clearly register her criticism of the restrictive views held by those she refers to as bigoted "dabblers":

> Religion, pure source of comfort in this vale of tears! how has thy clear stream been muddied by the dabblers, who have presumptuously endeavoured to confine in one narrow channel, the living waters that ever flow towards God-the sublime ocean of existence! What would life be without that peace which the love of God, when built on humanity, alone can impart? Every earthly affection turns back, at intervals, to prey upon the heart that feeds it; and the purest effusions of benevolence, often rudely damped by man, must mount as a free-will offering to Him who gave them birth, whose bright image they faintly reflect.[20]

Her argument is expedited in the *View*, where she suggests, "We must get entirely clear of all the notions drawn from the wild traditions of original sin: the eating of the apple, the theft of Prometheus, the opening of Pandora's Box, and the other fables, too tedious to enumerate, on which priests have erected their tremendous structures of imposition . . . we shall then leave room for the expansion of the human heart, and, I trust, find, that men will insensibly render each other happier as they grow wiser."[21]

This argument would have been deemed presumptuous, especially by those theologians who had spent years in doctrinal study: to these conformist preachers she laid the charge of restricting the Word of God to the letter, losing thereby the spirit. She was intent on lifting "impositions"—what she saw as fallacious teaching—and replacing it with the "purest effusions of benevolence," demanding a higher and more expansive love in place of the restrictive practices she considered were responsible for the duplicity at the heart of religion.

The conviction that inspired Wollstonecraft is evidenced in her attacks on repressive patriarchal ideologies and their construction of a female subordinate. Her literary texts register the complex issues surrounding the representation of women; they also mirror a developing sense of self that was intrinsic to her arguments. Her authorial identity, however, was ambiguous insofar as she wrestled with the cultural and political issues of the day. The tensions between reason and feeling in her texts reflected an accumulation of mental trappings. Barker-Benfield suggests, "She connected her adult misery to her own father's treatment of her as a child, she also explained it as the result of the conventional rearing and education of middle-class females, their sensibilities developed at the expense of reason." He goes on to observe that "Wollstonecraft insisted that women toughen themselves by fully entering the world and subjecting themselves individually to all of the experiences possible to men."[22]

Wollstonecraft did indeed fully enter the world, subjecting herself in the process "to all of the experiences possible to men." She was in France when war was declared on February 1, 1793, and this period had serious consequences for her. That year witnessed the execution of Louis XVI and the guillotining of Marie Antoinette, along with Madame Roland and Olympe de Gouges. The following registers her horror on seeing Louis driven to his execution: "I have been alone ever since; and, though my mind is calm, I cannot dismiss the lively images that have filled my imagination all the day. Nay, do not smile, but pity me; for, once or twice, lifting my eyes from the paper, I have seen eyes glare through a glass-door opposite my chair, and bloody hands shook at me . . . I am going to bed—and, for the first time in my life, I cannot put out the candle."[23]

The overthrow of government and social order, the violence and anarchy, the hopes and despairs are all recorded in the *View*, and it is this text, I would suggest, which marks the beginning of a sea change in her sociopolitical perspective. The demand for political liberty and political virtue was the nucleus around which Wollstonecraft's arguments were arranged in the *View*. She viewed the revolution in France as the exemplification of the age-old struggle between light and dark, truth and error, between superstition and the enlightened sentiments. "The revolution in France," she suggests, "exhibits a scene, in the political world, not less novel and interesting than the contrast is striking between the narrow opinions of superstition, and the enlightened sentiments of masculine and improved philosophy."[24]

The political and public world was the field upon which the battle for reform would be fought. Jane Rendall suggests that it is in the *View* that "Wollstonecraft's study of these 'grand causes' can be most clearly understood through her assumption and exploration of the masculine voice of the philosophical historian."[25] I would suggest further that it was the assumption and exploration of male values and logic that was to crystallize in Wollstonecraft's mind, a need to press for a purity of sentiment, a philosophy of thought that emphasized female values and spiritual ideals. The fault line at the heart of theological teaching and practice had already been exposed in *Vindication*. It was the unyielding nature of those who pursued these beliefs that drew severe censure from her pen.

Spiritual Wickedness

Vivid textual imagery is used by Wollstonecraft as she sought to highlight rampant spiritual wickedness at work in "high places." Referring to the practice of public worship she suggests, "As these ceremonies have the most fatal effect on their morals, and as a ritual performed by the lips, when the heart and mind are far away, is not now stored up by our church as a bank to draw on for the fees of the poor souls in purgatory, why should they not be abolished?" She refers to the perpetrators of these ceremonies as "indolent slugs" guarding their "snug place" by "sliming it over," thus enabling themselves to eat, drink, and make merry "instead of fulfilling the duties" of their vocation. She points to "rapacious priests of superstitious memory" as "idle vermin who two or three times a day perform in the most slovenly manner a service which they think useless," concluding that "nothing, indeed, can be more irreverent than the cathedral service as it is now performed in this country, [neither] does it contain a set of weaker men than those who are the slaves of this childish routine."

Wollstonecraft is slightly more sympathetic toward high mass on the continent, which she concedes "must impress every mind, where a spark of fancy glows," but juxtaposed with this acknowledgment is a criticism of the "theatrical pomp" that supports and surrounds a religious devotion that merely "gratifies the senses."[26]

These basic postulations pervaded the political, religious, and cultural systems of Great Britain, France, and the United States of America,[27] but Wollstonecraft identified "religion" as arguably the *chief* cause in "the grand causes which combine to carry mankind forward." The materialism that enveloped the teaching and practice of Christianity was the chief subject, therefore, that needed addressing if society was to be reformed and justice ratified.

A letter Wollstonecraft wrote to Joseph Johnson early in 1793 reflects her deep concerns that the eagerly anticipated "golden age" was at that very moment fading before her eyes. This led her to question, not the existence of God, but the power of the wiles of the devil to overcome good with evil. The opening paragraph reads:

> Before I came to France, I cherished, you know, an opinion, that strong virtues might exist with the polished manners produced by the progress of civilization; and I even anticipated the epoch, when, in the course of improvement, men would labour to become virtuous, without being goaded on by misery. But now, the perspective of the golden age, fading before the attentive eye of observation, almost eludes my sight; and, losing thus in part my theory of a more perfect state, start not, my friend, if I bring forward an opinion, which at the first glance seems to be levelled against the existence of God! I am not become an Atheist, I assure you, by residing at Paris: yet I begin to fear that vice, or, if you will, evil, is the grand mobile of action, and that, when the passions are justly poized, [*sic*] we become harmless, and in the same proportion useless.

Clearly, her cherished hopes for improvement of the race had been dashed during her residence in France; indeed the immorality she had witnessed during this time had worked to erode her utopian vision. It is important to observe, however, that even in this she is careful to emphasize her religious conviction; her faith in God is unwavering. It is her faith in man that appears diminished: moral arousal, enthusiasm for action—none was the panacea she had hoped. There is a trace of anticipation, however, as she concludes, "Whether a nation can go back to the purity of manners which has hitherto been maintained unsullied . . . I cannot give up the hope, that a fairer day is dawning on Europe."[28]

Wollstonecraft's "revolution" discourse still apparently promotes reason and rationality, over sensibility and feeling, as the route toward an egalitarian society. "Reason," she explains, "beaming on the grand theatre of political changes, can provide the only sure guide to direct us to a favourable or just conclusion."[29] Use of the word "theatre" in this context brings to mind some dramatic performance, adding to that sense of political melodrama. She may well have had in mind also the dramatic public performances being staged on the streets of Paris: the public guillotining and the dismantling of bourgeois society.

Wollstonecraft's writing at this period, however, mirrored her mounting misgivings in a system that appeared to be constructed on hypocritical values. Deceit in the corridors of power; dishonesty in the Church; rampant evil stalking purity, virtue, and goodness; these were the torments she wrestled with during her engagement with "all of the experiences possible to men." There was another drama unfolding in the life of Wollstonecraft at this time, however, and it was set to become equally dramatic for her personally, as the revolution had been collectively. This "experience" was largely responsible for the change in literary tone that surfaced.

Toward the beginning of 1793, Wollstonecraft met Gilbert Imlay, an American army captain whose beguiling manner enticed her completely, saving her from the waves of misfortune that had tossed and agitated her for most of her life. The relationship opened up a new chapter in her life, lifting her spirits, and as Godwin suggests, "Her confidence was entire; her love was unbounded. Now, for the first time in her life, she gave a loose to all the sensibilities of her nature."[30]

Tomalin suggests in her biography of Wollstonecraft that she idealized Imlay "into a worthy recipient for her love." She explains that "the pressure of circumstances helped her to do this" and that "the temptation to adore and cling to him" may well have been a result of the lonely situation in which she found herself at this time.[31] A step-by-step account of this period is not necessary: I simply wish to expose how the trauma of the revolution, a period of forced dependency on Imlay, and the birth of her first child served to inspire Wollstonecraft with a primitive impulse toward a romantic sublimity.[32]

Imlay was a disappointment. He publicly humiliated Wollstonecraft with his philandering, and his business acumen left a lot to be desired. However, when he summoned her, along with her child, to return to England, she did so, albeit with a sick heart and a weary soul. It was April 1795, and by June of that year she sought to end her life with a suicide attempt. It was at this low point that a plan emerged that resulted in Wollstonecraft and her daughter leaving England for Scandinavia on an "errand" for Imlay. Tomalin explains, "There is an almost sublime effrontery about sending off a discarded mistress, newly recovered from a suicide attempt and accompanied by a small baby, on a difficult journey into unknown territory, to recoup your financial disasters for you and leave you free to enjoy the company of her rival without reproach."[33]

Her *Letters* of this period, however, reflect a reengagement with the sublime; the beautiful forms of nature reignited the sentiments and nurtured her soul: "I forgot the horrors I had witnessed in France," she wrote, "which had cast a gloom over all nature, and suffering the enthusiasm of my character, too often, gracious God! damped by the tears of disappointed affection, to be lighted up afresh, care took wing while simple fellow feeling expanded my heart."[34]

The Golden Age: A Utopian Vision

A counterrevolutionary nature and insouciance of tone mark these letters, which are in distinct contrast to the "cool eye of observation" heretofore exhibited. The unrestrained enthusiasm emerges from a desire to evoke affection. Her letters, by her own admission, are an attempt to introduce the reader to their tender-hearted author: "if they do not wish to become better acquainted with me," she suggests, "I give them leave to shut the book." The letters are the result of impressions produced on her feelings: "I found I could not avoid being continually the first person—the little hero of each tale"; but though she tried to correct this "fault," she admits, "in proportion as I arranged my thoughts, my letter, I found, became stiff and affected: I, therefore, determined to let my remarks and reflections flow unrestrained . . . A person has a right, I have sometimes thought . . . to talk of himself when he can win on our attention by acquiring our affection."[35]

Letter One suggests that the "golden age"—that "more perfect state" to which she referred in her letter to Johnson as "almost eluding her sight"—may be found by going back to the "purity of manners which has hitherto been maintained unsullied."[36] "Amongst the peasantry," she indicated in this first impression, "there is, however, so much of the simplicity of the golden age . . . so much overflowing of heart, and fellow-feeling, that only benevolence, and the honest sympathy of nature, diffused smiles over my countenance."[37]

The civilization she had left behind with its refined culture and its sophisticated enlightenment had left her sad and disappointed "draining off the nourishment from the vital parts."[38] In this letter, she records, "I walked on, still delighted with the rude beauties of the scene; for the sublime often gave place imperceptibly to the beautiful, dilating the emotions which were painfully concentrated."

These literary images denote a sense perception that sees the hand of the creator in the beauty and sublimity of the landscape. This in turn inspires an expansive emotional response or sensibility in the nature of those who inhabit this pastoral region. References to the "heart," "feeling," "benevolence," and "sympathy" underscore the power of these feminine characteristics to invoke the golden age—a more perfect state of civilization.

Wollstonecraft's mistrust and dislike of fraudulent piety, spiritual wickedness even, in high places, has already been examined, and *Letter Nine* is a vivid portrayal and appreciation of a cult of religious feeling drawn from a utilitarian ideological perspective. Comparing this with the restrictive religious code of her own country, she observes,

> The people of every class are constant in their attendance at church; they are very fond of dancing: and the sunday evenings in Norway, as in catholic countries, are spent in exercises which exhilarate the spirits, without vitiating the heart. The rest of labour ought to be gay; and the gladness I have felt in France on a sunday, or decadi, which I caught from the faces around me, was a sentiment more truly religious than all the stupid stillness which the streets of London ever inspired where the sabbath is so decorously observed. I recollect, in the country parts of England the churchwardens used to go out, during the service, to see if they could catch any luckless wight playing at bowls or skittles; yet what could be more harmless? It would even, I think, be a great advantage to the English, if seats of activity, I do not include boxing matches, were encouraged on a sunday, as it might stop the progress of methodism, and of that fanatical spirit which appears to be gaining ground.[39]

The true religious sentiment that Wollstonecraft witnessed on her travels through Norway and the joyful impressions gleaned in France, juxtaposed with the often misguided enthusiasm of bigoted clergy in England, serves to expose the constructed nature of religious teaching and practice in her own country. "Observance of forms" points to the dishonesty and hypocrisy she believes has crept into this simulated religious creed. Gregory Dart suggests, "Throughout the Letters Wollstonecraft cultivates the language of solitary sensibility as a means of cajoling and berating the conscience of her readers."[40] Her letters argue for the reestablishment of natural religion, making a sharp distinction between a faith that inspires a truly religious sentiment and one that is purely ceremonial.[41]

Letter Fourteen emphasizes the value and importance she now places in the senses: "I am persuaded," she records, "If we wish to render mankind moral from principle, we must give a greater scope to the enjoyments of the senses, by blending taste with them. Just as dance and exercise in response to a joyous spirit promote a symmetry of form, so the outward manifestation of grace and refinement serves to pacify and settle the inner being, leading, in turn, towards the cultivation of a virtuous soul and an expansion of the heart."[42]

In similar vein, Wollstonecraft argues that while nature reflects the beautiful, grand architecture represents the sublime, and both produce an effect on the senses:

The same thought has struck me, when I have entered the meeting-house of my respected friend, Dr Price.—I am surprised that the dissenters, who have not laid aside all the pomps and vanities of life, should imagine a noble pillar, or arch, unhallowed. Whilst men have senses, whatever sooths them lends wings to devotion; else why do the beauties of nature, where all that charm them are spread around with a lavish hand, force even the sorrowing heart to acknowledge that existence is a blessing; and this acknowledgement is the most sublime homage we can pay to the Deity.[43]

Wollstonecraft's perspectives are encapsulated in these few lines of *Letter Fourteen*. Architectural grandeur could be said to represent a noble and elevated thought, while a pillar—that column which supported a superstructure—as a metaphor of the stern resolve and strength of character necessary to a virtuous society. These visual representations, just like objects of art, hinted at the creative power of the "first cause."

In gendered terms, the sublimity of fine architecture could be viewed as a masculine representation, while the beauty of nature delineates the feminine. As Ruskin argues in his essay "Of Queens' Gardens," "We are foolish, and without excuse foolish, in speaking of the 'superiority' of one sex to the other, as if they could be compared in similar things. Each has what the other has not: each completes the other, and is completed by the other."[44]

Wollstonecraft's travels enabled her to glimpse the promise behind the beautiful forms of nature; the landscape was to her a reflection of the Deity. The senses that were receptive to this heavenly influence were soothed, and soared to reach divine heights. The recognition and acceptance of this earthly blessing, she came to recognize, was the "most sublime homage we can pay to the Deity." Coalescence of the sublime and the beautiful and its ideological implications were at the heart of this aesthetic discourse.[45]

Wollstonecraft now appears to understand that a pursuit of reason and rationality at the expense of sensibility was not the route toward a more just society. She had already witnessed the demoralization in the ranks of the established church, how materialism and superstition had been allowed to take the place of pure religion. Through these letters she endeavored, as Dart suggested, to "cajole and berate the conscience of her reader."

Although conscious that a mind imbued with sensibility *and* reasoned thinking was a powerful instrument for reform, Wollstonecraft instinctively understood that education should be in tune with contemporary opinion. Maternal instinct drove her to protect her own daughter from what *she* had suffered as a pioneering woman, and she was clearly torn between enlarging her daughter's mind at the expense of her sensibility, or vice versa, as *Letter Six* identifies: "I dread lest she should be forced to sacrifice her heart to her principles, or principles to her heart. With trembling hand I shall cultivate sensibility, and cherish delicacy of sentiment, lest, whilst I lend fresh blushes to the rose, I sharpen the thorns that will wound the breast . . . I dread to unfold her mind, lest it should render her unfit for the world she is to inhabit—Hapless woman! what a fate is thine!"[46]

Wollstonecraft utilizes all the literary tools at her disposal to endorse the eminence of the feminine, drawing on the sentiments of the wits and philosophers. In *Posthumous Works* she expands on and develops Immanuel Kant's theory that "the Fair sex has just as much understanding as the male, but it is a beautiful understanding, whereas ours should be a deep understanding, an expression that signifies the sublime."[47]

Wollstonecraft explains, "Mr Kant has observed, that the understanding is sublime, the imagination beautiful—yet it is evident, that poets, and men who undoubtedly possess the liveliest imagination, are most touched by the sublime, while men who have cold, enquiring minds, have not this exquisite feeling in any great degree, and indeed seem to lose it as they cultivate their reason." She concludes, "I am more and more convinced, that poetry is the first effervescence of the imagination, and the forerunner of civilization."[48] Wollstonecraft appears to identify the "beautiful" as the highest mental state: precursor of intellectual, cultural, and moral refinement. This heightened mental state is that best equipped to activate the "sublime" for the purpose of promoting a more civilized and advanced state of social development.

Letter Twenty-three confirms Wollstonecraft's awareness, through personal experience, of the divisive nature of men who become infected with consumerism, losing sight of life's simple pleasures and family values: "A man," she suggests, "ceases to love humanity, and then individuals, as he advances in the chase after wealth; as one clashes with his interest, the other with his pleasures: to business, as it is termed, every thing must give way; nay, is sacrificed; and all the endearing charities of citizen, husband, father, brother, become empty names . . . Why, to snap the chain of thought, I must say farewell."[49] The "farewell" might refer to the severance of her relationship with Imlay, but on another level, severance from a chain of thought that seeks reform on masculine terms.

Wollstonecraft's pursuit of this "grand cause" was no longer ambivalent, but unequivocal. No longer was this frame of mind, according to Dart, "as it was in the *Vindication*, a faculty complicit with the institutions of patriarchy": it had now become "a utopian principle, an educative force, a symbol of the gap between the present state of society and one of true liberty and equality."[50] The negative "chain of thought," the "tightened cord of life or reason," snapped, and Wollstonecraft, as these *Letters* indicate, was set free to envision the golden age and inhabit the perfect state. The publication of these letters in 1796 was followed some months later by Wollstonecraft's death.

In 1798, Godwin published Wollstonecraft's *Postumous Works*, together with letters she wrote to Imlay, which together with his *Memoirs of the Author of A Vindication of the Rights of Woman* served to seal her fate as a corrupt libertine. Godwin's love and admiration for his wife were not shared by a public who came to regard her as the epitome of all that was worst in the female nature. Poems and novels were published using her life's example as a cautionary tale for other women who were tempted to step outside their sphere. Even in America her reputation was besmirched; publications that portrayed her as representing debauched femininity resulted in her writing being out of print for much of the nineteenth century.[51] Public rejection, however, was overturned with the emergence of the British and American suffrage movement, which regaled her as a feminist icon. Her influence crossed continents, reaching out and touching those minds that were sympathetic to the cause of women.

In the Image of God Created He Them

The challenging of religious bigotry became central to Stanton's reformist arguments; sharply critical of female subordination, resulting, she believed, from their status in the Bible, she wrote to deconstruct what Wollstonecraft had earlier identified as "fables": "notions" upon which "priests have erected their tremendous structures of imposition."[52]

Her *Reminiscences* mark her sorrow at the ignorance, superstition, and blind belief that, she believes, characterize the great religious denominations. While visiting the great cathedrals of France, she always left these monuments with "a feeling of indignation" due, she wrote, to "the generations of human beings who have struggled in poverty to build these altars to the unknown god."[53] The consequence of this ignorance at the heart of theological teaching was that "the whole performance was hollow and mechanical. People walked in, crossed themselves at the door with holy water, and, while kneeling and saying their prayers, looked about examining the dress of each newcomer, their lips moving throughout, satisfied in reeling off the allotted number of prayers in given time."[54] "Theatrical pomp" was how Wollstonecraft referred to this automated religious conduct.[55]

Connecting the earlier arguments with those of later writers confirms that "baton" effect already referred to. Mary Daly was clearly influenced by Stanton's arguments: "Elizabeth Cady Stanton was indeed accurate in pointing out the key role of the myth of feminine evil as a foundation for the entire structure of phallic Christian ideology . . . The myth of the Fall can be seen as a prototypic case of false naming . . . the myth takes on cosmic proportions since the male's viewpoint is metamorphosed into God's viewpoint."[56]

In disputing "the myth," Stanton labored indefatigably to identify woman and her rightful inheritance as an equal heir of God. In a tract written in May 1854, a text that remained in print for many years, and was advertised as *The Position of Woman as Woman, Wife, Widow, Mother*, Stanton argued with regard to the civil ceremony of marriage that "the signing of this contract is instant civil death to one of the parties."[57] She savaged the tyrannical behavior toward woman as wife:

> The woman who but yesterday was sued on bended knee, who stood so high in the scale of being as to make an agreement on equal terms with a proud Saxon man, to-day has no civil existence, no social freedom. The wife who inherits no property holds about the same legal position that does the slave on the southern plantation. She can own nothing, sell nothing. She has no right even to the wages she earns; her person, her time, her services are the property of another. She cannot testify, in many cases, against her husband. She can get no redress for wrongs in her own name in any court of justice. She can neither sue nor be sued. She is not held morally responsible for any crime committed in the presence of her husband, so completely is her very existence supposed by the law to be merged in that of another.[58]

This legislative discourse throws light on the incorrigible nature of the legal system as far as women's rights are concerned, and she points to the marriage ceremony as the instigator of woman being reduced to "chattel" status: "Nature has clearly made the mother the guardian of the child; but man, in his inordinate love of power, does continually set nature and nature's laws at open defiance." Stanton presses an argument that is hedged about with moral and spiritual law: citing the ancient philosophers, the Christian ethic, human conscience, the love of Heaven, and last but not least, the law of mother nature: "Would to

God you could know the burning indignation that fills woman's soul when she turns over the pages of your statute books, and sees there how like feudal barons you freemen hold your women."[59] Appealing to masculine moral and religious sentiment she concludes, "But if, gentlemen, you take the ground that the sexes are alike, and, therefore, you are our faithful representatives-then why all these special laws for woman? Would not one code answer for all like needs and wants? Christ's golden rule is better than all the special legislation that the ingenuity of man can devise: 'Do unto others as you would have others do unto you.' [Matthew 7:12 and Luke 6:31] This, men and brethren, is all we ask at your hands."[60]

Mingling political and religious discourse, she identifies the highest rule of law as that which promotes an inevitable equity and justice: Christ's golden rule. This perspective also emphasizes the mutual nature of her argument, a covert criticism of passivity, it is a call for reciprocal action: *do unto, as you would be done by.*

The introduction to Stanton's *Eighty Years and More* explains, "Women had an obligation to themselves and to that higher power that had made them to speak out on the basis of what their hearts and consciences told them to be true-about the evils of slavery and sexism, and the congenital narrowmindedness of those men who wrote Reverend and Doctor before their names."[61] A letter Stanton wrote to her friend Martha C. Wright reiterates, "If we love the black man as well as we love ourselves, we shall fulfill the Bible injunction."[62] She was clearly conscious that, while women had fought vociferously for the cause of abolition, they were slow to address injustices done their own sex.

REVOLUTION

In January 1868, Stanton, along with Anthony, founded a newspaper, *Revolution,* with the express purpose of becoming a public mouthpiece sensitive to suffrage and humanitarian causes. The title reflected the somewhat rebellious style of its author and its confrontational atmosphere led to inevitable conflict.[63]

A violent disagreement with Horace Greeley, editor of the New York *Tribune* led to his insisting, "I have given strict orders at the *Tribune* office that you and your cause are to be tabooed in the future."[64] This altercation resulted from a certain deviousness on the part of Stanton with regard to a petition drawn up and signed by Mary Cheney Greeley (wife of Horace Greeley). A Constitutional Convention at which Greeley was to present an adverse report on the question of woman suffrage, also included a petition in favor of suffrage. This petition, headed with the name Mary Cheney Greeley, was subtly changed by Stanton to ensure there might be no mistake over the authorship, thus Mr. Horace Greeley's opposition was succeeded by Mrs. Horace Greeley's petition of support, resulting in severe embarrassment to the editor of the *Tribune*.

The founding of the *Revolution*, though regarded by Stanton as one of the happiest periods of her life, nevertheless resulted in much soul-searching. The publication was to be representative of the higher causes in society: "We said at all times and on all subjects just what we thought, and advertised nothing that we did not believe in."[65] An editorial from the January 1868 edition makes plain its intent: "With the highest idea of the dignity and power of the press, this journal is to represent no party, sect, or organization, but individual opinion; editors and correspondents alike, all writing, from their own stand point, and over their own names. The enfranchisement of woman is one of the leading ideas that calls this journal into existence . . . With both man and woman in the editorial department, we shall not have masculine and feminine ideas alone, but united thought on all questions of national and individual interest."[66]

Much pressure was brought to bear on both Stanton and Anthony from those opposed to their reforming initiatives, and she notes, "I feel now that our patience and forbearance with our enemies in their malignant attacks on our good name, which we never answered, were indeed marvelous."[67] While this literary medium, with its wide appeal, appeared to offer opportunities hitherto unavailable to woman, nevertheless it brought severe censure from many of the leading political figures of the day. A letter written to Anthony on December 28, 1869, registers Stanton's strongly held views with regard the title of their newspaper:

MY DEAR SUSAN,-As to changing the name of the *Revolution*, I should consider it a great mistake. If all these people who for twenty years have been afraid to call their souls their own begin to prune us and the *Revolution*, we shall become the same galvanized mummies they are. There could not be a better name than *Revolution*. The establishing of woman on her rightful throne is the greatest revolution the world has ever known or ever will know. To bring it about is no child's play. You and I have not forgotten the conflict of the last twenty years—the ridicule, persecution, denunciation, detraction, the unmixed bitterness of our cup for the past two years, when even friends crucified us. A journal called the *Rosebud* might answer for those who come with kid gloves and perfumes to lay immortal wreaths on the monuments which in sweat and tears others have hewn and built; but for us and for that great blacksmith of ours who forges such red-hot thunderbolts for Pharisees, hypocrites, and sinners, there is no name like the *Revolution* . . . This field is ripe for the harvest . . . I would not see you crushed by rivals even if to prevent it required my being cut into inch bits.[68]

Stanton derogates her detractors in similar style to Wollstonecraft, referring to "galvanized mummies" where Wollstonecraft pointed to the "indolent slugs" who clogged the wheels of advancing society. Both images highlight a heavy hand of oppression intent on blocking reforming initiative; juxtaposed with this portrayal is one that endorses the active ascendancy of woman toward a position from which to effectively liberate the oppressed. The inauguration of woman to her "rightful throne" echoes Eddy's allusion to woman's "dazzling crown" and "sceptered throne" in her poem *Woman's Rights*. Both use laudatory language to appropriate virtue and esteem to womanhood.

Biblical imagery reinforces Stanton's argument; drawing attention to the persecution, denunciation, and detraction that constituted the "bitterness of our cup"; "friends" who crucified them reminds the reader of those earlier Christian pilgrims who suffered at the hands of "Pharisees, hypocrites, and sinners." This portrayal works to link female suffering to Christian discipleship. Further reinforcing this sense of martyrdom, Stanton concludes, "I will wear the yoke a few months longer, bravely and patiently."

The life of the *Revolution* was not long (three years to be exact), but it brought Stanton to the conclusion that in spite of opposition toward her cause, the field was indeed "ripe for harvest."[69] Her own sphere was unconfined, mentally or physically; thus her scope for garnering support was extensive as she travelled freely throughout Europe as well as the American continent.

In an 1870 address, she explains, "The Bible, too, is so interpreted as to make woman the inferior and dependant of man. I ask a new interpretation of God's will, that shall make them joint heirs to the riches and fullness of earth and heaven . . . When woman holds the lofty position God meant she should as mother of the race, base men will find no woman base enough willingly to hand down their vices, diseases, crimes, their morbid appetites, low desire, their tainted blood, that fire in the veins that consumes the workers of unrighteousness."[70] This argument appropriates to woman what is *already* her "right" according to Romans 8:16 and 17: "And if children, then heirs; heirs of God, and joint-heirs with Christ."

There is an anticipatory tone as Stanton concludes: "The day is breaking; it is something to know that life's ills are not showered upon us by the Good Father from a kind of Pandora's box, but that it is His will that joy and peace should be ours. By a knowledge and observance of His laws the road to health and happiness opens before us, and Paradise will be regained on earth"[71] (similar terminology again to Wollstonecraft's "Pandora's box").

A law of God supports Stanton's argument, and it is evidently through an appreciation of God's feminine nature that "maternity [will] acquire a new sacredness and dignity, and a nobler type of manhood and womanhood will glorify the earth" This understanding will in turn lead to man inhabiting this heavenly kingdom here on earth. Stanton explains, "When, in the new development of the race, we shall have true marriage—a union of the great souls masculine and feminine—love, wisdom, justice, mercy, liberty, equality, fraternity, will gladden our earthly pilgrimage, and the Adams and Eves, so long wanderers in the great wilderness of life, will regain their lost Paradise, and live obedient to eternal law."[72]

> One night on the train from New York to Williamsport, Pennsylvania, I found abundant time to think over the personal peculiarities of the many noble women who adorn this nineteenth century, and, as I recalled them, one by one, in America, England, France, and Germany, and all that they are doing and saying, I wondered that any man could be so blind as not to see that woman has already taken her place as the peer of man. While the lords of creation have been debating her sphere and drawing their chalk marks here and there, woman has quietly stepped outside the barren field where she was compelled to graze for centuries, and is now in green pastures and beside still waters, a power in the world of thought.[73]

Stanton chose not to reside in "green pastures" or "beside still waters," as well she may have done approaching her eighth decade. She understood that if the barren nature of the spiritual landscape was ever to become fertile and fruitful again, the myth of the 'Garden of Eden' needed retelling. Woman needed her rightful name and nature restoring to her. This period witnessed, I would suggest, the mental birth of *The Woman's Bible* as a corrective to what Stanton saw as the years of misunderstanding that had led to the subjugation of woman. The next chapter will closely examine this radical literary text as it propelled Stanton toward becoming "a power in the world of thought."

The next section of this chapter will analyze More's later texts, attempting to discover if, as Stanton suggested, "the tact and intelligence of this woman completely turned the tide of opinion . . . and the wise ones of her day gloried in her success."[74]

The Living Christ and Practical Christianity

More was sixty-six years old when *Practical Piety* was published. It was her writing of this period that Hole suggested had "degenerated into decline" but that I will identify as eloquent, compelling, and influential—a result of her personal conversion experience. Smith notes that "there was a religious revival in the late eighteenth and early nineteenth century, with the result that a Christian emphasis infused many lives,"[75] but she pointed to religion as a major contribution toward the reinforcement of separate spheres.

More was undoubtedly disappointed with the "abysmal" (as Smith identifies) state of formal religion in England, especially its inability to confront and correct rampant immorality. The evangelical movement, with its religious enthusiasm and emphasis on moral reform, was embraced by Anglicans and dissenters alike in this period, in the United States as well as Britain. Biblical interpretation was central to this millenarian vision. The most characteristic feature was the personal spiritual awakening of its adherents, which involved probing the heart and searching the soul as a means of individual reform and salvation.

More's purpose as she undertook these later works was "to plant genuine unadulterated Christianity" in the hearts of her readers, to "correct mistakes in religion" and through religion "to give a peace which the world, with all its promises and blandishments, cannot give."[76] A powerful spiritual ethos pervades her discourse and this text was clearly a reflection of a life exemplified; it illustrates, from personal experience, how a "religion of the heart" impinged upon and exerted influence over the "conduct of the life." Authenticity, humility, and an instinctive discernment are what mark the tone of this work replacing the panegyrical discourse of her late-eighteenth century works.

The *politics* of religion through which she had attempted to reform fashionable society had been found wanting in the exigency of personal trauma. More argued that an external conformity to religious practices, even though right in themselves, may be adopted from human motives, and to answer secular purposes: "It is not a religion of forms, and modes, and decencies. It is," she now insists, "being transformed into the image of God. It is being like-minded with Christ." Pomp, pride, and ceremony had no place in this religion of the heart:

this religion was an "internal principle" demanding absolute conse-cration. Moreover, she recommended, "It is the desiring earnestly to surrender our will to his, our heart to the conduct of his spirit, our life to the guidance of his word."[77]

The Blagdon Controversy, 1799–1802

More's tortuous path in the immediate aftermath of the Blagdon crisis apparently led her to two conclusions. The first was the inherent poten-tial for cruelty in man and the abuse of the religious tenet "do unto another as you would have them do unto you." The second resulted from the protracted and malicious attack on her own name and nature, which brought her face-to-face with the need for *individual* reform. She had attempted to initiate social reform on a grand scale up to this point, but it was her own conversion experience that emphasized the need for a personal relationship with God. More feared that the spiritual barrenness she witnessed would eventually lead to the demise of the Church, submitting, "I too, really think the church is in danger, though in another and far more awful sense."[78]

This controversy will not be examined in too much detail: the point of introducing it is to shed light on the noticeable change of tone in More's later writing.

Briefly, the dispute began as a local affair in the year 1799; Wil-liam Wilberforce had encouraged More and her sisters to extend their community care to include the education of the children of the poor. They had responded eagerly, and a number of schools were estab-lished to provide education and moral discipline to the young. The schools quickly became popular and successful, and More was justifi-ably proud of their achievements. However, an incident occurred at the school in Blagdon that led to More being accused of treachery and disloyalty to the church and the state. There were many who questioned the wisdom of educating the lower orders at all, but the most serious allegation came in the form of an attack on her religious persuasion. Was Hannah More a Methodist? Were Methodist prin-ciples being taught in her schools, and was she contributing to the undermining of the doctrines of the Church of England?

The virulence of the dispute became a cause célèbre in the early years of the nineteenth century and culminated in accusations that More was pursuing Jacobinical politics as well as Methodist principles. The attacks on her person and writings were merciless and left More traumatized, humiliated, and broken in spirit.[79] Her diaries and letters testify the depths to which she plumbed and mark each weary step as she reemerged.

More wrote to Wilberforce from Cowslip Green in 1801, "Rachel is still weeping for her children, and refuses to be comforted because they are not instructed.[80] This heavy blow has almost bowed me to the ground." A glimmer of hope emerges however, as she continues, "I doubt not but that he who can bring much real good out of much seeming evil, will eventually turn this shocking business to his glory; and already a *little* light seems to be springing out of this darkness."[81]

In January 1803, a record in More's diary confirms her faith in redemption: "Lord, do thou sanctify to me my long and heavy trials. Let them not be removed till they have answered those ends which they were sent to accomplish . . . O Lord, grant that I may be more fixed in my thoughts, more frequent in self-examination, more heedful of the emotions of my own mind . . . O, Lord, I resolve to begin this year with a solemn dedication of myself to thee."[82]

The evangelical creed included punishment as a means of atonement, and More's diaries and letters chronicle the transformation as it took place in her heart. Her diaries record, in Herbert's words, how she "dressed and undressed her soul" night and day to discover her wrongdoing. In 1804, her atonement was complete: "I have had a life of so much prosperity that I needed powerful correction . . . a comfortable evidence of growth in grace, the desert years are over."[83]

Christianity: An Internal Principle

The preface to *Practical Piety* exhibits the tone and voice More has now chosen through which to exert influence; it is far removed from the dictatorial and authoritative tone of the earlier days: "The writer has endeavoured to address herself as a Christian who must die soon . . . She writes not with the assumption of superiority, but with a deep practical sense of the infirmities against which she has presumed to caution others. She wishes to be understood as speaking the language of sympathy rather than of dictation, or feeling rather than of document."[84] Prior to her conversion experience she spoke the *letter* of Christianity; now she expressed its *spirit*. Sympathy and feeling having replaced dictation and document.

More is keen to establish a basis on which true Christian principles may be constructed. She is clearly disillusioned with the superficiality of outward worship and its potential for perversion of true religion, but is aware of her own limitations: "To point out with precision all the mistakes which exist in the present day, on the awful subject of Religion, would far exceed the limits of this small work."[85]

A letter More wrote to Rev. Richard Hart-Davis in 1821 usefully portrays her firm allegiance to the church establishment. It identifies her awareness of those who allow pernicious political purposes to outweigh the spirit of true religion and gives the reader an intimate glimpse into her own position. Acclaiming a work written by her friend, Mr. Wilks, joint preacher at Bentinck Chapel, that he dedicated to Lord Liverpool, she writes, "Its object [is] to prove the value of a Church Establishment and the vast superiority of the Church of England Establishment. It is a most able, interesting work. The general view very comprehensive . . . very judicious, the style animated and perspicious. He is a zealous friend to the Church, but very candid and blessed, free from all party spirit and virulence."[86]

Practical Piety is a text that emerges from a chastened heart: "The Sacred Writings," More suggests, "frequently point out the analogy between natural and spiritual things. The same Spirit which in the creation of the world moved upon the face of the waters, operates on the human character to produce a new heart and a new life. By this operation the affections and faculties of the man receive a new impulse . . . Genuine religion demands not merely an external profession of our allegiance to God, but an inward devotedness."[87] More's explication credits the heart as an *active* center of spiritual life; mental and physical regeneration begin with a change of heart, and her clear distinction between genuine and professed piety mirrors her sensibility argument.

The Encyclopedia of Religion, quoting Pascal, would appear to define More's argument: "But it is, in addition, the organ that knows an order superior to that of reason: 'It is the heart that feels God and not reason: this is what faith is, God susceptible to the heart and not to reason . . .' Pascal means that reason is not useless, but that it remains insufficient, for it belongs to the natural order, whereas 'the heart has reasons that reason knows not.'"[88]

Challenging doctrinarism she exposes the "pernicious purposes" of the fanatic, and the "pious error of holy men" in her espousal of "genuine piety."[89] More uses this word "genuine" repeatedly in her text: "What doctrine of the New Testament has not been made to speak the language of its injudicious advocate," she proclaims, "and turned into arms against some other doctrine which it was never meant to oppose?"[90] The search for "divine truth" can never be found by what More refers to as "formal religionists"—those who, she suggests, have "probably, never sought, and, therefore, never obtained any sense of the spiritual mercies of God" and consequently "conclude that there is, therefore, no such state."[91]

The Fall

Implicit within the argument of Chapter 1 in *Practical Piety* is the need to get back to a first cause and fixed principles: "The mistake of many in religion appears to be that they do not begin with the beginning."[92] The "beginning" creative account in Genesis 1 recounts, "In the beginning God created the heaven and the earth . . . And God saw every thing that he had made, and, behold, it *was* very good." It concludes, "Thus the heavens and the earth were finished." Could More be hinting at a suggestion that possibly that second creative account, which introduces original sin, is not the place to start? "It is a very bold charge against God's goodness," she suggests, "to presume that he had made beings originally wicked, and against God's veracity to believe, that having made such beings he pronounced them 'good?'"[93]

The "original sin" assumption and its locating of female culpability in the fall of man is fundamental to an argument for female approbation. Wollstonecraft grappled with this position, and clearly More deems it to be an inappropriate and incongruous imputation that a good God could create wicked children *in His image.*

More's "heart religion"[94] is expanded upon in *The Encyclopedia of Religion*: "The discovery of the heart therefore reestablishes human nature in its original state, before the Fall, in rediscovering the energy of the Holy Spirit given by baptism, and in becoming the temple of God once again."[95]

Distancing herself from the damaging notion of woman as the source of sin, More effectively uses "the fall" as the very essence or source of man's redemption:

> When we see how graciously he has turned our very lapse into an occasion of improving our condition; how from this evil he was pleased to advance us to a greater good than we had lost; how that life which was forfeited may be restored; how, by grafting the redemption of man on the very circumstance of his fall, he has raised him to the capacity of a higher condition than that which he has forfeited, and to a happiness superior to that from which he fell.-What an impression does this give us of the immeasureable wisdom and goodness of God, of the unsearchable riches of Christ![96]

The impression left with the reader is that the "lapse" of woman, if it is she who must bear responsibility for the fall, preceded great growth in grace, ultimately preparing her heart for reception of the Christ child. As Walter Gardini argues, "Mary is transformed into the abode of the Spirit, the place of his presence and his action in the world. The Spirit spiritualizes her and makes her divine to enable her to be the mother of God in the flesh."[97]

Atonement and repentance are the keynote of More's brand of Christianity. Her own "fall" from grace has clearly influenced her spiritual perspective, and she now witnesses to the restorative nature of a chastened heart. The strength of humility, the gentleness of mercy and the beauty of virtue are qualities fundamental to this religion of the heart. Taking up the cross requires constant self-examination and self-renunciation on the part of the follower, and these Christly qualities are the nucleus around which More's arguments are arranged.

The advancement of women in society depended upon the influence they were able to exert as guardians of the nation's morals, and More was intent on giving to this influence a holy edict. Speaking on behalf of those subjugated followers of Christ who had been taught to regard themselves as responsible for the sins of the world, she offered hope: "We must not, however, think falsely of our nature, we must humble, but not degrade it." Her claim that "our original brightness is obscured, but not extinguished"[98] seems to be a covert renunciation of "original sin" as the putative responsibility of the female.

This polemic offers a reading that enables woman to be glimpsed in her original glory. Its argument is from a covert feminist position, and while a suggestion of More as a "feminist" is a rather precarious one, the spiritual subtext to the arguments she "humbly" proposes subscribe to the spiritual equality of the sexes. The métier and raison d'être behind More's arguments in this later period of her life, reflect her concern at the injudicious religious advocates whose "pernicious purposes" have promoted a distortion of true Christianity:

> The religion which it is the object of these pages to recommend, has been sometimes misunderstood, and not seldom misrepresented. It has been described as an unproductive theory, and ridiculed as a fanciful extravagance. For the sake of distinction it is here called, *the religion of the heart. There* it subsists as the fountain of spiritual life; *thence* it sends forth, as from the central seat of its existence, supplies of life and warmth through the whole frame; *there* is the soul of virtue, *there* is the vital principle which animates the whole being of a Christian.
>
> This religion has been the support and consolation of the pious believer in all ages of the Church. That it has been perverted both by the cloystered and the uncloystered mystic, not merely to promote abstraction of mind, but inactivity of life, makes nothing against the principle itself.

But if it has been carried to a blameable excess by the pious error of holy men, it has also been adopted by the less innocent fanatic, and abused to the most pernicious purposes.[99]

This argument makes a clear distinction between Christ's Christianity—or the religion of the heart—and its "injudicious" fallacious representation. These basic definitions take More's "sensibility" argument, examined in Chapter 3, onto a higher plane, reflecting the ascending argument of this chapter. Constructing a tangible alternative perspective to that "pious error of holy men," More depicts a womblike place, a space of origination and development from which flows out an active influence. This "central seat" could easily refer to woman herself or the private sphere from which emanates this "life and warmth" of heartfelt (or internal) religion. Spiritual responsiveness was the mark of genuine piety, and honest investigation *from* the pure in heart, allowed the challenging of mistaken or misunderstood doctrine.

Subtly nuanced within More's discourse is a hint that the subjugating of *pure* Christianity may not be so far removed from the oppression and hostility faced by virtuous women who fostered these operative spiritual values: "They seize every occasion to represent it as if it were criminal, as the foe of morality; ridiculous, as the infallible test of an unsound mind; mischievous." For "it" read "she" and the portrayal begins to sound like that of misogynous writers of the period who portrayed woman in similar terms.[100]

More links Christianity with sensibility, sensibility with femininity, and femininity with spirituality. Her connections between the heart as the "central seat of existence" or source of spiritual life and the mother as the nucleus of family life, compellingly substantiate her argument for the exaltation of women and their equal spiritual status with men.

If the reformation of male manners through female influence was the thrust of her early works, when social reform was to be on the basis of the all-pervading cult of sensibility, she *now* seized the initiative to identify and promote a feminized Christianity. Her distinctive theological naming, so there should be no mistake, of *the religion of the heart*, and the inculcation of the maternal with its compassion, tenderness, and fundamental empathy, within religious doctrine, witnesses this. According to More, the "enemies" of this intuitive spiritual awareness or "internal religion" would appear to be those "holy men" who have not only misconstrued "the Word" but also through their ineptitude allowed the noxious and what she refers to as "less innocent fanatic" to distort its message.

More's argument in effect highlights the struggles within the church to enforce orthodoxy. Barker-Benfield explains, "The vision of a barbaric and cruel God, worshipped by cruel forefathers, opposed to a benevolent and sympathetic one, worshipped by more refined and humane congregants of people with 'native Tenderness' in 'their own bosom[s]' corresponded to the struggle between opposing definitions of manhood."[101]

More's very visual discourse clearly defines a God of compassion, radiating love and tenderness to His flock, and this definition aesthetically reinforces the beatitude admonition: "Blessed are the pure in heart: for they shall see God."[102] This perception works to consolidate an image of a first parent who as the source of maternal tenderness effectively authorizes a definition of manhood that embraces femininity. Divine revelation, according to More, is a practical, operative principle, and it is revealed not through "rational persuasion" or "arbitrary compulsions" but rather "require[s] the influence of that Spirit which dictated them"; in other words, revelation or the word of God speaks to the heart made ready:

> Not withstanding that all the truths of religion, all the doctrines of salvation, are contained in the Holy Scriptures, these very Scriptures require the influence of that Spirit which dictated them to produce an influential faith. This Spirit, by enlightening the mind, converts the rational persuasion, brings the intellectual conviction of divine truth, conveyed in the New Testament, into an operative principle . . . A mere historical faith, the mere evidence of facts, with the soundest reasonings and deductions from them, may not be that faith which will fill him with all joy and peace in believing.[103]

More's identifying of the necessary "influence of that Spirit which dictated" Scripture to "produce an influential faith" works to degender spiritual communication. Eddy put it this way: "The divine Science taught in the original language of the Bible came through inspiration, and needs inspiration to be understood. Hence the misapprehension of the spiritual meaning of the Bible, and the misinterpretation of the Word in some instances by uninspired writers, who only wrote down what an inspired teacher had said."[104]

This position became central to the arguments of these women reformers and this intrinsic and elemental standpoint had a dual role: first, it allowed the questioning of centuries-old doctrine, dead rites, and patriarchal interpretation of Scripture; but second, and of equal importance, it emphasized the "native tenderness" or matriarchal nature inherent in God; and the female as well as male, created "in His image."

Practical Piety is infused with religious argument that reinforces the spiritual worth and hence status of women and while the restrictive nature of *this* work makes it impossible to closely examine each chapter, a pronouncement from the preface brings sharply into focus More's identification of Christianity in the feminine: "Christianity may be said to suffer between two criminals, but it is difficult to determine by which she suffers most."[105]

Creating strong analogies, More reinforces her argument: onto the dramatic event of the crucifixion, she carefully superimposes her perspective. The two criminals More referred to were "uncharitable bigotry" and "indiscriminate candour." The first "disguises *her* Divine character, and speculatively adopts the faggot and the flames of inquisitorial intolerance," while the second, "by stripping *her* of her appropriate attributes, reduces *her* to something scarcely worth contending for; to something which, instead of making *her* the religion of Christ, generalizes *her* into any religion which may choose to adopt her.— The one distorts *her* lovely lineaments into caricature, and throws *her* graceful figure into gloomy shadow; the other, by daubing *her* over with colours not *her* own, renders *her* form indistinct, and obliterates *her* features. In the first instance, *she* excites little affection; in the latter, *she* is not recognized."[106]

More's gendered portrayals are particularly persuasive in their promotion of a feminized Christianity, and they mark the ascending scale of her reforming arguments. This form of gendered referencing was not unique to More; William Wilberforce was also writing in similar vein, suggesting, "Christianity has of late years been attacked. Had *she* not been wholly unarmed for the contest, however, *she* might have been forced from *her* untenable posts, and compelled to disembarrass *herself* from *her* load of encumbrances, *she* never could have been driven altogether out of the field by *her* puny assailants."[107]

It needs to be acknowledged that this feminized representation was a controversial one, however; the more typical claims that theology was the preserve of the male were endorsed by men such as Rev. Philip Doddridge. Supporting a tradition of female subordination, he argued in his biblical commentaries that because of her contribution to the "fall," woman should be "less forward in attempting to be guides to others."[108]

More's feminized portrayal of Christianity was also in sharp contrast to that notion of "muscular Christianity" promulgated by authors such as J. J. Rousseau, William Howitt, Maria Edgeworth, and Harriet

Martineau, among others of the period.[109] As the century progressed, this overt masculinization of Christianity was to become more pronounced through writers such as Charles Kingsley (1819–75) and Thomas Hughes (1822–96) when "Christian manliness" became "a common Victorian preacher's catchphrase."[110] *Practical Piety* nevertheless pressed the reforming potential of a feminized Christianity and spiritual vision: "The mists of vanity are dispersed," she writes in the concluding chapter. "The films are removed from *his* eyes."[111]

A high-minded humility marks More's later literary publications. The pride of earlier years, acknowledged by More herself in a letter to Wilberforce—"I mean to re-read, for the fiftieth time, your chapter on the over valuing of human-estimation"[112]—has been replaced by Christian humility. It could be said that "the mists of vanity" have indeed been dispersed and More now writes with a spiritual *insight*, which state could not be further removed from the diminution and regression suggested by Hole. To assist an understanding of More's growth in grace, this chapter will now examine some, as far as I have been able to ascertain, unpublished material discovered at the Bristol Record Office.

A New Tongue

In June 1824, Anna Victoria Inman, wife of Major Little, wrote to her friend Caroline Swaine (later the wife of William C. Bowly), "The Manuscript of Mrs. Hannah More, which I have fastened into this little Book, was obtained for you my dear Caroline under the following circumstances." (Inman had fastened an essay given to her by Hannah More into a small pocket book.)

The essay discusses the attributes of the Bible, and while only a short work, includes a suggestion that I shall argue introduces an important and unique proposition. Before examining this work, a record of the circumstances under which it was obtained will be inspected for the purpose of disputing an image of a woman lacking in mental energy. Inman's letter portrays Hannah More as a woman who at the age of seventy-nine, though suffering some physical decline, expresses great mental activity. Her great number of visitors keep her up to date and abreast of current affairs:

> On the 20 May accompanied by Miss M W I left Redland for Barley Wood—its venerable and interesting mistress having previously sent me an invitation . . . She received us with an encouraging smile of welcome and alluded to her friendship for my late Grandfather in very gratifying

terms—but we were scarcely seated, when a large party arrived from Clifton, they were wholly unexpected & appeared to disturb her a little, as she had just told me a Gentleman from London had already been with her and she hoped we should remain uninterrupted. I should before have told you that her Eyes are remarkably quick & searching, indeed her whole appearance denotes great mental activity . . .

When the visitors entered, the conversation became general—letters were read from Lord Bexley—Montgomery, the Book etc. etc.,—some engravings were handed about.—The Bible Society—family prayer . . . We withdrew.[113]

Upon their return, Inman and More spent some time alone, Inman sharing some lines written by her friend with More. So impressed was she with these that she insisted Inman take something for the author: "I must send something of my own to the authoress." This record of circumstances gives a valuable firsthand account of More, physically and mentally at this late stage of her life. The "something of her own" was the following essay, signed and dated at Barley Wood, May 1824:

The *Bible* is with the most significant emphasis called *The Book*, as containing in itself the sum and substance of all Truth. The Antiquary may admire it as the *oldest* book in the world; the Divine as teaching the only rational and consistant [*sic*] scheme of Theology. The Moralist may consult it as containing the only perfect system of Ethics, the man of taste as abounding with the most sublime and exalted Imagery: the afflicted christian as affording the only source of Consolation.- Other Books may teach us the knowledge of the world, the Bible alone can teach us the knowledge of ourselves. Other Books represent Man according to the peculiar views of the Writer the Bible represents him in his Fall and his Restoration. Other Books may give us the history of the World, the Bible records the History of its Creation, and the prediction of its end. Other Books may teach human Sciences, the Bible alone can teach the Science of Salvation thro' the blood of *Christ*. Other Books may assist in forming us for this transitory Life; the Bible only, can fit us for that Life which will have no end. Other Books may make us wise for Time, the Bible makes us wise for Eternity. When all other Books shall be burnt up in the consuming fire of the great globe itself, the Bible shall survive, in the Souls of the millions it has saved.[114]

This essay confirms that More considers the Bible to be the source-book for life; its message meeting the needs of all humanity. As a piece of work it is entirely representative of More's religious perspective. However, as has already been suggested, More is not averse to secreting deeper meanings that become clear only through close analysis of her texts. Her proposal that "the Bible alone can teach the *Science* of Salvation thro' the blood of Christ"[115] seems at odds somewhat with her portrayal of the intuitive nature of a heart religion.

The term "Science" indicates an organized body of knowledge, a state of knowing or understanding, as opposed to "belief." "Belief," on the other hand, is a concomitant of intuition, something unlearned or spontaneous. Could More be suggesting that a prerequisite to an understanding of the "scientific" sacred teachings is that intuitive spiritual state of pure Christianity? Her juxtaposing of these apparently opposing perspectives needs closer investigation.[116]

One explanatory route might be found through linking More's proposal that "the Bible alone can teach the Science of Salvation" with some of Wollstonecraft's observations: "Mr Kant has observed that the understanding is sublime,"[117] she says, identifying knowledge and judgment in masculine terms. Natural religion or Christianity, on the other hand, is closer to the "intuition" or the "imagination of the beautiful" implicit within the feminine. Taking this argument to its conclusion, More and Wollstonecraft would appear to concur: Wollstonecraft's "men who undoubtedly possess the liveliest imagination, are most touched by the sublime"[118] parallels More's view that "the Science of Salvation" can be reached "thro' the blood of Christ." Put another way, science or true understanding, she seems to be suggesting, is illuminated through the inspired spiritual nature at the heart of pure Christianity.

This explanation would support More's argument that "Christianity has exalted women to true and undisputed dignity . . . equally with men redeemed by the blood of Christ."[119]

Seen in this light, More's argument for the spiritual equality of the sexes is cleverly reinforced, using the Bible as a literary signifier. I would like to suggest that More's purpose was simple, yet profound: close reading of her texts suggest that she did indeed intend to represent spiritual equality through a unique religious understanding. What more powerful way to confirm the status of women than through the book itself: the patriarchal perspective of the Old Testament married to the matriarchal milieu of the New?[120] The two Testaments standing in relation to each other as representations of the highest ideals, offering an equipoise that could be achieved through an understanding of their commensurate value. It could be suggested that, as the beauty and sublimity of the landscape were *physical* representations of their creator, so the Holy Scriptures could be viewed as *literary* portrayals of the understanding (sublime) *and* inspiration (beautiful) of their author.

If this reading was More's intention, she appears to identify the inspirational thought as the higher state. This exegetical perspective contributes to More's desire to disperse the mists of confusion and restore "the purity of a perfect law."[121] Viewed in this light, "The Book" could indeed be said to contain "the sum and substance of all Truth."

"The Scriptures were illumined; reason and revelation were reconciled"[122]
Sensibility's promotion of woman as a repository of spiritual values worked to challenge arguments for her innate sinfulness, and the chapter will now examine an essay, "Man and Woman," written by Eddy in response to masculine claims of "feminine instability."[123] The essay, written in December 1900, will be examined for its particular relevance to the argument of this chapter. It exhibits her careful deconstruction of those critical "truths" shaped according to gendered epistemological values, and displays her conviction as to her own "calling" as well as the equal status of the sexes.

Eddy was already an influential figure, and this essay was written in response to Judge Joseph Clarkson's attempts to impose patriarchal authority on the religious movement she founded.[124]

Clarkson was serving on the Christian Science Board of Lectureship at the time and feared that "feminine instability" would negatively affect its future development.[125] In light of her achievements, which were considerable—author, lecturer, publisher, the establishment of a worldwide church and international daily newspaper all standing to her credit—his desire to usurp her position would appear to reflect contemporary patriarchal opinion.

Eddy, however, was certain she had witnessed a divine order of creation that, when understood, would revolutionize traditional hierarchical arguments. Her intention to publish—"I know of no greater, more valuable, legacy to give to Christian Scientists . . . than the following essay on Christian Science relative to man and woman"—is clear. Why she changed her mind is not so clear. It may well have been that she considered her views too progressive for that period. This essay, arguing for the divinely ordained equality of the sexes offers some rather intriguing perspectives:

"Man and Woman" (c. December 1900)
"God is All in all. He is masculine, feminine, neuter. He is the Father and Mother of the universe . . . The equality of man and woman is established in the premises of this Science. God made them male and female from the beginning, and they were in His image and likeness—not images, but *image*. In the divine Mind there is no sex, no sexuality,

and no procreation; the Infinite Mind includes all in Mind." Eddy's argument for the equality of male and female is absolute: her declaration is unqualified in its insistence that this is a *divinely* ordained paradigm. There is no room for dissension or negotiation in her edict: "Divine modes or manifestations are natural, beyond the so-called natural sciences and human philosophy, because they are spiritual and coexist with the God of nature in absolute Science . . . Inductive or deductive reasoning is correct only as it is spiritual, induced by love and deduced from God."[126]

The essay goes on to say that while "the masculine element has had precedence in history," this "element must not murmur if at some period in human history (the word 'time' is inserted here but crossed through in the original) the verdict should take a turn in behalf of woman, and say, Her time has come."

> At such a juncture I would not dislike to be referee;-I would declare that one was not less, nor more, important in God's sight than the other, and that in the divine order they both originated in One and as one, and should continue thus without taint of sexuality. Why, you admit that God's order has been infringed, and made to represent two sides of a sphere so called, instead of the round whole. This digression came from *suggestion*, even the lie, and the liar that from the beginning was the father of the lie . . . And the question of woman's wrongs and woman's rights sprang from the dire effect of one lie producing another, till the offspring of error mooted these questions to relieve its own creation.

This is an interesting passage; Eddy could have been forgiven if, as referee, she had favored the woman over the man, claiming "her time has come." She rather took the opportunity to emphasize their already equal status according to "divine order" and confirmed this through recourse to the Genesis 1 record of creation: "Originated in One and as one." She identifies any suggestion as to woman's inferiority as mythical, built upon a story that was allegorical, belief in which had led to discrimination against half the human family. While she clearly favored an ideology of separate spheres—"Fulfilling the different demands of their united spheres"[127]—as her earlier writing has shown, this essay argues that she believes it is ultimately only through an understanding of the simultaneous nature (thus equal status) of creation, that religious bigotry will be diffused. At this point, enfranchisement arguments will have been superseded and become irrelevant: "Now, then, let us return to God, to the divine Principle of the universe including the genus man:—we shall find therein no occasion for departure, no occasion for strife, no suggestion of preeminence, or dis-severance of the masculine and feminine elements of God's creating—no question of whom shall be the greatest."

Eddy's essay validates equality; identifying this as a natural outcome of the Divine creative Principle allows her to dismiss any suggestion of hierarchy, but she is not afraid to criticize either sex where she sees the need:

> The feminine weakness that talks when it has nothing to say, that gossips, slanders, unwittingly or unconsciously, that envies or scorns where it should only pity, is out of line with being in Science, and in line with the masculine element that robs innocence of purity, and peoples of liberty and life, in the name of the rights of might. These are indeed dark stains on the brighter disk of humanity. But God's dear love washes away these plague spots, and Divine Science makes clean the inside of the platter, unselfs the human, and gives back the Divine. "To err is human, to forgive, divine."

According to Eddy, "woman's wrongs" or "woman's rights" were not really the issue; she simply took the argument to a higher perspective. She was keen to point out that no one sex had proprietorial rights to divinity. Immoral behavior whether in the form of feminine weaknesses or masculine cruelty, were "dark stains" on the human character; absolution could only be obtained through "God's dear love," which washed away the "plague spots" of evil.

Through scientific argument, Eddy exposed a reading of Scripture that routed that patriarchal doctrine upon which theologians had built their defense of female subjugation. The essay is important in that it allows her to clarify disputed doctrinal issues, but having addressed the wider issues, "the scene shifts" and Eddy now moves to defend her position as leader of the movement she founded.

The sharp distinction between the two faces of the feminine is overtly emphasized. When comparing "feminine weakness," which was what Eddy had been accused of, with the diligent industrious woman who never left her post, but toiled indefatigably to share her message of God's love for humanity, *her* right to *her* seat, she argues, is unequivocal. This "right" has nothing to do with feminist issues; this "right" has been earned. Expression of those Christly qualities have allowed her to transcend the feet of clay. Having spiritually identified the *woman* of God's creating, Eddy is keen to ratify what she believes to be her own divinely bestowed position: "But the scene shifts, and behold a woman! The almond blossom upon her head, busy hands and pen, never leaving the post of duty, but week after week, month after month, and year after year, toiling, watching, praying, and sending forth messages of God's dear love over all the earth. No remuneration, save the blessing it brings to mankind, compensates such a life."[128]

Why is the woman represented with "almond blossoms upon her head"? At first reading this may seem a rather fanciful, even frivolous image, but on closer analysis, this figurative emblem, I would suggest, is used to authorize and authenticate her appointment. It is drawn from Scripture: the book of Numbers records how it is God who appoints and anoints. It explains how the Lord spoke to Moses telling him how *He* will choose those whom He wishes to minister for Him. Twelve rods, one from each eligible family, should be brought to the tabernacle, "and it shall come to pass, that the man's rod, whom I shall choose, shall blossom." The conclusion to this verse is revealing: "and I will make to cease from me the murmurings of the children of Israel, whereby they murmur against you."[129] The chosen rod, Aaron's rod in that case, did indeed bloom blossoms, and yield almonds, and under the circumstances it would seem a perfectly plausible reading of the text.

This essay was a potent rebuke to dissenters, to those men who considered that the church was their domain and required male leadership.[130] At the same time, it was a powerful proclamation of the equal status of the sexes, a panegyric to woman as a force for good; her right to revelation being an inevitable result of her birthright.

Eddy's conviction resulted from a close relationship with her God and with His Word. The Bible was central to her study: "The Bible" she claims, "is the learned man's masterpiece, the ignorant man's dictionary, the wise man's directory,"[131] and to confirm its centrality to her perspectives, I include a brief essay she wrote, titled simply "Bible":

> It is a book of laws to show the right and wrong
> It is a book of wisdom that condems all folly
> It is a book of Truth that condems all error
> It is a book of Life that shows the way from everlasting death
> It will puzzle the surest most skillful Anatomist and critic
> It exposes the subtle sophist, and drives diviners mad
> It is the best covenant that was ever agreed to, the best deed that was ever sealed
> It is a complete code of laws, a perfect body of divinity—an unequalled narrative

There are close similarities to More's essay: More's description of the Bible as "containing in itself the sum and substance of all Truth" is matched by Eddy's explanation of the book as "wisdom that condemns all folly," "Truth that condemns all error," and "Life that shows the way from everlasting death," which links closely with More's claim that "the Bible only, can fit us for that Life which will have no end." More's identification of its appeal to "the Antiquary . . . the Divine . . . the Moralist" is matched by Eddy's reference to the "Anatomist," the "sophist," and the "divines."

Most importantly, however, is their equal and unequivocal recognition of its primacy. "It is the best covenant that was ever agreed to, the best deed that was ever sealed / It is a complete code of laws, a perfect body of divinity an unequalled narrative," says Eddy. More identifies it as the book that contains "the only perfect system of Ethics . . . the most sublime and exalted imagery . . . the only source of Consolation."

This leaves possibly only two key distinguishing features between the edicts: the first is that Eddy's is unpunctuated; this literary device has the effect of leaving the reader with an "unconfined" impression rather than that sense of closure a period might bring to a message. Second, and this is a major point, Eddy did not sign the piece with her own name as had Hannah More, but concluded with "Author-God."[132] Might this have been in recognition of God as author of the Bible, or was Eddy pointing rather to the revelatory nature of its inception, as with her text *Science and Health*? "The Scriptures were illumined," she wrote, "reason and revelation were reconciled . . . No human pen nor tongue taught me the Science contained in this book."[133]

This is a key issue in terms of the argument of this chapter, building upon that earlier linking of spiritual sensibility with divine vision. This vision or "right to revelation" according to these authors, is not the prerogative of either sex but rather the result of a spiritual awakening (a genderless spiritual awakening) what More referred to as "genuine religion." The sanctioning of a "feeling" heart effectively authorized these spiritual seers to bring fresh insights to what More identified as "misrepresented" religion, biased views that had promoted a dereliction of God's feminine side in favor of the masculine.

The importance of the Bible to the religious outlook of each author is unequivocal, but their analytical techniques differed; this is most evident in the case of Eddy and Stanton's perspectives. The publishing of *The Woman's Bible* brought a sharp riposte from Eddy in the form of a short literary composition titled simply "Womans Bible": "The woman's man's Bible is the womans bible," she proclaims. "We cannot have two if the sexes are equal."[134] These perspectives will be closely examined in the next and final chapter.

CONCLUSION

In this chapter, I have pointed to "corrupt interpretations" of Scripture as possibly the chief conduit of misinformation relating to woman and her spirituality.

Paying close attention to what appears to be a recurring theme in the arguments of the authors—what they refer to as "wild tradition," "fallacious and mistaken" doctrine, in terms of accepted religious belief—I have identified the deleterious effects of a bigoted religion bound by "an observance of forms." Exposing the core masculinity of this dogma and contrasting its negative influence with a true religious sentiment of natural revealed religion, what More termed "unadulterated Christianity," a God in the feminine has been identified. This recognition has sanctioned and authorized womanhood.

New England preacher Reverend Joseph Richardson in "A Sermon on the Duty and Dignity of Woman" outlined the privileged confinement of the female sex: "The world concedes to you the honor of exerting an influence, all but divine; but an influence you lose the power to exert, the moment you depart from the sphere and delicacy of your proper character."[135]

The final chapter will examine how Eddy and Stanton attempted to exert this divine influence through two key reformative religious texts. Operating outside their "sphere" but maintaining that sensitivity of character, *Science and Health with Key to the Scriptures* and *The Woman's Bible* will be examined in the light of their identification of a Deity in the feminine.

Figure 5. A likeness of Elizabeth Cady Stanton by Sharon Winter

Figure 6. A likeness of Mary Baker Eddy by Sharon Winter

CHAPTER 5

WOMAN, THE ELECT OF GOD?

SLAVES, SALVATION, AND MATRIARCHAL MINISTERS

Jesus Christ raised women above the condition of mere slaves, mere ministers to the passions of men, raised them by His sympathy, to be Ministers of God . . . there shall arise a woman, who will resume, in her own soul, all the sufferings of her race, and that woman will be the Saviour of her race.

—Florence Nightingale, *Cassandra*

Undermining centuries of religious tradition in terms of the status of women in society, Stanton and Eddy inverted theological argument and created an interpretative space from which to challenge a singular definition concerning creation in Genesis and prophecy in Revelation. Identification of the maternal nature of the Godhead allowed them to represent God in feminine terms, destabilizing centuries of historically accepted patriarchal argument. The writers' identification of "elect" womanhood in these two books, the first and the last of the Bible, will form the nucleus of the argument of this final chapter.

THE WOMAN QUESTION

Women's suffrage was an important issue in nineteenth-century Boston, and while the aim of women reformers was to determine the rights of women in social and political life, there were in fact different groups, and different approaches to this issue, within the movement as a whole. In spite of inevitable connections between the groups, there are nevertheless some key divergences. Possibly the most important of these, for the purpose of this work, is that of Biblical interpretation.

"The Word" and its "Re-Wordings" needs close examination in the light of the authors' arguments for the "elect" nature of womanhood.

Wollstonecraft and More had both challenged Scriptural authenticity: Stanton and Eddy also identified the levels of distortion they believed crept into Biblical exegesis. Stanton, quoting Disraeli suggests there were 150,000 blunders in the Hebrew, and 7,000 in the Greek.[1] Eddy referred to "the thirty thousand different readings in the Old Testament, and the three hundred thousand in the New."[2]

Had dissenting religious attitudes paved the way for these radical reformers, and was the time now right for the publication of two textual challenges to historical theological interpretation? A key touchstone in dealing with these issues will be distinctions made between "religion" and "spirituality," between religious "belief" and spiritual "understanding," what Eddy refers to as "the warfare between this spiritual idea and perfunctory religion, between spiritual clear-sightedness and the blindness of popular belief."[3]

Contemporary public opinion exposes the religious constraints to which they were subject. George Keely, a nineteenth-century Baptist minister, defined the political, religious, and cultural parameters of female participation in American society when he proclaimed, "That woman appears to me lost to modesty and prudence, who has boldness enough to teach or exhort where men are present. If she were a relative of mine, I should request her to change her name and remove to a distance where her connections were not known."[4]

New England preachers chose their Bible texts with care; women were stepping outside their sphere and seizing for themselves an autonomy that some religionists were not comfortable with and in an attempt to reaffirm masculine superiority, they emphasized texts from the Bible, which they considered preached female subordination.[5]

Juxtaposed alongside this restrictive religious perspective, a more spiritual cultural era was emerging: the period from 1828 to 1865 was known as the American Romantic period, the American Renaissance, or the Age of Transcendentalism. Mirroring the philosophical arguments for the inspiration, vision, and transcendence that marked British Romanticism, this literary and philosophical movement was centered around Boston. Adherents included Ralph Waldo Emerson, A. Bronson Alcott, Margaret Fuller, and Elizabeth Peabody. M. H. Abrams suggests that "in all the major literary genres except drama, writers produced works of an originality and excellence not exceeded in later American history."[6]

This movement was highly influential in promoting a religious "feeling" and emotional mood that emphasized "free thought" and was antipathetical to the rigid religious rationalism that had marked earlier periods. American writing had its roots in European literary history, and the literary arguments of the day mirrored the political and religious debates across the Atlantic.

The Transcendentalists believed in "the validity of knowledge that is grounded in feeling and intuition." Abrams suggests that Samuel Taylor Coleridge was an "intellectual antecedent of American Transcendentalism."[7] They believed that a limited human sense could be literally transcended through an intuitive relationship with a divine first cause. The influence of the Romantics on this philosophical movement was evident in their arguments for "original innocence" over "original sin" and a poetic promotion of the natural world over corruption and materialism.

While didactic tracts in a variety of genres had been written by female reformers in their attempts to influence society, it was the moralistic novels of writers such as Frances Hodgson Burnett, Louisa May Alcott,[8] and Harriet Beecher Stowe that were perhaps more representative of American literary didacticism. This somewhat uncontroversial style of writing was deemed a suitable genre for women writers, and allowed the authors to promote their pious ideals through the drawing room. It did not, however, lift that heavy patriarchal hand of theological oppression. This task required a foray into that more masculine genre of theological discourse, a genre into which few women writers had ventured.

Toward a Discourse of Transfiguration

The religious inclinations of women had received public impetus in the wake of the cult of sensibility, and in spite of attempts to curtail those *bold* enough to teach or preach, their natural endowments and sensibility of disposition made them fitted to minister to a society losing its way.

A *Woman's Bible* and a *Key to the Scriptures* were, however, by any stretch of the imagination, a radical venture for these nineteenth-century authors: they smacked of rebellion and laid them open to charges of heresy—indeed the titles alone would have been considered provocative. These texts marked a critical strategy that drew on the "head" as well as the "heart"; they were powerful in that they reflected the personal struggles and emerging spiritual self-identification of their authors. Their breaking with ecclesiastical tradition reflected a scholarly and academic praxis on the part of their authors. Originality marked the arguments, bringing sharply into focus the subtextual implications of earlier works. Challenging patriarchal values and meanings of sacred texts, they deconstruct discriminatory theological doctrine, registering a Protestantism with a unique critique of biblical history.[9]

Eddy spent three and a half years writing *Science and Health with Key to the Scriptures*; it was published in 1875 by a small Boston printer, W. F. Brown & Co, who printed and bound the first 1,000 copies.[10] She constantly revised her book over the next few years in an attempt to refine its meaning. In 1889, putting aside her other activities, Eddy spent some two years preparing the fiftieth edition; the book evolved through some 400 editions.[11]

It is recorded that "after the publication of *Science and Health*, Mrs. Eddy sent copies to libraries and various people of note, including Bronson Alcott . . . Alcott, well aware of the hardships that fame can bring to pioneering thinkers, visited Mrs. Eddy, saying, 'I have come to comfort you.'"[12] His written response to the text usefully contributes to the argument of this chapter: "The sacred truths which you announce sustained by facts of the immortal Life, give to your work the seal of inspiration-reaffirm in modern phrase, the Christian revelation." Clearly a progressive thinker, he concluded, "And my joy is heightened the more when I find the blessed words are of woman's divinings."[13]

It is worth noting that to date this book has sold some ten million copies, been translated into seventeen languages including Braille, and in 1992 was listed by the Women's National Book Association as one of the seventy-five books by women whose words have changed the world.[14] Eddy's argument was not an overtly feminist one; she believed, as had More, that an enlightened understanding of Scripture was the most effective means by which to authorize the spiritual equality of the female. Her critical approach, I would suggest, had more in common with More's *Practical Piety*, than *The Woman's Bible*.

The hallmark of *Science and Health* was its innovative use of language. Acknowledging the originality of her diction, she declared, "The liberty that I have taken with capitalization, in order to express the 'new tongue,' has well-nigh constituted a new style of language."[15] She used the Bible as a means of inspiration for her new language, incorporating this into a poetic prose that in some instances imitated the rhythms and cadences of the Scriptures. She confirmed the inspired nature of its inception: "No human pen nor tongue taught me the Science contained in this book, SCIENCE AND HEALTH; and neither tongue nor pen can overthrow it."[16]

The Woman's Bible conversely was the production of a committee of women and was in itself a "scientific" exercise. Focusing on textuality, its purpose was to expose inconsistencies, as it searched for truth and authenticity in regard to female identity. In 1882, Stanton explained "I tried to organize a committee to consider the status of women in the *Bible*, and the claim that the Hebrew Writings were the result of divine inspiration. It was thought very presumptuous for women not learned in languages and ecclesiastical history to undertake such work. But as we merely proposed to comment on what was said of women in plain English, and found these texts composed only one-tenth of the Old and New Testaments, it did not seem to me a difficult or dangerous undertaking." She was to learn otherwise, but was pragmatic as the following confirms: "Like other 'mistakes,' this too, in due time, will be regarded as 'a step in progress.'"[17]

The idea of collaboration is interesting: Stanton possibly hoped this route might deflect hostile attention to individuals. Stanton's feminist and religious principles were, however, to cost her dearly: her father disinherited her, and the women who had revered her as a leading campaigner for women's rights ostracized her as author of *The Woman's Bible*. Marla Selvidge points out, "Unfortunately this critical approach to the Bible caused so much negative criticism that it was never taken seriously by any of the societies within the women's movement."[18]

WOMAN AND THE WORD

The original language of the Bible came through inspiration, and needs inspiration to be understood.

—Mary Baker Eddy, *Science and Health with Key to the Scriptures*

Diversity and conflict of opinion have surrounded scriptural interpretation for 2,000 years. *The Encyclopedia of Religion* suggests that "powerful intellectual currents have brought hermeneutics once again to the fore, so that interest in it has burgeoned among literary critics . . . and students of religion."[19]

Expanding on this subject of hermeneutics, Friedrich Schleiermacher (1768–1834), who is widely acknowledged to be the founder of modern hermeneutics, presented a compelling argument. Referred to as the "Kant of hermeneutics," Schleiermacher argued that "the nature of language was the crucial theoretical issue confronting hermeneutical theory, because one could gain access to another person's meaning only through the medium of language." Under the subheading "Authorial Intention," *Encyclopedia of Religion* explains,

Schleiermacher's hermeneutical theory is organised around two foci: (1) the grammatical understanding of any characteristic modes of expression and the linguistic forms of the culture in which a given author lived and which conditioned that author's thinking and (2) the technical or psychological understanding of the unique subjectivity or creative genius of that author. Both these foci reflect Schleiermacher's own indebtedness to Romantic thinkers who had argued that any individual's mode of expression, however unique, necessarily reflects a wider cultural sensibility or spirit (*Geist*). A correct interpretation requires not only an understanding of the cultural and historical context of an author, but a grasp of the latter's unique subjectivity. This can be accomplished only by an "act of divination"—an intuitive leap by which the interpreter "relives" the consciousness of the author.[20]

Spiritual discourse drew on a literary tradition that promoted a transcendency of the human mind as a prerequisite state. The Romantic poets, Coleridge, Barbauld, Wordsworth, and Charlotte Smith, for example, evidenced this style of linguistic emotionalism that marked them as poetic intermediaries, opening the way for a religious idealism built on free thought principles instead of doctrinal religious dictate.

Ian Finseth suggests in his thesis "Liquid Fire Within Me" that in this era "Doctrinal niceties and complicated theological disputations gave way to a simpler, more 'authentic' form of language that would move people emotionally." He pointed out that both Transcendentalists and Evangelicals "participated in a shift from a traditional form of discourse in which language primarily served the function of scriptural exegesis to one in which language operated to spark religious emotion. In this move from linguistic rationalism to linguistic emotionalism, both movements engaged in what has come to be understood as a realignment from an Enlightened to a Romantic understanding of language."[21]

While not suggesting that Stanton or Eddy belonged to either movement, it would seem safe to assume that the Age of Transcendentalism did for their arguments what the Age of Sensibility had done for their predecessors, offering in effect, a cultural space from which to challenge a biblical interpretation that Selvidge pointed to as "riddled with errors."[22]

The problem facing female religious reformers was inevitably one of communication; that women were receptive to divine inspiration had become acceptable, but the linguistic promotion of their religious ideals required a unique, some might say, virgin idiolect. Eddy explains, "In its literary expression, my system of Christian metaphysics is hampered by material terms, which must be used to indicate thoughts that are to be understood metaphysically."[23]

Sallie McFague suggests, "The last word as well as the first word in theology is surrounded by silence. We know with Simone Weil that when we try to speak of God there is nothing which resembles what we can conceive when we say that word."[24]

The task, then, that these women took upon themselves was to develop a vernacular through which to effectively communicate their fresh Scriptural insights, what Eddy termed "the language of Spirit." Through this new tongue, they attempted to make the Deity discernible, and to disclose the divine rights of that feminine representation, created simultaneously with the masculine, in the image and likeness of their creator.

Between the years 1866 and 1869 Eddy wrote a 600-page manuscript titled "The Bible in Its Spiritual Meaning." Expanding on the question "What is the language of Spirit?" she explained, "Certainly it is spiritual. The German talks the German language the Frenchman the French and the Englishman the English . . . Science has . . . one tongue namely the idiom of God—the spiritual language of Spirit."[25] Drawing on "linguistic rationalism *and* linguistic emotionalism," Eddy's "language of Spirit" might well be identified in terms of what McFague refers to as a "New Sensibility."

Schleiermacher's explanation of "the various religions as culturally conditioned forms of an underlying and universal religious sensibility" supports this theory and contributes to an argument that through a heightened state of consciousness, a clear-sighted spirituality, women could become divine intermediaries.[26]

In her text *Models of God*, McFague devotes a chapter to "A New Sensibility" pointing to "the value of deconstruction's critique of Western metaphysics for the new sensibility needed to do Christian theology."[27] Eddy's "language of Spirit" certainly "does" Christian theology, disputing and deconstructing oppressive theological dictate.

In a paper titled "Understanding Mary Baker Eddy," Thomas Johnson suggests that "those inclined to take her spiritual perspective more seriously, and patient enough to wrestle with the language in which she labored to convey it, saw something more akin to what the secular writer George Steiner described in the radical twentieth century French convert to Christianity Simone Weil: 'intimations of a common thirst for light on the other side of reason, but rationally urged and somehow communicable, sensible to human thought and discourse.'"[28]

The New Sensibility

There is "an obvious continuity between [Eddy's] earliest and her latest religious experiences, as they are reflected in her writing" according to Peel in his biography of Eddy, "and she herself felt that in one sense she was only seeing more deeply into the Christian faith she had had since girlhood."[29]

Engaging with and expanding then that "sensibility" debate over the nature of God—that identification of God as sympathetic and tender, rather than harsh patriarchal dictator—Eddy portrayed God as Mother as well as Father, suggesting even, "In divine Science, we have not as much authority for considering God masculine, as we have for considering Him feminine, for Love imparts the clearest idea of Deity."[30] The portrayal of God's motherhood in these terms allowed Eddy to identify and expand on the spiritual status of womanhood. "The ideal woman," she suggests, "corresponds to Life and to Love."[31]

Eddy wrote to Clara Choate in terms that identified her expectations of this "ideal woman": "It is glorious to see what the women *alone* are doing here for temperance, more than ever man has done." Confirming her faith in the *religious* reforming potential of women, and in a tone that mirrors that of Hannah More, she concludes, "This is the period of *women, they* are to move and to carry all the great moral and Christian reforms."[32]

Emphasizing her sympathies with the movement of women, she is careful to locate their "rights" in their spirituality: "Let it not be heard in Boston that woman, 'last at the cross and first at the sepulchre,' has no rights which man is bound to respect. In natural law and in religion the right of woman to fill the highest measure of enlightened understanding and the highest places in government, is inalienable, and these rights are ably vindicated by the noblest of both sexes. This is woman's hour, with all its sweet amenities and its moral and religious reforms."[33]

> "This is the period of women."[34]
>
> "This is woman's hour."[35]
>
> "The right of woman to fill the highest places . . . in government, is inalienable."[36]
>
> "Women are to move and carry all the great moral and Christian reforms."[37]

These arguments, while exuding female potential, are not unlike those earlier ones put forward by both Wollstonecraft and More.

The real ideological shift came through a unique identification of women's spiritual and God-given nature, and it was to the Bible that Eddy turned for literary confirmation of her compelling alternative to woman's subservient station. Searching for "light on the other side of reason," she drew on logic and inspiration: "In this revolutionary period," she wrote, "like the shepherd-boy with his sling, woman goes forth to battle with Goliath."[38] The analogy is interesting: Goliath with all his male might was deposed by the stone and the sling of a simple shepherd-boy.

"In the beginning..."

So God created man in His own image, in the image of God created He him; male and female created He them.

—Genesis 1:27

And the Lord God (Jehovah) formed man of the dust of the ground . . . And the Lord God (Jehovah, Yawah) caused a deep sleep to fall upon Adam, and he slept: and He took one of his ribs, and closed up the flesh instead thereof; and the rib, which the Lord God (Jehovah) had taken from man, made He a woman.

—Genesis 2:21, 22

Eddy possibly saw patriarchal theological opposition in terms of Goliath proportions; how was she to break down the tremendous weight of opposition to female spiritual equality? Her "stone," I would suggest, could be likened to her word or expression, while her sling might be identified as representing the precipitate launching of her edict or proclamation on a society that oppressed the weaker sex.

In *Practical Piety*, More had argued that "the mistake of many in religion appears to be, that they do not begin with the beginning."[39] Eddy moved precipitately to target and dispute the establishment of an inferior female identity "in the beginning." "The infinite," she suggests, "has no beginning. This word *beginning* is employed to signify *the only*."[40] A dictionary definition of this word "only" is "unique by virtue of being superior,"[41] and this explanation could be applied to her argument for the inimitable nature of the first record of creation that she refers to as "the spiritual record of creation, to that which should be engraved on the understanding and heart 'with the point of a diamond' and the pen of an angel."[42]

Impressed in this way on the sense *and* sensibilities, historically and "culturally conditioned" religious views could be challenged through an enlightened discernment, a clear-sighted spirituality.

This perspective has the effect of liberating scripture from doctrinal dictate, of shifting the argument from a doctrinal to a spiritually inspired one, confirming distinctions between religion and spirituality. It was to this higher "sense" that Eddy credited her ability to differentiate between what she considered to be the spiritual and material, accounts of creation: "Through spiritual sense you can discern the heart of divinity, and thus begin to comprehend."[43] She admits, "Mortal thought does not at once catch the higher meaning, and can do so only as thought is educated up to spiritual apprehension."[44]

Earlier chapters have already examined the writers' arguments as they distinguished between the two representations of sensibility: the spiritual with its potential promise for femininity and its material and potentially destructive opposite. The succeeding argument, it could be suggested, mirrors the style of that earlier one. Differentiating between the two representations of womanhood—that made in the image of God, and the allegorical creature taken from man's rib— allows identification of a spiritual hierarchical order, one that legitimizes a female elect.

Original Sin

Central to an argument for female election is the authors' explication of the account of creation; there is no doubt that an account in which woman is taken *from* the bone of man and created as helpmeet *to* man, suggests a subserviency. Their "beginning" arguments will therefore be examined closely; it is worth noting that both Stanton and Eddy argue the validity of the record in Genesis 1, pointing to the strictly allegorical nature of the subsequent account. Deconstruction of historically accepted arguments for female subservience vis-à-vis, the "afterthought" nature of her creation, and her culpability in the fall of man, are therefore central to attempts to grant her sanctified status.

Their claim is especially interesting in the light of its effective disputation of other authors' "original sin" arguments; arguments like those in Aemilia Lanyer's "Salve Deus Rex Judacorum," which sought to blame Adam as the *source* of Eve's derivation: "If any Evill did in her [Eve] remaine, Beeing made of him [Adam], he was the ground of all [*sic*]"[45] and Hannah More's "atonement" perspective: "When we see how graciously he has turned our very lapse into an occasion of improving our condition."[46]

The Woman's Bible and *Science and Health*, through a literal and figurative discourse, deconstruct that latter record, the one as the work of a "highly imaginative editor" whose purpose was to prove woman's inferiority,[47] the other suggesting, "Spiritually followed, the book of Genesis is the history of the untrue image of God, named a sinful mortal."[48] "Original sin" arguments viewed in this light would therefore be simply symbolic, mythical, and parable.

Eddy's "spiritual interpretation" involved that awareness or intuition associated with women, by the cult of sensibility, confirming the "underlying religious sensibility" as cited by Schleiermacher. Indeed, she writes, "Spiritual sense, contradicting the material senses, involves intuition."[49] By its very nature, this argument authorizes the feminine on two levels: the first is to emphasize female receptivity to messages from God, the second is that through this higher state of consciousness or spiritual discernment, confirmation of essential religious truths that *support* her supremacy is uncovered. Eddy explains, "Divine logic and revelation coincide. If we believe otherwise, we may be sure that either our logic is at fault or that we have misinterpreted revelation."[50]

Close attention to sacred texts allows Eddy to develop an argument through which to challenge epistemological "truths": "The Scriptures are very sacred," she says. "Our aim must be to have them understood spiritually, for only by this understanding can truth be gained."[51] Exposing a belief system constructed upon masculine values, she identifies a parallel reading through which to legitimize the hereditary spiritual status of women. Explaining the term "man" as generic, Eddy argues that "masculine, feminine, and neuter genders are human concepts."[52]

Gillian Gill, quoting from the first edition of *Science and Health*, submits that "[Eddy] distinguishes sharply between Genesis 1 and 2, accepting the former as the word of God, and rejecting the latter as the revisionist work of timid scribes: 'they spake from error, of error, and from the standpoint of matter attempted to define Spirit, which accounts for the contradistinctions in that glorious old record of creation.'"[53]

Gill concludes that "Mrs. Eddy reads Genesis 1 to say that gender is primary in man since God is both male and female . . . Male and female cannot be one in person, but are one in Principle, and if God is a person his gender would be both male and female, these being the likenesses of Him, as the Scripture informs us . . . Gender is embraced in Spirit, else God could never have shadowed forth from out Himself, the idea of male and female."[54]

Gill assumes an incredulous note: "With even more daring she claims that woman is the higher of the two since she was the latter to be created: 'We have not as much authority in science, for calling God masculine as feminine, the latter being the last, therefore the highest idea given of Him.'"[55]

Spiritual Semantics

The elusive nature of words in conveying higher concepts was of particular concern to Eddy, and Gill identifies Eddy's idiolectic use of a semantic code as similar to that of the French philosopher, psychoanalyst, and feminist, Luce Irigaray.[56] She points to "the circular, oracular, repetitious, strongly metaphorical progression of Mrs. Eddy's text," together with "its exploration of the semantics of typography," demanding the reader's "active participation." This literary style was in itself antithetical to the rigid staticity that marked the ancient ceremonials and points to a charged and vital author-reader relationship. Through fresh and innovative argument, Eddy juxtaposed the "blindness of popular belief"[57] with intuitive divine vision, suggesting, "This Soul-sense comes to the human mind when the latter yields to the divine Mind. Such intuitions reveal whatever constitutes and perpetuates harmony."[58]

Finseth pointed to the "advance of scriptural 'higher criticism'" in this period, "which held that the language of the Bible did not possess absolute authority but, as a product of human endeavour, filtered through the imperfect medium of the human mind, could only approximate those Christian truths which did possess absolute authority. In effect," he concluded, "the evidence of truth was not the words themselves, but the intuitive feeling that what the words attempted to express was truth."[59]

Eddy writes, "Human reason and religion come slowly to the recognition of spiritual facts." [60] She suggests, "The Judaic religion consisted mostly of rites and ceremonies. The motives and affections of man were of little value."[61] Interpretation, then, of those Christian truths through a higher criticism, was Eddy's route to spiritual explication: "Inspired writers interpret the Word spiritually, while the ordinary historian interprets it literally."[62] Here we have what is possibly the clearest signal yet of the state of sensibility necessary to "do" Christian theology. Drawing on Protestant sensibilities to differentiate between "religious belief" and "spiritual understanding," Eddy is careful to distinguish between objective religious truths based on history and patriarchy, and that active vital connection with the Deity, through which spirituality is discerned.

"Ritualism and creed," she argues, "hamper spirituality."[63] If, therefore, she can successfully portray the *receptive* thought as the highest in terms of its ability to commune with God, her own dissenting arguments will inevitably carry more weight.

Clearly, both Eddy and Stanton were of the opinion that a religious sensibility, rather than dead rites and dogma, was the route to spiritual truth: "Even the Christian Church itself is not based upon Christ as a Saviour," says Stanton, "but upon its own teachings that woman brought sin into the world, a theory in direct contradiction, not only to the mysteries, but to spiritual truth."[64] She concludes, "The canon law, the Scriptures, the creeds and codes and church discipline of the leading religions bear the impress of fallible man, and not of our ideal great first cause, 'the Spirit of all Good.'"[65]

The foregoing encourages the legitimizing of an argument that Scriptural illumination proceeded from a space that transcended the public academic and civic space. Eddy identifies this instinctive state: "ANGELS. God's thoughts passing to man; spiritual intuitions, pure and perfect."[66] This intuitive state, or transcendental wisdom, Finseth suggests, allowed the speaker to "act as a kind of organ-pipe for immutable spiritual principle," concluding that "since his language took as its reference this principle his auditor would automatically sense its truth."[67]

Attempting, then, to recover "those Christian truths which did possess absolute authority," Eddy strove to distinguish between contradictory biblical representations of femininity. Juxtaposing biblical narratives, and sifting between what she understands to be truth and allegory, she points to human hypotheses as having "darkened the glow and grandeur of evangelical religion."[68]

Linguistic communication of transcendental thought was essential if she was to furnish that theological "silence" referred to by McFague. Eddy begins this task in logical form and inspirational style, attributing to the creator and His creation tangible and identifiable qualities:

GOD. The great I AM; the all-knowing, all-seeing, all-acting, all-wise, all-loving, and eternal; Principle; Mind; Soul; Spirit; Life; Truth; Love; all substance; intelligence.[69]

MAN. The compound idea of infinite Spirit; the spiritual image and likeness of God; the full representation of Mind.[70]

In her paper "God in the Feminine," Mulder points to Feuerbach's description of God as "the mirror of man";[71] Eddy inverts this portrayal, describing man as the mirror of God: "Now compare man before the mirror to his divine Principle, God. Call the mirror divine Science, and call man the reflection."[72] This explanation registers the resemblance of man to God, preempts any suggestion of original sin, and effectively sets the seal on gender equality, the male and female of His creating: "Note how true," she says, "is the reflection to its original."

Original Innocence

Gender ideologies have flourished through acquaintance with the second, rather than the first chapter of Genesis, and for the purpose of qualifying the status of woman, Eddy confirms this first record as the unique and only beginning. She illustrates the inevitable equality of man, made "in our image, after our likeness" (Gen. 1:26). Identifying "man" as "the family name for all ideas, the sons and daughters of God,"[73] she verifies her argument:

> God fashions all things, after His own likeness. Life is reflected in existence, Truth in truthfulness, God in goodness, which impart their own peace and permanence. Love, redolent with unselfishness, bathes all in beauty and light. The grass beneath our feet silently explains, "The meek shall inherit the earth." The modest arbutus sends her sweet breath to heaven. The great rock gives shadow and shelter. The sunlight glints from the church-dome, glances into the prison-cell, glides into the sick-chamber, brightens the flower, beautifies the landscape, blesses the earth. Man made in His likeness, possesses and reflects God's dominion over all the earth. Man and woman as coexistent and eternal with God forever reflect, in glorified quality, the infinite Father-Mother God . . . The ideal woman corresponds to Life and to Love. In divine Science, we have not as much authority for considering God masculine, as we have for considering Him feminine, for Love imparts the clearest idea of Deity.[74]

This figurative discourse identifies the masculine and feminine natures that, Eddy believes, are expressions of God; aesthetic binaries allow her to characterize the masculine and feminine through gendered landscape imagery. This richly descriptive passage is of a typically "romantic" genre and has echoes of William Blake's style: it takes the traditional language of the Bible and through visual imagery creates a sensory perception. Abrams identifies Blake's "Songs of Innocence" as using a "technique of compressed metaphor and symbol which explode into a multiplicity of references"[75] and this metaphorical style of signification is valuable in making the intangible tangible.

In her text *Metaphorical Theology*, McFague explains, "Poets use metaphor all the time because they are constantly speaking about the great unknowns—mortality, love, fear, joy, guilt, hope, and so on. Religious language is deeply metaphorical for the same reason and it is therefore no surprise that Jesus' most characteristic form of teaching, the parables, should be extended metaphors. Less obvious, but of paramount importance, is the fact that metaphorical thinking constitutes the basis of human thought and language."[76]

"Metaphorical thinking" is an important element in the promotion of Eddy's theological argument. The foregoing passage identifies linguistically "Love" in feminine terms. Unselfishness, meekness, and modesty; these are silent exclamations that all signify the wife, the mother, the daughter, the nurse. "The modest arbutus," when contrasted with "the great rock" that gives "shadow and shelter," usefully appropriates discourse of the sublime and beautiful, identifying the male and female of His creating and the meritorious qualities of each. Masculinity is associated with rocks and mountains that stand for solid and grand ideas signifying strength, elevation and resolve.

Using nature to illustrate her argument for spiritual reflection she describes "the oracular skies, the verdant earth—bird, brook, blossom, breeze, and balm—are richly fraught with divine reflection," concluding, "And how is man, seen through the lens of Spirit enlarged, and how counterpoised his origin from dust, and how he presses to his original, never severed from Spirit."[77]

Building on this metaphorical imaging, the "lens of Spirit" could be seen as focusing and dispersing the light of truth, with the prism of poetic interpretation diffusing this light into the spectrum of spiritual understanding. The man of dust, seen through this "inspirational" lens, is shown to be a deception, allowing the male and female man of His creating to appear, confirming the Bible text "Let us make man in our image . . . and let *them* have dominion."[78] If "man" was not created "male and female," the text would surely have been in the singular: "and let *him* have dominion."[79]

Legitimizing her unique scriptural perspectives, Eddy explains, "Divine Science is not an interpolation of the Scriptures . . . it only needs the prism of this Science to divide the rays of Truth, and bring out the entire hues of Deity, which scholastic theology has hidden."[80] It was the rigidity of theological intellectual conformity that Eddy saw as responsible for clothing "religion in human forms"; it was "superstition and creeds"[81] that had allowed gendered discrepancies to flourish, and she was intent on disputing what she saw as a restricting of the Word to the letter. She sought to authorize her argument through spiritual means: "The lens of Science magnifies the divine power to human sight; and we then see the supremacy of Spirit"[82] It was the witnessing of this "Spirit" that allowed a transcending of material limitations, and ultimately gave such authority to Eddy's hegemonic discourse.

Father-Mother God

The marginalization and suppression of the female sex had been aided by patriarchal exposition of sacred texts. The male as head was intrinsic to this hierarchical order. The portrayal of a masculine God effectively maintained this order, perpetuating an argument for male superiority; the exclusion of women from theological scholarship preserved a domain in the masculine.

One of the earliest challenges to this singular definition of the Deity can be found in the *Revelations* of fourteenth-century Anchoress, Julian of Norwich; her argument for a God in the feminine justifies Eddy and Stanton's perspectives. In her text *God is our Mother*, Jennifer Heimmel writes, "Julian of Norwich clearly devoted great effort and creativity to a complete cyclical development of this image of a Christian feminine God for the first time in its long history." Heimmel identifies her as "the fourteenth century woman who was responsible for the great cyclical vision of Christian mother-God . . . One further discovers," she writes, "that she was also a skillful literary artist whose style is made to faithfully reflect and recreate the near twenty year experience of her struggles and beliefs as though occurring spontaneously within the text."[83]

The *Revelations* were apparently spiritually inspired, of an instinctive and spontaneous nature, reflecting a true religion of the heart and her depiction of the Trinity reinforces an image of the feminine in the Godhead: "and of the mother 'Christ, in whom oure hyer party is groundyd and rotyd' and 'our moder' who is 'the / seconde person of the trynyte [*sic*].'"[84]

Some five centuries later, Eddy was to identify God in the feminine:[85] "Father-Mother," she explained, "is the name for Deity, which indicates his tender relationship to His spiritual creation."[86] Eddy's respective mode of identification of God as Mother as well as Father was an important step in authorizing the status of woman. Her discourse consolidates a sense of the inevitable femininity in a God who created "female" in His image.

Eddy was not a feminist per se, but her identification of woman as "Love," which she understood to be the highest concept of the Deity, is a powerful indication of her spiritual hierarchical ordering. Gendered sanctions that saw female exclusion from schools of divinity may well have worked to women's benefit: their minds being less doctrinally inhibited, they were more open to divine influence, and as Eddy pointed out, through this "prism of Science," the "rays of Truth" were divided, allowing her to witness the "entire hues of Deity."

The Bible, as has already been identified, was central to Eddy's study, and it was her close reading of this text that instigated her fresh insight and revelatory new meaning to Scriptural language.

Linguistic Metaphor

In a paper titled "God Language as Two-Way Traffic," under the subheading "The Birth of New Meaning," Kune Biezeveld suggests that "the task of metaphor is to shock the patriarchal symbolic order."[87]

The concept of "God Language as Two-Way Traffic" is an interesting one, suggesting an operating in either of two directions, a mutuality: challenging finitude, this idea lends credence rather to the infinite nature of God's Word, which, like spirituality, cannot be restricted or confined. This idea effectively opens the sacred texts to different interpretative strategies and Eddy identifies the importance of substituting "the spiritual for the material definition of a Scriptural word," which, she suggests, allows "the meaning of the inspired writer" to be elucidated.[88] Her exposition of those "allegorical" rivers flowing out of the Garden of Eden is quite unique and would no doubt have shocked the "patriarchal symbolic order."

Eddy begins, not so unusually, by identifying the word "river" as a metaphor for "channel of thought: When smooth and unobstructed it typifies the course of Truth, but *muddy*, foaming, and dashing, it is a type of error."[89] This explanation brings to mind Wollstonecraft's: "Religion, pure source of comfort in this vale of tears! how has thy clear stream been *muddied* by the dabblers."[90] Landscape imagery was a useful means of substantiating the intangible, but Eddy's interpretation of the different rivers, as we shall see, appears to be quite distinct from conventional metaphorical discourse and the reader might question how she arrived at her unique explanations.

Throwing light on her methodology, she suggests, "The two largest words in the vocabulary of thought are 'Christian' and 'Science.' The former is the highest style of man; the latter reveals and interprets God and man; it aggregates, amplifies, unfolds, and expresses the ALL-God."[91] Juxtaposing this idea with More's pronouncement that "the Bible alone can teach the Science of Salvation thro' the blood of Christ,"[92] allows credence to my earlier tentative suggestion that a prerequisite to an understanding of the "scientific" sacred teachings is that intuitive spiritual state of pure Christianity. With that in mind, Eddy's interpretation of the four rivers will be examined.

The river Euphrates, Eddy explains, symbolizes "Divine Science encompassing the universe and man; the true idea of God," [93] the Hiddekel represents "Divine Science understood and acknowledged,"[94] and the Pison represents "the love of the good and beautiful, and their immortality."[95] Her explanation of the river Gihon, however, is most startling; this river, according to Eddy, represents "the rights of woman acknowledged morally, civilly, and socially."[96]

Nadia Neidzielska, in an essay titled "The Rights of Women Sustained by Divine Law," asks, "Don't these definitions correspond to states of spiritualized consciousness able to bring about improved human conditions?" She points to Eddy's prediction: "Through discernment of the spiritual opposite of materiality, even the way through Christ, Truth, man will reopen with the key of divine Science the gates of Paradise which human beliefs have closed"[97] suggesting, "Wouldn't, then, the definition of 'Gihon' indicate that one of the conditions for attaining this Paradise is the acknowledgement of the rights of women?"[98]

The foregoing explanation contributes toward a compelling argument that the rights of woman are indeed enshrined in Scripture; a paradigm shift in critical theory has revealed interpretative discrepancies to which each author has referred. The "damaging notion of original sin" and belief that woman was literally taken from the bone of man, Wollstonecraft had earlier disputed: "Yet, as very few, it is presumed, who have bestowed any serious thought on the subject, ever supposed that Eve was, literally speaking, one of Adam's ribs, the deduction must be allowed to fall to the ground."[99] Eddy furthers this argument.

A Kind of Man from the Dust of the Ground

Eddy, like Wollstonecraft, did bestow "serious thought on the subject" of Eve's derivation from one of Adam's ribs, and her disputation of "accepted" doctrine appears in this case, to register a shift from the revelatory to the scientific. As identified earlier in this chapter, Eddy points to this "second" account of creation as being merely symbolic and no part of "the beginning" as already recorded in Genesis 1. It is rather, she argues, "mortal and material."[100] "Man reflects God; *mankind* represents the Adamic race, and is a human, not a divine, creation."[101]

The determining, by patriarchal religious authority, of female subordination on the basis of this second creative account, Eddy contests. Having made the crucial distinction between the man of God's creating and the Adamic race, she identifies these beings, created from dust, in the following terms:[102]

ADAM. Error; a falsity; the belief in "original sin," sickness, and death; evil; the opposite of good—of God and His creation; a curse; a belief in intelligent matter, finiteness, and mortality; "dust to dust," red sandstone, nothingness; the first god of mythology; not God's man, who represents the one God and is His own image and likeness . . . The name Adam represents the false supposition that Life is not eternal, but has beginning and end.[103]

EVE. A beginning; mortality; that which does not last forever; a finite belief concerning life, substance, and intelligence in matter; error; the belief that the human race originated materially instead of spiritually— that man started first from dust, second from a rib, and third from an egg.[104]

Having distinguished between "man" and "mankind," she proceeds, through analysis of syntactical convention and the "dissection and definition of words," to promote her argument for the untrue image, the progeny of Adam and Eve who, she believes, represent the fallen race. "The word *Adam*," she explains, "is from the Hebrew *adamah*, signifying the *red color of the ground, dust, nothingness.* Divide the name Adam into two syllables, and it reads, *a dam*, or obstruction . . . It further suggests the thought of that 'darkness . . . upon the face of the deep,' when matter or dust was deemed the agent of Deity in creating man . . . Here *a dam* is not a mere play upon words; it stands for obstruction, error, even the supposed separation of man from God."[105]

This argument leads Eddy to the following conclusion: "Jehovah declared the ground was accursed; and from this ground, or matter, sprang Adam, notwithstanding God had blessed the earth 'for man's sake.' From this it follows that Adam was not the ideal man for whom the earth was blessed. The ideal man was revealed in due time, and was known as Christ Jesus."[106]

Eddy presents a credible case in defense of her perspective; adroitly reidentifying the creator and his progeny, she negotiates a position for woman commensurate with her "elect" spiritual status. Eddy's claim that woman, whom she identifies as "Love," was the highest in the order of creation and her proposition that Jesus rather than Adam was "the ideal man for whom the earth was blessed"[107] marks a radical departure from traditional doctrinal argument.

Submissions for the mutual status of male and female are supported by the style of her critical discourse. Indeed, a key feature of Eddy's writing is the way her ideological positions seem to be linguistically supported by her adept movement through an agency of "manly" argument and the aesthetics of a feminine discourse. Identifying her own spiritual awakening she articulates in "feminine" style: "Sweet music" is how she describes this divine disclosure, which "ripples in one's first thoughts of it like the brooklet in its meandering midst pebbles and rocks, before the mind can duly express it to the ear—so the harmony of divine Science first broke upon my sense, before gathering experience and confidence to articulate it."[108]

Aidan Day points to "the forms of the material world [which] may be read as emblems of a profounder, spiritual reality transcending nature, time and space . . . Nature," he writes, "is important insofar as it manifests the same transcendental energy as informs the human mind and at the same time provides an objective, material barrier which allows the individual subject to recognize transcendence without being overwhelmed by it."[109]

Eddy refers to this divine articulation as "Earth's hieroglyphics of Love."[110] Her "Voices of Spring" represent an argument for a natural hierarchical order reflecting the divine, and notably it is to the "housewife" she gives the task of setting the "earth in order."

> Mine is an obstinate penchant for nature in all her moods and forms, a satisfaction with whatever is hers . . . In spring, nature like a thrifty housewife sets the earth in order; and between taking up the white carpets and putting down the green ones, her various apartments are dismally dirty. Spring is my sweetheart . . . Spring passes over mountain and meadow, waking up the world . . . The alders bend over the streams to shake out their tresses in the water-mirrors; let mortals bow before the creator, and looking through Love's transparency, behold man in God's own image and likeness.[111]

DISCOURSE OF AESTHETICS: "A TRANSCENDENCE IN THE FEMININE"[112]

Epistemological argument and religious "truths" have historically been shaped by masculine values and gendered discourse. Patriarchal ideologies have therefore held sway, and while earlier chapters have identified female receptivity to divine signals, the literary expression of these signals or "revelations" inevitably required a "new tongue" through which to elucidate its representation.

Religions and Discourse identifies the need "for a 'house of language' which is open to the ongoing dialogue about values we want to live by, as well as an example of this dialogue."[113] In her paper "A God in the Feminine," Anne-Claire Mulder identifies the need for feminine terms. Drawing on Irigaray's linguistic and philosophical arguments, she explains that "women need a God in the feminine."

She quotes from Irigaray's "Divine Women":

> If women have no God, they are unable either to communicate or commune with one another . . . without a divine which suits her, a woman cannot fulfil her subjectivity according to an objective which corresponds with her. She lacks an ideal that would be her goal or path in becoming . . . According to Irigaray women have to do more than criticize the representation of Woman within the dominant order of discourse in order to become free subjects. They have to construct an identity or images of an identity that present them as free and autonomous subjects . . . Hence Irigaray's question 'This God, are we capable of imagining it as a woman?'[114]

Eddy's "house of language" has worked to construct a convincing spiritual identity for woman. Challenging modes of identification that had served to scripturally confirm her subjection, Eddy's arguments destabilized what she understood to be a prejudiced, hegemonic religious structure. Focusing on "the beginning" Word, Eddy identified the inevitable equal status of the sexes, created simultaneously, by a first parent who was the origin of male and female.

This "beginning" *does* indeed allow God to be identified, imagined, and understood "as a woman" and as such, answers Irigaray's question absolutely and in the affirmative.

The New Woman

Having identified a "God in the feminine" and thus, scriptural advocacy for the equal status of the sexes, what role does Eddy envision for these new "heavenly" incumbents?

Gill notes, "The metaphysical and theological notions of woman's equality with, or even ontological superiority to, man which Mrs. Eddy elaborates in *Science and Health* are echoed on a much smaller scale in the very short and fragmentary chapter she devotes to marriage . . .

Mrs Eddy," she suggests, "was no political activist and no worker in the vineyards of female suffrage. Her role, she believed, was to provide with her science a new theoretical and spiritual advocacy for the primary equality of the sexes, and the mother-fatherhood of God."[115]

Eddy's arguments tend toward the upholding of traditional roles for women, reinforcing More's earlier proposal: "To you, is made over the awfully important trust of infusing the first principles of piety." But there is an added impetus, an urgency and potency to these activities, that results, I would suggest, from the linking of motherhood with the Godhead, from that portrayal of a "God in the feminine."

Identifying the maternal as the highest representation of Deity, and justifying this ideal through textual analysis of scripture, Eddy accords to the space inhabited by this "new woman" a powerful authority. Exalted and dignified through a fresh understanding of her birthright and relationship to God, "the new woman" was effectively given permission to stand as a free, autonomous, and equal heavenly citizen.

A press cutting from *The New Century*, Boston, February 1895, one of many around the time of Eddy's newly erected Church edifice, records,

> We all know her—she is simply the woman of the past with an added grace—a newer charm . . . She is the apostle of the true, the beautiful, the good, commissioned to complete all that the twelve have left undone . . . 'The time of times' is near when 'the new woman' shall subdue the whole earth with the weapons of peace. Then shall wrong be robbed of her bitterness and ingratitude of her sting, revenge shall clasp hands with pity, and love shall dwell in the tents of hate; while side by side, equal partners in all that is worth living for, shall stand the new man with the new woman.[116]

The Mother Church Was Consecrated in Boston on January 6, 1895

As well as being the year Eddy's Church was consecrated, 1895 also witnessed the publication of *The Woman's Bible*. While no communication has been traced between the two women, in spite of Stanton's address being found in Eddy's personal address book, they inevitably had mutual acquaintances.[117] A review written by Eddy and titled "Womans Bible" [*sic*], however, shows her disapproval of the text: "The woman's man's Bible is the womans bible. We cannot have two if the sexes are equal and we would not if we could separate the interests of Soul and body from their fraternity in both and give to either prominence of perfectibility beyond the other. Man is the generic term for both men and women and even the most radical suffragist could not cannot ask or would receive a greater emolument than to be made in the image and likeness of God"[118]

Religious Revolution and Weapons of Peace

An essay written by Elizabeth Cady Stanton and published in the *North American Review* of 1885, titled "Has Christianity Benefited Woman?" was a searing attack on the treatment of women in the name of religion: "The assertion that woman owes all the advantages of her present position to the Christian church, has been repeated so often, that it is accepted as an established truth by those who would be unwilling to admit that all the injustice and degradation she has suffered might be logically traced to the same source."

That woman's subjugated status results from religious misunderstanding has now become Stanton's clarion call; in epideictic[119] style she argues, "A consideration of woman's position before Christianity, under Christianity, and at the present time, shows that she is not indebted to any form of religion for one step of progress, or one new liberty; on the contrary, it has been through the perversion of her religious sentiments that she has been so long held in a condition of slavery."[120]

Misinterpretation and misrepresentation are identified in this persuasive proclamation as responsible for female subjugation. Sharply critical of "*accepted*" established truths, "truths" approved at a period in history when the sociopolitical structure reflected the predominance of men, Stanton sought to dispute what she believed to be distorted dogma: Jewish-Christian traditions built upon a masculine structure controlled and administered by men.

There was always a fear (as Wollstonecraft was quick to counter) of atheistic accusations when criticizing religious doctrine, and while Stanton *is* sharply critical, it is a criticism of "*accepted*" interpretations of "established truths." Distorted and discriminatory perceptions had allowed for female collusion in their enslavement, and the reader can witness the progression in Stanton's arguments, culminating in *The Woman's Bible*. In this text, her persona, tone, and voice all contribute toward a powerful discourse of deconstruction. Her purpose is to challenge "historically accepted truths": her method is through close critical analysis of the Bible, paying special attention to sections relating to women. Stanton and her team of researchers attempted to throw fresh light on male interpretations that *his*tory had sanctioned, anticipating a restructured society, based on justice and equality for all, as a result of their "Re-Wordings." Stanton is convinced that women's political and social degradation is "an out-growth" of their status in the Bible. An "entire revolution in all existing institutions" is inevitable, she believes, if woman is ever to gain her independence.

Newsom and Ringe suggest in their introduction to *The Women's Bible Commentary,*

> Although women have read the Bible for countless generations, we have not always been self-conscious about reading *as* women. There are many reasons why it is important that women do so. Women have distinctive questions to raise about the Bible and distinctive insights into its texts: our experiences of self and family, our relationship to institutions, the nature of our work and daily lives, and our spirituality have been and continue to be different in important respects from those of men. But there is another reason, too. Because of its religious and cultural authority, the Bible has been one of the most important means by which woman's place in society has been defined.
>
> During the women's movement of the late nineteenth and early twentieth centuries there emerged a clear sense of the need for women to read the Bible self-consciously as women. Just over a hundred years ago Frances Willard, president of the Woman's Christian Temperance Union, made this appeal: "We need women commentators to bring out the women's side of the book." To that end she urged "young women of linguistic talent . . . to make a speciality of Hebrew and New Testament Greek in the interest of their sex."[121]

It is these "distinctive insights" the chapter will now examine as *The Woman's Bible* seeks to "bring out the women's side of the book."

In this text, the language of political feminism has been indelibly fused with that of theological feminism. The introduction marks this: "From the inauguration of the movement for woman's emancipation the Bible has been used to hold her in the 'divinely ordained sphere,' prescribed in the Old and New Testaments. The canon and civil law; church and state; priests and legislators; all political parties and religious denominations have alike taught that woman was made after man, of man, and for man, an inferior being, subject to man. Creeds, codes, Scriptures and statutes, are all based on this idea. The fashions, forms, ceremonies and customs of society, church ordinances and discipline all grow out of this idea."[122]

Stanton's argument brings an intellectual matriarchal perspective to patriarchal sacred texts, drawing at the same time on the inner or private space experiences of women from which to influence the outer public sphere. Her *approach* to Scripture bears little resemblance to

Eddy's, which had argued for the inspirational nature of the sacred writings. Stanton argued she did not believe "that God inspired the Mosaic code, or told the historians what they say he did about woman."[123] "Does anyone seriously believe that the great spirit of all good talked with these Jews, and really said the extraordinary things they report? . . . Do they think that all men who write the different books were specially inspired?"[124]

The Woman's Bible was to provoke a diatribe of opposition.[125] In January 1896, a gathering of the Woman's Suffrage Movement in The Church of our Father witnessed this. The tide of opinion had turned with the publication of Stanton's latest work and a resolution had come before the assembly in the form of a direct rebuke. The resolution was to distance the members from Stanton's theological publication. In spite of, or perhaps because of the public furor, the book proved to be immensely popular, going through seven printings in six months and translation into several languages.

Churchmen came out in strong opposition; Stanton noted in her memoirs, "The clergy denounced it as the work of *Satan*, though it really was the work of Ellen Battelle Dietrick, Lillie Devereux Blake, Rev. Phebe A. Hanaford, Clara Bewick Colby, Ursula N. Gestefeld, Louisa Southworth, Frances Ellen Burr, and myself." "Extracts from it," Stanton continues, "and criticisms of the commentators, were printed in the newspapers throughout America, Great Britain, and Europe. A third edition was found necessary, and finally an edition was published in England."[126]

Fitzgerald notes, "Stanton's sustained ideological assault on religious orthodoxy, especially her publication of The Woman's Bible in 1895 and 1898 represented her last but not least controversial attempt to lessen the influence of what she believed constituted the ideological basis for women's subordination in nineteenth century America."[127]

Stanton's religious beliefs and faith in God, however, overshadowed her faith in man and her thrust to promote religious reform became an overriding concern. As Fitzgerald noted, Stanton spoke "directly to the more conservative suffragists through the pages of The Woman's Bible, arguing that their inability to grasp the importance of critiquing traditional religion was either a sign of ignorance or an act of 'cowardice' disguised by talk of political pragmatism and fear of religious opposition."[128]

Female Interpretation of Paradisaical Indictment

Sharply critical of interpretations that suggested it was "woman brought sin and death into the world," woman who "precipitated the fall of the race," and woman who "was arraigned before the judgment seat of Heaven, tried, condemned and sentenced," Stanton was intent on recovering a valid interpretation, and turning this "object of pity into an exalted, dignified personage, worthy our worship as the mother of the race."[129] "The canon law," she argued, "the Scriptures, the creeds and codes and church discipline of the leading religions bear the impress of fallible manhood and not of our ideal great first cause, 'the Spirit of all Good.'"[130]

Female emancipation she now believed to be impossible without a credible feminized Scriptural exegesis, and to this end, she and her committee of women scrutinized the Scriptures. Firmly convinced that the root cause of female subjection was misinterpretation of the Old and New Testaments, Stanton resolved to reverse this perverted application. Where she led, other activist women followed and Murphy notes, "This conception of the nature of the Bible's challenge—that the problem was not the document itself but errors in the reading and application of it—was in fact explicitly endorsed at the Seneca Falls Convention in these words: '*Resolved*, That woman has too long rested satisfied in the circumscribed limits which corrupt customs and a perverted application of the Scriptures have marked out for her.'"[131]

Chapter 1 pays critical attention to the first account of creation in Genesis: "Here is the sacred historian's first account of the advent of woman; a simultaneous creation of both sexes, in the image of God." Close textual analysis leads her to argue,

> It is evident from the language that there was consultation in the Godhead, and that the masculine and feminine elements were equally represented. Scott in his commentaries says, "this consultation of the Gods is the origin of the doctrine of the trinity." But instead of three male personages, as generally represented, a Heavenly Father, Mother, and Son would seem more rational.
>
> The first step in the elevation of woman to her true position, as an equal factor in human progress, is the cultivation of the religious sentiment in regard to her dignity and equality, the recognition by the rising generation of an ideal Heavenly Mother, to whom their prayers should be addressed, as well as to a Father.
>
> If language has any meaning, we have in these texts a plain declaration of the existence of the feminine element in the Godhead, equal in power and glory with the masculine. The Heavenly Mother and Father!

"God created man in his *own image, male and female.*" Thus Scripture, as well as science and philosophy, declares the eternity and equality of sex . . . The masculine and feminine elements, exactly equal and balancing each other, are as essential to the maintenance of the equilibrium of the universe as positive and negative electricity, the centripetal and centrifugal forces, the laws of attraction which bind together all we know of this planet whereon we dwell and of the system in which we revolve. E. C. S.[132]

This logical exegesis invokes a number of disciplines in its attempt to credit an account of creation in which male and female are equal: science, philosophy, theology, language, history, even the laws of physics are used to emphasize this important first principle. It is notable, however, that while Stanton insists on ratiocination and "pure reason" in her interpretation, it is the notion of sensibility that marks the paragraph, demanding recognition of the dignity and equality of woman. "The cultivation of the religious sentiment" she points to as "the first step" toward the elevation of woman and a prerequisite in the acceptance of an image of God as Heavenly Mother as well as Father. A representation of God as "Mother" is at the heart of authorizing the feminine and is of primary importance as Stanton proceeds to unravel "accepted" theological perspectives:

In the great work of creation the crowning glory was realized, when man and woman were evolved on the sixth day, the masculine and feminine forces in the image of God, that must have existed eternally, in all forms of matter and mind. All the persons in the Godhead are represented in the Elohim the divine plurality taking counsel in regard to this last and highest form of life. Who were the members of this high council, and were they a duality or a trinity? Verse 27 declares the image of God male and female. How then is it possible to make woman an afterthought? We find in verses 5–16 the pronoun "he" used. Should it not in harmony with verse 26 be "they," a dual pronoun? We may attribute this to the same cause as the use of "his" in verse 11 instead of "it." The fruit tree yielding fruit after "his" kind instead of after "its" kind. The paucity of language may give rise to many misunderstandings.[133]

Semantic criticism is brought into play as Stanton draws attention to the potential for misunderstanding due to the limits of language, but even bearing in mind the "paucity of language," her argument is entirely sustainable in its recognition of the simultaneous creation of male and female. Masculine pronouns were an inevitable result of patriarchal historicism and tend to obfuscate the principal argument.

"The above texts," Stanton proclaims, "plainly show the simultaneous creation of man and woman, and their equal importance in the development of the race."[134]

A clear understanding in the premise of the equal status of male and female is essential in highlighting the dubious nature of conclusions drawn from that subsequent account. "As to woman's subjection," she fulminates, "on which both the canon and the civil law delight to dwell, it is important to note that equal dominion is given to woman over every living thing, but not one word is said giving man dominion over woman." Her conclusion: "No lesson of woman's subjection can be fairly drawn from the first chapter of the Old Testament."[135]

Ellen Battelle Dietrick adds her contribution in Comments on 'Genesis.' This account as well as being critical of literary interpretation, points out practical and historical problems that contribute to misunderstanding:

> The most important thing for a woman to note, in reading Genesis, is that that portion which is now divided into "the first three chapters" (there was no such division until about five centuries ago), contains two entirely separate, and very contradictory, stories of creation, written by two different, but equally anonymous, authors. No Christian theologian of today, with any pretensions to scholarship, claims that Genesis was written by Moses. As was long ago pointed out, the Bible itself declares that all the books the Jews originally possessed were burned in the destruction of Jerusalem, about 588 B.C. . . . When it is remembered that the Jewish books were written on rolls of leather, without much attention to vowel points and with no division into verses or chapters, by uncritical copyists, who altered passages greatly, and did not always even pretend to understand what they were copying, then the reader of Genesis begins to put herself in position to understand how it can be contradictory. Great as were the liberties which the Jews took with Genesis, those of the English translators, however, greatly surpassed them.[136]

Dietrick's contribution illustrates the differences in strategy and style between *The Woman's Bible* and *Science and Health with Key to the Scriptures*. Eddy's claim that "inspired writers interpret the Word spiritually, while the ordinary historian interprets it literally"[137] is evidenced here *by* the voice of the reasoned historian, as she dismantles patriarchal sacred texts; but again, this reinforces that coalescence that emerges through each perspective.

Important historical and philosophical detail is introduced in the above passage, which, through critical analysis of the book of Genesis reveals not only a literary ambivalence, but works to throw doubt on its authorial authenticity. This critical route allows seeds of suspicion to germinate as the writer concludes, "Now it is manifest that both of these stories cannot be true; intelligent women, who feel bound to give the preference to either, may decide according to their own judgement of which is more worthy of an intelligent woman's acceptance" Dietrick's own opinion was "that the second story was manipulated by some Jew, in an endeavour to give 'heavenly authority' for requiring a woman to obey the man she married."[138]

A further stratum in the dismantling process is introduced by Lillie Devereux Blake, allowing the reader to become conscious of the intricate, interwoven nature of their critical approach to this first book of the Bible. The different threads of the events and circumstances in the accounts of creation are woven into a linguistic tapestry that exhibits a totally different design from that time-honored patriarchal picture. Blake's very visual argument is profound in its simplicity, yet its conclusion has far-reaching implications: "In the detailed description of creation we find a gradually ascending series. Creeping things, 'great sea monster,' (Chap. I, v. 21, literal translation). 'Every bird of wing,' cattle and living things of the earth, the fish of the sea and the 'birds of the heavens,' then man, and last and crowning glory of the whole, woman. It cannot be maintained that woman was inferior to man even if, as asserted in chapter ii, she was created after him without at once admitting that man is inferior to the creeping things, because created after them."[139]

It is the simple logic of the foregoing argument that makes it especially persuasive; it succeeds, where allegory and metaphor might struggle, in representing an ascending hierarchical system that credits the sovereignty of the feminine. The clarity and lucidity of the arguments in *The Woman's Bible* work on a number of levels to dispute any suggestion of female inferiority. The power of this text emerges through the passionately held beliefs of its authors as they deconstruct doctrine detrimental to the female sex.

Stanton and Eddy agree on the allegorical nature of that "creation" account, so long used as a means of confirming a secondary status for women: "As the account of the creation in the first chapter is in harmony with science, common sense, and the experience of mankind in natural laws, the inquiry naturally arises, why should there be two contradictory accounts in the same book, of the same event? It is fair to infer that the second version, which is found in some form in the different religions of all nations, is a mere allegory, symbolizing some mysterious conception of a highly imaginative editor."[140]

"There is something sublime," Stanton writes, "in bringing order out of chaos; light out of darkness; giving each planet its place in the solar system; oceans and lands their limits" and her syntactical strategy in this passage, I suggest, works to reinforce this ideal.

That image of harmony in relation to the first account of creation, and the linking of this creative order with science, common sense, and natural law allows the disputation of a second "contradictory" account. Why would a Creator whose work was complete in terms of the universe, solar system and the creation of mankind in His image, need to resort to what she refers to as a "petty surgical operation to find material for the mother of the race"? As it accords with neither science, natural law nor common sense, it must be an allegorical representation: "It is on this allegory that all the enemies of women rest their battering rams, to prove her inferiority."[141]

Mirroring the logic of Blake's argument in pointing to the fact man was not "first" in the order of creation, Stanton introduces an enigmatic tone: "Accepting the view that man was prior in the creation, some Scriptural writers say that as the woman was of the man, therefore, her position should be one of subjection. Grant it, then as the historical fact is reversed in our day, and the man is now of the woman, shall his place be one of subjection?"[142] It is an interesting point.

"Truth for authority, and not authority for truth"

Close critical analysis of Stanton's epic work (and I don't think "epic" is too strong a word to describe this text, embodying as it does the conception of a nation's religious history) reveals a language and style intent on provoking "direct action." Difficult issues and technical terms are effectively transposed through the innovative use of linguistic strategies: epithets with previously designated connotations are renegotiated. Sensitive analysis of the written word combined with the challenging of historically defined gender parameters, results in textual evidence that reveals palpable discrepancies in exegesis.

Literature that argued a moral or religious doctrine, expounding its theme by allegory and example, became known in this period as "propagandist literature." Writing women made an immense contribution through persuasive rhetoric toward this form of literature. Abrams identifies this style of didactic literature as "written to move the reader to assume a specific attitude toward, or to take direct action on, a pressing social, political, or religious issue of the time at which the work is written."[143]

The conclusion to Chapter V does indeed "move the reader to assume a specific attitude": "But that the Scriptures, rightly interpreted, do not teach the equality of the sexes, I must be permitted to doubt. We who love the Old and New Testaments take 'Truth for authority, and not authority for truth.'"[144] "It is no wonder that woman's true relation to man and just position in the social fabric has remained unknown . . . Their religious nature is warped and twisted through generations of denominational conservatism . . . So long as they mistake superstition for religious revelation, they will be content with the position and opportunities assigned them by scholastic theology."[145]

"The Bible," this polemic argues, "from the beginning to end teaches the equality of man and woman, their relation as the two halves of the unit, but also their distinctiveness in office. One cannot take the place of the other because of the fundamental nature of each. The work of each half in its own place is necessary to the perfect whole." The writer suggests further that "unintentionally women have been and will continue to be bigoted until they allow a higher ideal to penetrate their minds; until they see with the eye of reason and logic, as well as with the sentiment which has so long kept them the dependent class." The argument is clear: "woman's sense of duty and religious sentiment have been operative according to a false ideal."[146]

Working then to replace this "false ideal" of "authority for truth" with that higher one of "truth for authority," *The Woman's Bible* expands: "Like the tables of stone the Bible is written on both sides."[147]

This is an important idea, and not unlike Johnson's argument when identifying the spiritual perspectives of Eddy as "intimations of a common thirst for light on the other side of reason."[148] This portrayal links well with that earlier one with regard to More's essay "The Bible." More's intimated linking of the patriarchal perspective of the Old Testament with the matriarchal milieu of the New and her identification of the Bible as "the sum and substance of all Truth" allows credence to a suggestion that the sacred text itself might be viewed as a literary signifier of sexual equality.

The Woman's Bible builds on this suggestion, attempting to recover "an interior spirit or meaning" from the "letter which is its exterior," and this is explained in the following terms: "The exterior or male half is outermost, the interior or female half is covered by the outer. One is seen, the other has to be discerned."[149]

The text goes on to suggest, "The man has more prominence than the woman in the Bible because the masculine characters in their succession represent man as a whole-generic man." A suggestion, however, that "the book of Genesis is the substance of the whole Bible, its meaning is the key to the meaning of the whole" needs closer investigation. "The book of 'Genesis,'" says *The Woman's Bible*, "is the skeleton around which the rest is built." It concludes, "If the remainder of the Old Testament were destroyed its substance could be reconstructed from Genesis. As the bony structure of the physical body is the framework which is filled in and rounded to symmetrical proportions by the muscular tissue, so Genesis is the framework which is symmetrically rounded and filled by the other books which supply the necessary detail involved in basic principles."[150]

Using metaphoric symbolism, this passage seems to suggest that for the purpose of identifying "truth for authority" over "authority for truth," the "beginning" argument needs clarification and confirmation.

Identifying the Bible as a textual representative of the male and female of God's creating builds upon the "separate sphere" ideology, arguing the necessity of the two halves of the whole, each fulfilling its unique purpose. It symbolically equates the *text* to "the exterior or male half," the half that is visible, but that is effectively hiding within its *pages* an interior female half, something that has to be discerned. Identifying the "harmonious relativity" of the two halves of the whole that make up "man," it works to effectively confirm the necessity of the feminine aspect in the *understanding* and *explaining* of the text or outer part.

The book of Job 38:36 locates wisdom: "Who hath put wisdom in the inward parts?" and Proverbs 4:5–8 suggests, "Get wisdom, get understanding . . . Forsake *her* not, and *she* shall preserve thee; love *her*, and *she* shall keep thee . . . Exalt *her*, and **she** shall promote thee . . . Hear, O my son." (added emphasis) This gendered referencing promotes the qualities of wisdom and understanding in feminine terms, and note how the masculine is instructed to pay attention.

Ursula N. Gestefeld corroborates, suggesting, "The first chapter of Genesis is not the record of the creation of the world. It is a symbolical description of the composite nature of man, that being which is male and female in one. The personal pronoun 'He' belongs to his exterior nature; and the characters which illustrate this nature and the order of its development are men. The pronoun 'She' belongs to the interior nature, and all characters—fewer in number—which illustrate it, are women. 'Male and female created he them.'"[151]

Frances Ellen Burr argued, "And now that we are coming to understand the Bible better than to worship it as an idol, it will gradually be lifted from the shadows and the superstitions of an age when, as a fetich, [*sic*] it was exalted above reason, and placed where a spiritually enlightened people can see it in its true light," and, she continued, "in view of the rapid steps which we are taking in these latter years, we can almost feel the breath of the new cycle fan our cheeks as we watch the deepening hues of the breaking dawn."

There is a palpable anticipation, excitement even as this writer goes on to portray woman "on a perfect equality in the Godhead." The "breaking dawn" suggests a new beginning, a "genesis" through which "a spiritually enlightened people can see it [the book] in its true light." This religious requisition of old dogma and superstition thus allowed the "stately Hebrew Kabbalah, hoary with antiquity," to sanction this insight: "For better authority than that one can hardly ask."[152]

I asked at the beginning of this chapter if dissenting religious attitudes had paved the way for these radical reformers. Was the time right for the publication of two textual challenges to historical theological interpretation? The *Woman's Bible* identifies that "the close of this century has long been pointed to by scholars, by writers and by Prophets, within the Church and out of it, as the close of the old dispensation and the opening of the new one,"[153] and the arguments of these two texts lead me to suggest they have made an effective, and timely, contribution to the opening of a new and more spiritually enlightened dispensation.

RE-VEILINGS

The Woman's Bible has pointed to "the book of Genesis [as] the substance of the whole Bible," its meaning the key to the whole, and the foregoing arguments have promoted compelling evidence that "the beginning" creation account does indeed accord equal status to woman. An earlier chapter has hinted that through More's treatment of the New Testament, it might be viewed as a literary signifier for the feminine, and I will now examine how the arguments of Stanton and Eddy support this theory.

"Does the New Testament bring promises of new dignity and of larger liberties for woman?" asks Stanton.[154] Certainly it offered, through the life of Christ Jesus, a route through which the native qualities of the female could be appreciated; his tenderness, humility, and ministration to those in need were all representative of the maternal nature. His radical questioning of religious dogma brought him into dispute with those who claimed the name without the nature of pure and undefiled religion.

An anonymous writer in *The Woman's Bible* notes that "Jesus was the great leading Radical of his age. Everything that he was and said and did alienated and angered the Conservatives, those that represented and stood for the established order of what they believed to be the fixed and final revelation of God."[155] Stanton herself could have been portrayed in this light; she alienated and angered the conservatives, those men who "represented and stood for the established order," and her challenging of the "fixed and final revelation of God" led to accusations that her ideas were the work of Satan.

"And there appeared a great wonder in heaven; a woman clothed with the sun, and the moon under her feet"[156]

The book of Revelation makes a considerable contribution to an understanding of the power and authority of the female in the scheme of things. Feminine imagery is used to confirm woman's spiritual powers. *The Woman's Bible* suggests, "It is a purely esoteric work, largely referring to woman, her intuition, her spiritual powers, and all she represents. Even the name of its putative author, John, is identical in meaning with 'dove,' the emblem of the Holy Ghost, the female principle of the Divinity." It points to the proper title of this book as "Re-veilings" and suggests, "It is not then strange that such a profoundly mystic book as Re-Veilings should be so little understood by the Christian Church as to have been many times rejected from the sacred canon."[157]

Feminine Divinity

Clothed with the sun, woman here represents the Divinity of the feminine, its spirituality as opposed to the materiality of the masculine; for in Egypt the sun, as giver of life, was regarded as feminine, while the moon, shining by reflected light, was looked upon as masculine. With her feet upon the moon, woman, corresponding to and representing the soul, portrays the ultimate triumph of spiritual things over material things, over the body, which man, or the male principle, corresponds to and represents.

"There was war in heaven." The wonderful progress and freedom of woman, as woman, within the last half century, despite the false interpretation of the Bible by the Church and by masculine power, is the result of this great battle; and all attempts to destroy her will be futile. Her day and hour have arrived; the dragon of physical power over her, the supremacy of material things in the world, as depicted by the male principle, are yielding to the spiritual, represented by woman. The eagle, true bird of the sun and emblem of our own great country, gives his wings to her aid; and the whole earth comes to help her against her destroyer. And thus must Re-Veilings be left with much truth untouched, yet with the hope that what has been written will somewhat help to a comprehension of this greatly misunderstood yet profoundly "sacred" and "secret" book, whose true reading is of such vast importance to the human race.

—Matilda Joslyn Gage, *The Woman's Bible*

These are complex issues and this descriptive passage provides an original perspective on matters that were of such relevance to woman.

Rational argument and sympathetic symbolism identify her spiritual supremacy: "Her day and hour have arrived" suggests the above-writer, linking with Eddy's pronouncement "This is woman's hour."[158] Both writers believed that the promotion of virtuous womanhood through religious metaphor and confirmed by sacred text would result in recognition of the "divinity of the feminine." Woman, this text argues, would be responsible for the ultimate triumph of the spiritual over the material.

Biblical misinterpretation had promoted masculine power at the expense of woman, and the re-vision of this book allowed the divinity of the feminine to be identified and acknowledged. This effective and authoritative argument identifies the "war in heaven" as prophetic of woman's liberation, pointing to the futility of attempts to destroy her.

The Woman's Bible promotes an ideal that, far from the female sex being subordinate to the male, "true reading" of this "greatly misunderstood yet profoundly 'sacred' and 'secret'" text reveals the opposite. While this was undoubtedly a controversial proposition, the writers' close textual analysis of St. John's vision or prophetic transcript appears to support this perspective. "Here," Stanton suggests, "is a little well intended respect for woman as representing the Church. In this vision she appears clothed with the sun, and the moon under her feet, which denotes her superiority, says the commentator, to her reflected feebler light of the Mosaic dispensation."[159]

Eddy and the Apocalypse

Eddy wrote a manuscript of seven chapters that dealt with a number of key doctrinal issues. Chapter V was titled "The Interpretation of Revelation," and it was suggested that this chapter was written in response to contentions that Eddy "viewed herself literally as the Woman of the Apocalypse."[160]

"The Apocalypse," she suggests, "like all holy vision, when left to mortals' interpretation or application to identify its meaning, is susceptible of abuse owing to one's ignorance of another's mood and mode of thinking. I am not capable of applying St. John's far-reaching thoughts only as type and shadow," and marking the ephemeral nature of St. John's vision, she goes on to say, "I would as soon undertake to catch a sunbeam in my hand . . . I have but a glimpse of the full meaning of his sublime vision."[161] This glimpse, nevertheless, witnessed through an intuitive state or divine inspiration, allows for explanations that contribute toward a fresh and innovative interpretation of this text.

Eddy's apocalyptic argument identifies a hierarchical system dependent, not on gender, but on mental states. She points to a system that extols and honors matriarchal virtues as the highest, yet these characteristics, she is clear, are not the sole prerogative of either sex: "Love is impartial and universal in its adaptation and bestowals."[162]

Her interpretation of Revelation makes plain that this "vision" does *not* refer to her as an individual, or even woman collectively: "What St. John saw in prophetic vision and depicted as 'a woman clothed with the sun and the moon under her feet' prefigured no specialty [*sic*] or individuality." She explains, "His vision foretold a type and this type applied to man as well as to woman." It was this explanation that ultimately allowed her to identify the superiority of the feminine. The "type" she refers to, is the quality or character of "purity"; it was this pure state of which the highest representation of motherhood, the virgin mother, was the exemplar: "The character or type seen in his vision," she suggests, "*illustrated* purity."[163]

The reader is witnessing, through Eddy's argument, a weakening of rigid religious belief systems through innovative spiritual ideals, which work to effectively shift and reshape the boundaries of prohibitive religious gender identification. "I say what I mean," she writes, "so far as I can express my meaning, and I am careful to say what I understand and perceive spiritually."[164]

Identification of a "higher nature" rather than a "higher sex" becomes a key issue in Eddy's argument. Just as the quality of "sensibility," so associated with the feminine, has been identified as the highest mental condition, so the state of "purity" has been promoted by Eddy as the highest representation of the Deity: this line of argument does confirm a hierarchy, but it is a hierarchy of mental qualities, available to be claimed by either sex.

"The Woman in the Apocalypse," Eddy writes, "symbolizes generic man, the spiritual idea of God; she illustrates the coincidence of God and man as the divine Principle and divine idea. The Revelator symbolizes Spirit by the sun. The spiritual idea is clad with the radiance of spiritual Truth, and matter is put under her feet." Effectively lifting the veil of obscurity, Eddy announces, "As Elias presented the idea of the fatherhood of God, which Jesus afterwards manifested, so the Revelator completed this figure with woman, typifying the spiritual idea of God's motherhood. The moon is under her feet."[165]

The argument, it could be said, has come full circle, as the man of Genesis and the woman of Revelation are both identified in generic terms.

An article published in the *Boston Herald* encapsulates Eddy's redefining of historical gender divisions: "Look high enough, and you see the heart of humanity warming and winning. Look long enough, and you see male and female one—sex or gender eliminated; you see the designation *man* meaning woman as well, and you see the whole universe included in one infinite Mind and reflected in the intelligent compound idea, image or likeness, called man, showing forth the infinite divine Principle, Love, called God—man wedded to the Lamb, pledged to innocence, purity, perfection."[166]

CONCLUSION

Woman was not made in the image of God.

—Gratian (quoting words attributed to St. Augustine),
Women in the World's Religions

Come, come, my conservative friend, wipe the dew off your spectacles, and see that the world is moving. Whatever your views may be as to the importance of the proposed work, your political and social degradation are but an outgrowth of your status in the Bible.

—Elizabeth Cady Stanton, *The Woman's Bible*

In this chapter, I have called into question the credibility of time-honored religious interpretation. I have suggested that while "religion" was the umbrella or aegis under which grouped those believers in a supreme being, "spirituality" was the active agency that made it proactive and practical. This was a power beyond belief, and it was accessible to those minds that were receptive to divine inspiration. This pervading influence, with its innate power for moral and religious reform, has been identified as a feminine consciousness by each writer. Stanton and Eddy's texts have simply taken an argument to its ultimate conclusion. Reason and revelation merged in their quest for "Truth for authority," allowing a revised and biblically authorized status for woman. Their scriptural exegesis came to light through a unique idiolect not provided for by earlier examples.

Despite anticipated "rapid steps" toward a "new cycle" and the "breaking dawn" referred to in *The Woman's Bible*, dawn has been slow to break; first light, however, while being a gradual process is an inevitable one. These women were pioneers, and Eddy notes, "It is the task of the sturdy pioneer to hew the tall oak and to cut the rough granite . . . A book introduces new thoughts, but it cannot make them speedily understood . . . Future ages must declare what the pioneer has accomplished."[167]

National American Woman Suffrage Association

Member National Council of Women

Honorary President, SUSAN B. ANTHONY, 17 Madison Street, Rochester, N. Y.

President, CARRIE CHAPMAN CATT,
180 Bay 31st St., Bensonhurst, N. Y.
Vice-President-at-Large, REV. ANNA H. SHAW,
7128 Devon Street, Mt. Airy, Philadelphia, Pa.
Corresponding Secretary, KATE M. GORDON,
1800 Prytania Street, New Orleans, La.

Recording Secretary, ALICE STONE BLACKWELL,
3 Park Street, Boston, Mass.
Treasurer, HARRIET TAYLOR UPTON,
Warren, Ohio.
Auditors { LAURA CLAY, Lexington, Ky.
{ MARY J. COGGESHALL,
664 Seventh Street, Des Moines, Iowa.

NATIONAL HEADQUARTERS,
WARREN, OHIO

NATIONAL PRESS COMMITTEE, ELNORA BABCOCK, DUNKIRK, N. Y.

OFFICE OF HONORARY PRESIDENT, 17 MADISON ST., ROCHESTER, N. Y.

June 19, 1905.

Mrs. Mary D. E. Glover Eddy,

Concord, N. H.

My Dear Mrs. Eddy,-

I find your name on our Suffrage books way back in the olden time and I believe you must be still interested in the subject. I know many of your followers are friends of the cause, so I take the liberty of sending you Vol. IV of the History of Woman Suffrage. If you do not wish it yourself, will you put it in some high school, normal school or public library?

I remember of hearing you speak in the Chicago Music Hall a good many years ago; that is the only time I remember of seeing you.

Very sincerely yours,

Susan B. Anthony

Appendix 1. Letter from Susan B Anthony

Appendix 2. Letter from A Bronson Alcott

Appendix 2: Letter from A Bronson Alcott (*continued*)

Boston, *Oct. 30* 1875

Mr Edward Hitchings & Geo. W. Barry.

To W. F. Brown & Co., Dr.

Job, Card, and Book Printers,

W. F. BROWN.
C. M. N. TWITCHELL.

No. 50 Bromfield Street.

For Composition, Plates & Binding	
1000 Copies Science & Health	
430 pp as per Contract	1000 00
Com + Plates 24 pp Extra	31 70
Paper for 24 " "	14 64
Com + Plates on 5 to pp Cancelled	697 41
At Hardy 121 hours alterations 60	72 60
2 Sets Hardy Proofs	11 00
10 Byer	10 00
90¼ hours Extra Corrections office	452 00
	$2285 35
1875	
Feb 9 Cr By Cash H. & B. 500. as per notes	
aug 14 " " " B & N (200 " " "	700
	$1585 35
Nov 12 " " " as per note	500
	$1085 35

Appendix 3: Printer's Bill for publication of first edition of *Science & Health with Key to the Scriptures*.

CONCLUSION

SOCIAL REFORM TO
SPIRITUAL REDEMPTION

The challenging of patriarchal theological authority has been at the heart of attempts to recover, reclaim, and retrieve salvation, emancipation, and liberation for women.

In her text *Divine Women*, Irigaray argued, "Only a God in the feminine can look after and hold for us this margin of liberty and power which would allow us to grow more, to affirm ourselves."[1]

Witnessing the remarkable attempts by More, Wollstonecraft, Stanton, and Eddy to reclaim that "margin of liberty and power" to effectively "affirm" themselves as equal members of society has been a privilege. The lives of these women have told a story that, though lived in a previous century, holds significance for the woman of today. Their confirmation of "a God in the feminine" has been truly liberating.

There are inherent problems for those seeking to do academic work on women and the Bible, one of which has to do with that "distinction between deriving an interpretation from a text and reading an interpretation into a text."[2] This particular problem has been overcome, I would suggest, by the total diversity—disparity even—among the four women, and their distinctive "interpretative" strategies.

The importance to women in particular and society as a whole in establishing Scriptural authority for sexual equality cannot be overstated. Selvidge writes in *Notorious Voices*, "This collection of analyses is only the beginning of an area of research that must be pursued . . . The textual history of the Bible must also be investigated through feminist critical eyes."[3] That has been my aim; indeed, feminist *and* antifeminist "critical eyes" have been cast over the Bible and its textual history in an attempt to identify "truth for authority" over "authority for truth."

It has been an amazing journey, and I hope it has enabled you, the reader, to become better acquainted with the reformers as individuals. I have tried to identify the route these women took, as humanitarian thinkers, which led them to argue with such proficiency for spiritual gender equality: the causes that inspired them to put pen to paper in the name of reform.

Theirs was a long, often lonely, and frequently painstaking journey and I have pointed to the resultant spiritual autobiographical nature of their writing. I have tried to make the women "live" for the reader, to give a sense of how the *lives* of women qualified them to dispute patriarchal arguments for subservience.

In each century, there have been women of insight who have been prepared to speak out, often at detriment to themselves, for justice and equality. While these women undoubtedly wrote ahead of their time, I would suggest that in this "future age" there *are* glimpses of that breaking dawn referred to. A recently published teaching document, *The Gift of Scripture*, by the Roman Catholic Church, supports this suggestion and is a clear indication of a doctrinal shift taking place: "Modern insights about the nature of language have explored and clarified the potential of the written word to give rise to new meanings and insights."[4]

A study of the life and writings of these women has revealed the means by which they attempted, through "new meanings and insights" to reshape political, cultural, and ultimately religious history. Identifying the innate spirituality of woman and her divine ordinance has allowed her to be placed at the heart of Holy Scripture. Though linked, each contribution has been unique, and it is this "collective" uniqueness that gives such credence to ultimate conclusions.

Literary attempts to rectify negative notions of femininity and shift parameters, so restrictive to the influence of women in the public world, and affairs of society have been groundbreaking. Critical analysis of their writing has allowed not only identification of the cultural and political interrelations between Britain and America, but also the philosophical legacy passed from one generation of female reformers to the next.

Religious argument has been identified as running like fine threads through all their writings: in their demand for the freedom of black slaves, better conditions for the poor, or emancipation for women. The didactic writing of their early years, whether in the form of poetry, story, political tract, or indeed any of the different genres they employed to exert influence, had a powerful proselytizing effect. Fusing sensibility with evangelism, a humanitarian reforming zeal surfaced that undoubtedly contributed toward the abolition of the slave trade, Barbauld confirmed, "nothing . . . for centuries past, has done the nation so much honour."[5]

These women used literature as a reforming tool; while that glass ceiling perpetually hampered their progress, the cult of sensibility was a fundamental element in raising public awareness of the benefits female Christian reformers could bring to reforming male manners, societal inhumanity, and injustice. Through this cult, a literary space was created that effectively mirrored the "private sphere" values of women. The writers' identification of the "spiritual" nature at the heart of this cult promoted an image of saintly sisterhood and led to a veneration of womanhood.

Personal trauma and public opposition were key elements in the literary shift witnessed in their later writing. Disappointed with the hypocrisy they observed in the public sphere of politics and religion, their later writings marked the emergence of a Christian romanticism; language that drew on nature to articulate spiritual truths effectively furthered a feminization of Protestantism. Religious prose and didactic discourse were common genres for reforming women writers of the period; what distinguished these authors from their peers was their intensive interest in the doctrinal aspect of theology and their ultimate pressing of arguments that were at distinct odds with contemporary theological opinion.

Each writer whose works have been examined had an agenda, and I have been careful to identify ambiguities as well as affinities in both their writing styles and arguments. Their lifetime achievements were notable and their legacies reflect a common commitment to societal reform: Hannah More and Mary Baker Eddy, both identified as antifeminist, left tangible evidence of their public influence. More has been described as "the most influential female philanthropist of her day."[6]

Eddy became one of the most well-known women in the United States, founding a worldwide religious movement. Clara Barton, founder of the American Red Cross said that she "looked upon Mrs. Mary Baker Eddy as the one person, regardless of sex, living to-day, who has done the greatest good for her fellow-creatures."[7] Mary Wollstonecraft, as one of the earliest feminists, became recognized as the founder of the British women's rights movement, and Elizabeth Cady Stanton's lifetime commitment to reform was evidenced in her leadership of the American women's rights movement.

A deep love of the Bible has been at the heart of this work and a total conviction that a re-vision of Biblical language would allow woman and man to be identified in equal spiritual terms.

The disputation of an "original sin" beginning, for that of "original innocence" has been key to this work. This "original" re-identification has allowed the *rights* to *spiritual revelation* to be recognized as genderless rights; *rights* freely available to be claimed by either sex. Identification of a hierarchical system based on the concept of a higher nature, rather than a higher sex, is significant; it offers a unique "new beginning" place from which to *re*-view an argument for spiritual equality.

Through distinctive interpretative strategies, each author identified God as Mother as well as Father; distinguished between truth and allegory in "Genesis"; through "reason" *and* "revelation" identified the "elect" status of woman in St. John's prophetic vision. Language that celebrates the visionary heavenly city was represented through a vernacular of particular relevance to woman; pointing to her implicit connection with spiritual power, it marked her as a "chosen vessel" and it was this identification that Stanton and Eddy believed should finally result in some "well intended respect for woman as representing the Church."[8]

Portrayal of the Bible itself as a textual signifier of sexual equality—that is, the two Testaments standing in relation to each other, the patriarchal Old with the matriarchal New—has interesting implications for female spirituality.

The foregoing perspectives are powerfully persuasive and lead me to conclude that, in spite of, and possibly because of, the authors' multifarious perspectives and different literary devices, an argument for "Woman's Right to Revelation" is sustainable. As an inhabitant *of* that "future age" referred to by Eddy, I would suggest that the accomplishments of these spiritual pioneers have been impressive and effectual.

"This *is* the period of women, they *are* to move and to carry all the great moral and Christian reforms."[9]

NOTES

INTRODUCTION

1. E. S. Fiorenza, *Searching the Scriptures: A Feminist Introduction*, (London: SCM Press, 1994), 1.
2. G. Lerner, *The Creation of Feminist Consciousness*, (New York: Oxford University Press, 1993), 165.
3. D. Spender, *Women of Ideas (And What Men Have Done to Them): From Aphra Behn to Adrienne Rich* (London: Routledge & Kegan Paul, 1982), 8.
4. M. J. Selvidge, *Notorious Voices: Feminist Biblical Interpretation, 1500-1920* (London: SCM, 1996), 8.
5. C. Murphy, *The Word According to Eve: Women and the Bible in Ancient Times and Our Own* (London: Penguin, 1998), xxiii.
6. British Age of Sensibility approx. 1744–98, Romantic Period approx. 1785–1832. American Romantic/Transcendental Period approx. 1828–65, which incorporates the American Renaissance, literature of Sensibility and the Sentimental.
7. M. B. Eddy, *Prose Works* "Miscellaneous Writings" (Boston: Trustees under the Will of Mary Baker G. Eddy, 1896), 262.
8. M. Wollstonecraft, *A Vindication of the Rights of Woman* (London: Joseph Johnson, 1792), 120, vol. 6. Wollstonecraft's writings are included in *The Works of Mary Wollstonecraft*, edited by Janet Todd and Marilyn Butler, published (London: William Pickering, 1989) and referencing of all her texts, throughout the work, will be identified by their volume number in these Works.
9. R. B. Shoemaker, *Gender in English Society 1650-1850* (London: Longman, 1988), 209.
10. *Vindication*, 120.
11. H. More, *Strictures on the Modern System of Female Education. With a View of the Principles and Conduct Prevalent among Women of Rank and Fortune* (London: Cadell & Davies, 1799), 62–64.
12. H. More, *Practical Piety: or The Influence of the Religion of the Heart on the Conduct of the Life* (London: Cadell & Davies, 1825), 5; emphasis added.
13. W. Roberts, *Memoirs of The Life and Correspondence of Mrs. Hannah More* (London: R. B. Seeley and W. Burnside, 1834), 103, vol. 2.
14. *Practical Piety*, vii.

15. *Memoirs of the Life and Correspondence of Mrs. Hannah More*, 371, vol. 2.

16. *Vindication*, 115. It is interesting that Wollstonecraft is so gender determinate in her identification of the quality of "reason."

17. Ibid., 273.

18. L. Colley suggests in *Britons, Forging the Nation 1707–1837* (New Haven, CT: Yale University Press, 1992), 274: "Feminists have never quite known what to do with More, sometimes applauding her as one of themselves, sometimes dismissing her as a reactionary and apostate."

19. "The Daily Inter-Ocean," Chicago, December 31, 1894, reported, "Mary Baker was the daughter of Mark and Abigail (Ambrose) Baker, and was born in Concord, N. H. . . . On her father's side Mrs. Eddy came from Scotch and English ancestry, and Hannah More was a relative of her grandmother."

20. K. W. F. Stavely, *Puritan Legacies, Paradise Lost and the New England Tradition 1630–1890* (Ithaca, NY: Cornell University Press, 1987), 210.

21. S. Wilbur, *The Life of Mary Baker Eddy* (Boston: The Christian Science Publishing Society, 1907), 206.

22. See appendix for copy of this letter.

23. Elizabeth Cady Stanton, *The Woman's Bible* (Boston: Northeastern University Press, 1993 (1895, 1898), 8, part 2.

24. E. C. Stanton, *The Woman's Bible*, xxvii. Fitzgerald suggests that we might never have seen *The Woman's Bible* in print had Stanton not become so intensely and righteously frustrated with the political suffrage perspective of Anthony. "Stanton's constant attempts to bring the issue of women and religion to the public" she suggested "reveal a death-grip effort to continue the tradition of radical individualism that had undergirded her feminist theory." *The Woman's Bible*, xxvii.

25. More introduced *Cheap Repository Tracts* in 1795, Stanton established *Revolution* in 1868, and Eddy established *The Christian Science Monitor* in 1908.

26. In February 1999, The National Foundation for Women Legislators honored Mary Baker Eddy, as founder of this newspaper, with a media award. Compton's Interactive Encyclopedia Deluxe 1999 (The Learning Company, 1999) writes: "One of the most highly respected newspapers published in the United States is the *Christian Science Monitor*."

27. M. B. Eddy, *Prose Works* "Miscellaneous Writings," 274.

28. J. Melnyk (ed.), *Women's Theology in Nineteenth-Century Britain*, (New York: Garland, 1998)xi.

29. For example see, *Religions and Discourse, Towards a Different Transcendence, Feminist Findings on Subjectivity, Religion and Values*, P. Lang (ed.) (European Academic Publishers, Bern, 2001, vol. 9).

30. R. Hole, *Selected Writings of Hannah More* (London: William Pickering, 1996), xv.

31. W. S. Lewis (ed.), *The Correspondence of Horace Walpole*, 48 Volumes (London: Oxford University Press, 1961), xxxi, 397.

32. M. Twain in his text *Christian Science* (Buffalo, New York: Promethus Books, 1993).

33. J. Todd (ed.), *A Wollstonecraft Anthology* (Bloomington, IN: Indiana University Press, 1977), 266.

34. J. Milton, *Paradise Lost*, (1658) (London: Addison Wesley Longman, 1968), 521.

35. *The Woman's Bible*, 10.

36. See the chapter "The Sorcerer's Apprentice" in Cullen Murphy's text, *The Word According to Eve* (London: Penguin Press, 1999), 21.

37. *Practical Piety*, 11–14.

38. The term "Revelation" is used as a double entendre; as well as referring to the last book of the Bible it infers "revealed" religion as the disclosure, by God, of ideas that are not arrived at by reason or intellect alone.

39. "O fairest of creation, last and best of all God's works, creature in whom excelled whatever can to sight or thought be formed. Holy, divine, good, amiable or sweet!" John Milton, *Paradise Lost*, 521 (line 896).

40. J. Melnyk (ed.) *Women's Theology in Nineteenth-Century Britain: Transfiguring the Faith of their Fathers* (New York: Garland Publishing 1998), xi.

41. *The Woman's Bible*, p. xxix.

CHAPTER 1

1. R. Shoemaker, *Gender in English Society 1650–1850*, 6.

2. At a council meeting held in Macon, France in the year AD 585. Church leaders tussled with the question of women's humanity; sixty-three delegates were present, and women were declared human by one vote—thirty-two voted "yes" and thirty-one voted "no." This legend now granted mythological status. See "Do Women Have Souls" by Professor Michael Nolan, University College, Dublin, which nevertheless hints at the myth, mist, and confusion that has encouraged patriarchal bias to flourish. The Church in History Information Centre. www.Churchinhistory.org.

3. More's poem *The Bas Bleu* written in celebration of the Bluestockings, emphasized the equal educational opportunities necessary for a cultivated society. It reinforced Enlightenment theory that rational conversation was a mark of civilized society. Her *Slavery: A Poem* equally contributed to an Enlightenment debate on the nature of humanity. Anne Stott elaborates on this suggestion in *Hannah More the first Victorian* (Oxford: Oxford University Press, 2003).

4. "Bright Montagu" was marked for praise in *The Bas Bleu*.

5. M. G. Jones, *Hannah More* (Cambridge: Cambridge University Press, 1952), 16.

6. H. More, *Thoughts on the Importance of the Manners of the Great to General Society* (T. Cadell & W. Davies, in the Strand, 1818), ix.

7. K. W. F. Stavely, *Puritan Legacies, Paradise Lost and the New England Tradition 1630–1890* (Ithaca: Cornell University Press, 1987), 14.

8. This work was published anonymously, fearing retribution from her fashionable friends.

9. W. Roberts, *Memoirs of The Life and Correspondence of Mrs. Hannah More*, 226, vol. 2.

10. R. Hole, *Selected Writings of Hannah More* (London: William Pickering, 1996), xxix.

11. H. More, *An Estimate of the Religion of the Fashionable World* (Dublin: Printed for P. Wogan, P. Bryans, J. M. Moore, J.J. Jones, A. Grueber, and 5 others in Dublin1791), 62–101.

12. C. Krueger, *The Reader's Repentance: Women Preachers, Women Writers and Nineteenth-Century Social Discourse* (Chicago: The University of Chicago Press, 1992), 94–124.

13. *Strictures*, 1, 14, vol. 2.

14. *Strictures*, 34, vol. 1.

15. R. Hole, *Selected Writings of Hannah More*, xv.

16. The Bristol Record Office allowed me to access boxes of uncataloged material given to them by Adam Hart-Davis, a descendant of Richard Hart-Davis, Member of Parliament for Bristol 1812–1831, and recipient of some three hundred letters from Hannah More.

17. See Claire Tomalin, *The Life and Death of Mary Wollstonecraft*, (London: Weidenfeld and Nicolson, 1974), 18.

18. K. N. Cameron (ed.), *Shelley and his Circle 1773–1822* (Cambridge, MA: Harvard University Press, 1961), 935, vol. 11. Fourteen letters written to Miss Jane Arden from Mary Wollstonecraft and not previously published were acquired by The Carl H. Pforzheimer Library. A copybook bearing the title "Unpublished Letters of Mary Wollstonecraft" was passed to them when Volume 1 of the above mentioned work, *Shelley and his Circle 1773–1822*, was already in plate proof. These letters provide valuable resource material in assisting biographical research of her early years. Wollstonecraft married Godwin in March 1797.

19. M. Wollstonecraft, *Maria, or The Wrongs of Woman: A Fragment in two volumes*, 124, vol. 1.

20. Letter from Wollstonecraft to Arden June 4, 1773–November 16, 1774? K. N. Cameron, *Shelley and his Circle 1773–1822*, 957, vol. 11.

21. C. Tomalin, *The Life & Death of Mary Wollstonecraft*, 16–18.

22. M. Wollstonecraft, *Mary, A Fiction*, 11, vol 1.

23. Ibid., 6.

24. J. Todd (ed.), *A Wollstonecraft Anthology*, (Bloomington, IN: Indiana University Press, 1977), 6.

25. *Mary*, 73. See Matthew 22:30 "For in the resurrection they neither marry, nor are given in marriage, but are as the angels of God in heaven."

26. H. More, *The Works of Hannah More*, Vol. 1, Poems, (London: Cadell and Davies, 1818), 167–87, vol. 1.

27. *Mary*, 11.

28. Ibid., 14.

29. C. Tomalin, *The Life & Death of Mary Wollstonecraft*, 31.

30. M. H. Abrams (ed.), *The Norton Anthology of English Literature* (New York: W. W. Norton & Company, 1962). Manuscript copy of Locke's *A Discourse of Natural and Revealed Religion in Several Essays*, confirmed this particular perspective: "God is one or rather very oneness." Ms. Locke c. 27. Duke Humphrey's Library, University of Oxford.

31. W. Godwin, *Memoirs of Mary Wollstonecraft* (London: Constable, 1928), 27.

32. C. Tomalin, *The Life and Death of Mary Wollstonecraft*, 51.

33. J. Todd (ed.), *A Wollstonecraft Anthology*, 23.

34. A letter written to Johnson in the summer of 1788 records the depth of her feeling for him: "You are my only friend—the only person I am intimate with—I never had a father, or a brother." *Letters to Johnson*, 358, vol. 6.

35. Wollstonecraft fell passionately in love with Henry Fuseli, though he did not return her affections.

36. It has been suggested that Godwin fell in love with her as a result of her *Letters from Sweden*. He wrote, "A book of travels that so irresistibly seizes on the heart, never, in any other instance, found its way from the press." W. Godwin, *Memoirs of Mary Wollstonecraft*, 84.

37. C. Kegan Paul, *William Godwin: His Friends and Contemporaries* (London: Henry S. King, 1876), 191–92.

38. Boris Ford (ed.), *The New Pelican Guide to English Literature*, Vol. 9: *American Literature* (Harmondsworth, England: Penguin, 1988), 19.

39. Ann D. Gordon (ed.), *The Selected Papers of Elizabeth Cady Stanton and Susan B. Anthony* (New Brunswick, NJ: Rutgers University Press, 1997), 107–8, vol. 1.

40. T. Stanton and H. Stanton Blatch (eds.), *Elizabeth Cady Stanton As Revealed in Her Letters Diary and Reminiscences* (New York: Harper & Brothers Publishers, 1922), 1–3, vol. 1.

41. Ibid., 6.

42. Ibid., 9.

43. Ibid., 19.

44. Ibid., 20.

45. Ibid., 23.

46. Ibid., 23.

47. Ibid., 23.

48. Ibid., 26.

49. Ibid., 34.

50. Ibid., 26.
51. Ibid., 48.
52. Ibid., 49.
53. More will be written on the newspaper she founded, in further chapters.
54. A. D. Gordon (ed.) *The Selected Papers of Elizabeth Cady Stanton and Susan B. Anthony*, 98, vol. 1.
55. Ibid., 206.
56. S. Wilbur, *The Life of Mary Baker Eddy* (Boston: The Christian Science Publishing Society, 1907), 16.
57. Eddy's paternal grandmother was a descendant of the McNeils of Edinburgh, whose parents went to America seeking religious liberty. It was through this bloodline that Eddy was believed to be related to Hannah More.
58. *The Life of Mary Baker Eddy*, 14.
59. Ibid., 27.
60. Her first cousin, H. H. Smith, suggested, "Her brother Albert was one of the ablest lawyers of New Hampshire; but Mary was deemed the most scholarly member of her family." *The Life of Mary Baker Eddy* 8.
61. Ibid., 31.
62. M. B. Eddy, *Prose Works* "Retrospection and Introspection," 22.
63. *The Life of Mary Baker Eddy*, 32.
64. Ibid., 35.
65. Exhibit No. L02678. Used by permission of The Mary Baker Eddy Collection. Emphasis in original.
66. M. B. Eddy, *Poems* (Boston : Trustees under the Will of Mary Baker G. Eddy, 1910), 34.
67. M. Wollstonecraft, *Mary, A Fiction*, vol. 1, 73.
68. M. B. Eddy, *Prose Works* "Miscellany," 149. A paper presented to the New England American Studies Association held at the Massachusetts Historical Society, Boston, April 28, 2002, titled "Understanding Mary Baker Eddy" by Thomas Johnson suggests, "the very circumstances which seemed crushing in her life became a driving force behind her break with theologies which held at arm's length (or so it seemed to her) the immediacy of the divine reality, 'We are hungry for Love,' she wrote in a Christmas message in the 1890s; 'we are tired of theoretic husks.'"
69. *Prose Works* "No and Yes," 46.
70. H. More, *The Works of Hannah More*. *"Essays on Various Subjects Principally Designed for Young Ladies"* (New York: Harper & Brothers, 1836), 552, vol. 2.

Chapter 2

1. "Why must the female mind be tainted by coquetish arts to gratify the sensualist?" asks Mary Wollstonecraft in *A Vindication of the Rights of Woman*, 100.

2. *The Works of Hannah More*, (London: Cadell and Davies, 1818), xxiii, vol. 1.

3. William Wilberforce 1759–1833—Yorkshire Member of Parliament from Hull. He was the leading layman of the evangelical "Clapham Set" and powerful campaigner for the cause of abolition.

4. *The Works of Hannah More*, 371.

5. Ibid., 372.

6. *Oroonoko* or *The Royal Slave* was an antislavery play written by Aphra Behn. More was influential in persuading the manager of the Drury Lane Theatre to perform *Oroonoko* as a way of reaching 3,000 people each performance.

7. *The Works of Hannah More*, 374.

8. Ibid., 375.

9. Ibid., 377.

10. Ibid., 380.

11. Galatians 3:28.

12. *The Works of Hannah More*, 389 This poem clearly builds upon an earlier one *Slavery, A Poem* (London: T. Cadell in the Strand, 1788).

13. See Clare Midgley: *Women Against Slavery: The British Campaigns 1780–1870* (London: Routledge, 1994).

14. R. Hole, ed., *The Selected Writings of Hannah More* (London: William Pickering, 1996), xxviii.

15. C. Krueger, *The Reader's Repentance: Women Preachers, Women Writers and Nineteenth-Century Social Discourse* (Chicago: The University of Chicago Press, 1992), 94.

16. G. J. Barker-Benfield, *The Culture of Sensibility: Sex and Society in Eighteenth-Century Britain* (Chicago: The University of Chicago Press, 1992), 224. Bishop Porteous wrote to More on January 16, 1797, "I hear from every quarter of the globe. To the West Indies I have sent shiploads of them. They are read with avidity in Sierra Leone, and I hope our Scottish Missionaries will introduce them into Asia." *Memoirs of the Life and Correspondence of Mrs Hannah More* (London: R. B. Seeley & W. Burnside, 1834), 5 vol. 3.

17. M. A. Schofield and C. Macheski, (eds.), *Fetter'd or Free?: British Women Novelists 1670–1815*. M. Myers, "Hannah More's Tracts for the Times: Social Fiction and Female Ideology" (Athens, OH: Ohio University Press, 1986), 265.

18. N. F. Cott, *The Bonds of Womanhood "Woman's Sphere" in New England 1780–1835* (New Haven, CT: Yale University Press, 1977), 126.

19. B. Ford, (ed.) *The New Pelican Guide to English Literature: Vol 9: American Literature* (Harmondsworth, England: Penguin, 1988), 167.

20. K. W. F. Stavely, *Puritan Legacies, Paradise Lost and the New England Tradition 1630–1890* (Ithaca: Cornell University Press, 1987), 201.

21. This subject of female influence on their menfolk is reminiscent of More's earlier arguments.

22. Mary M. Glover (Eddy), "Oddfellowship," *The Covenant*, Vol. V, No. 11, November, 1846. 581–583. Held at The Mary Baker Eddy Library.

23. A paper by David J. Hufford, PhD, identifies the centrality of the notion of woman as minister, mother, and nurse in Eddy's writings "documents show that, nurse, like mother, had become a central aspect of her thinking . . . these make it clear that for Mrs. Eddy the idea of nursing, is inextricable from that of motherhood and love, metaphoric and literal, often poetic, permeates her thinking from an early age." The Mary Baker Eddy Library Core Collection, "Spirituality and Health, A Preliminary Assessment," May 2003. It is interesting that Florence Nightingale (1821–1910) suggested that had she not gone into nursing, she would have founded a religion.

24. Mary M. Glover (Eddy), *The Covenant*, Vol V, No. 1, September, 1847, No. 5 "Erin, the Smile and the Tear in thine Eyes," 409. Held at MBEL.

25. G. J. Barker-Benfield, *The Culture of Sensibility, Sex & Society in Eighteenth-Century Britain*, (Chicago: The University of Chicago Press, 1992), 352.

26. Exhibit No L02683. Mary Baker Eddy to Maj. Gen. Benjamin Butler, August 17, 1861. Used by permission of The Mary Baker Eddy Collection.

27. General Benjamin F. Butler's remarks can be found in his letter to Eddy dated August 20, 1861, written by his Aid-de-camp on his behalf (Incoming Correspondence File No. 653). Held at MBEL.

28. M. B. Eddy, *Poems, The New Century*, 22.

29. *The works of Hannah More, The Black Slave Trade*, 387

30. L. Davidoff and C. Hall, *Family Fortunes: Men and women of the English middle class 1780–1850* (London: Routledge, 1987), 335.

31. See N. F. Cott, *The Bonds of Womanhood, "Woman's Sphere" in New England 1780–1835* (New Haven, CT: Yale University Press, 1977), 133.

32. O. Cromwell, *Lucretia Mott* (New York: Russell & Russell, 1958), 29.

33. See O. Banks, *Faces of Feminism: A Study of Feminism as a Social Movement* (Oxford: Martin Robertson, 1981), 32.

34. Susan B. Anthony (1820–1906) Leader of the American suffrage movement. It is worth noting that Anthony took formal instruction in the new religion founded by Mary Baker Eddy. *Christian Science Sentinel*, October 30, 2002, p. 20.

35. Lucretia Mott wrote to Elizabeth Cady Stanton in 1851, "It is from the pen of a woman too, in great part, which adds to the interest of the article—for no man can write on woman's wrongs, as an intelligent sufferer of our own sex can." Cromwell notes in *Lucretia*

Mott, "Following the English pioneer, Mary Wollstonecraft, American women had not been silent." Indeed, Catharine Beecher was an eloquent orator on behalf of women's rights and Sarah Grimke suggested, "the inferior status of women could be traced to faulty interpretations of the Scriptures." O. Cromwell, *Lucretia Mott* (New York: Russell & Russell, 1958), 150.

36. M. Wollstonecraft, *The Female Reader*, 56, vol. 4. J. Todd and M. Butler (eds.) *The Works of Mary Wollstonecraft* (London: William Pickering, 1989).

37. The inclusion of William Cowper's poem *On Slavery* confirms this. *The Female Reader*, 297, vol. 4.

38. L. Davidoff and C. Hall, *Family Fortunes: Men and women of the English middle class 1780–1850* (Routledge: 1987), prologue.

39. M. Wollstonecraft, *Original Stories from Real Life; with Conversations, calculated to Regulate the Affections, and Form the Mind to Truth and Goodness*, 360, vol. 4.

40. M. Wollstonecraft, *Contributions to the Analytical Review 1788–1797*, 14, vol. 7.

41. Ibid., 100.

42. G. J. Barker-Benfield, *The Culture of Sensibility: Sex and Society in Eighteenth-Century Britain*, 224.

43. Ibid., 225

44. M. Wollstonecraft, *A Vindication of the Rights of Man*, 50, vol. 5.

45. Ibid., 50.

46. M. Wollstonecraft, *A Vindication of the Rights of Woman*, 73, vol. 5.

47. *Vindication*, 147.

48. *The Works of Hannah More, The White Slave Trade*, 391–405, vol. 1.

49. Ibid., 391, 392.

50. Ibid., 392, 393.

51. The male author of "The Lawes Resolution of Women's Rights" (1632) exposes the loss of identity suffered by a woman on the occasion of marriage. E. Hobby, *Virtue of Necessity: English Women's Writing 1649–88* (Ann Arbor, MI: The University of Michigan Press, 1999), 4.

52. *The White Slave Trade*, 400.

53. Ibid., 395.

54. R. Hole (ed.), *Selected Writings of Hannah More*, xvi.

55. *The White Slave Trade*, 403, 404, 405.

56. *The Culture of Sensibility*, 224.

57. A. D. Gordon (ed), *The Selected Papers of Elizabeth Cady Stanton and Susan B. Anthony—In The School of Anti-Slavery 1840–1866* (New Brunswick, NJ: Rutgers University Press, 1997), xxiii, vol. 1.

58. Ibid., xxiii.

59. Frederick Douglass (1817–1895) was born into slavery, but escaped. William Lloyd Garrison was a tremendous influence in his life, but he in

turn became impressed with Douglass. As well as speaking on the rights of black Africans, he was a staunch supporter of women's rights.

60. Ibid., xxiii.
61. Ibid., xxiv.
62. Ibid., 26.
63. Ibid., xxxi. At a Women's Rights Conference at Seneca Falls in 1848, the American Declaration of Independence was specially adapted to reinforce the "inalienable rights" of women as well as men. Using language that emphasized inherent "natural rights" endowed on women as well as men, from their creator, a Declaration of Sentiments was initiated by Stanton and Mott.
64. Ibid., 16.
65. Ibid., 19.
66. E. C. Stanton, *Eighty Years and More Reminiscences 1815–1897* (New York: Schocken Books, 1971), 72.
67. This refers to the decision to exclude women from the podium.
68. *Selected Papers*, 29.
69. Ibid., 409.
70. Ibid., 410.
71. Ibid., 410.
72. Ibid., 414.
73. Ibid., 410.
74. Ibid., 414.
75. Ibid., 414.
76. Ibid., 415.
77. Ibid., 415.
78. Ibid., 416.
79. See "Manly Words on Mount Parnassus" and "Returning to the Beautiful," L. L. Runge, *Gender and Language in British Literary Criticism, 1660–1790* (Cambridge: Cambridge University Press, 1997), 1–39, 168–210.
80. *Selected Papers*, 416.
81. Ibid., 418.
82. W. Wilberforce, *A Practical View of the Prevailing Religious System of Professed Christians in the Higher and Middle Classes in this Country Contrasted with Real Christianity* (London: Griffith, Farran, Okeden and Welsh. 1797), 230.
83. Barbara Welter identifies in "The Feminization of American Religion 1800–1860" M. S. Hartman and L. Banner (eds.) *Clio's consciousness raised; new perspectives on the history of women* (New York: Harper & Row, 1974). See also R. B. Shoemaker, *Gender in English Society 1650-1850* (London: Longman, 1998), 216.
84. *The Culture of Sensibility*, 258.
85. P. Springborg (ed.) *Mary Astell, Some Reflections Upon Marriage, in Political Writings* (Cambridge: Cambridge University Press, 1996), 18.

CHAPTER 3

1. See "Exorcising Evil from Eve": Chapter 2 in *Beyond God the Father* by Mary Daly (London: The Women's Press Ltd., 1986), 44.
2. *Vindication*, 148.
3. Ibid., 84.
4. M. Wollstonecraft, *An Historical and Moral View of the Origin of The French Revolution and the Effect it Has Produced in Europe*, 23, vol. 4.
5. M. Wollstonecraft, *Thoughts on the Education of Daughters*, 25, vol. 4.
6. K. N. Cameron (ed.), *Shelley and his Circle 1773–1822*, 970. vol. 11. Cameron suggests that Wollstonecraft's correspondence with Jane Arden evidences: "signs of both her later rebellion and humanitarianism." (939).
7. Ibid., 957, 965.
8. *Thoughts on the Education of Daughters*, 12
9. Ibid 12
10. Proverbs 22: 6.
11. M. Wollstonecraft, *Elements of Morality*, 5, vol. 2.
12. Ibid., 7.
13. Ibid.,11.
14. *Vindication*, 263.
15. Ibid., 263.
16. Proverbs 31:10–28.
17. It is worth noting the gendered referencing to "wisdom": Proberbs 4: 5, 6, 8, 9: "Get wisdom, get understanding: forget it not; neither decline from the words of my mouth. Forsake *her* not; and *she* shall preserve thee: love *her*, and *she* shall keep thee. Exalt *her*, and *she* shall preserve thee: *she* shall bring thee to honour, when thou dost embrace *her*. *She* shall give to thine head an ornament of grace: a crown of glory shall **she** deliver to thee." (emphasis added)
18. Richard Polwhele (1729–1838) A miscellaneous writer who wrote regularly for the *Anti-Jacobin Review* and contributed to the *Gentleman's Magazine*.
19. R. Polwhele, *The Unsex'd Females: A Poem* (London: Cadell and Davies, 1798), 35n.
20. For examples, see writings of Laurence Sterne, *A Sentimental Journey* (1768); Samuel Richardson, *Pamela, or Virtue Rewarded*, (1740); Jean Jacques Rousseau, *Julie or The New Heloise* (1761).
21. Barker-Benfield noted: "If sensibility was a form of religion, the evidence suggests it was overwhelmingly a religion of women. Women's minds, bodies, and domestic spaces were its sanctums (one 'shrine' therein was the tea table), where it could be consolidated and developed into self-consciousness and authoritative convention, before issuing outward in demands for heterosocial politeness and, eventually, reform. Its fundamental intention was to reshape men." *The Culture of Sensibility*, 262.

22. E. Eger, C. Grant, C. O. Gallchoir, P. Warburton (eds.) *Women, Writing and the Public Sphere 1700–1830*, "The choice of Hercules: the polite arts and 'female excellence' in eighteenth-century London," (Cambridge: Cambridge University Press, 2001), 79.

23. A. Stott, *Hannah More The First Victorian* (Oxford: Oxford University Press, 2003), 83.

24. *The Works of Hannah More, Poems: Sensibility*, 179 vol. 1.

25. Ibid., 179, 180.

26. Ibid., 180.

27. See Sarah Scott's *The History of Sir George Ellison* (London: A. Millar, 1766), for an illustration of this, p. 25, vol. 1.

28. M. H. Abrams (ed.), *The Norton Anthology of English Literature* (New York: W. W. Norton & Company, 1962), 2274, vol. 1.

29. *Sensibility*, 181.

30. *The Culture of Sensibility*, 173.

31. *Strictures*, xii–xiii, vol. 1.

32. These issues are discussed more widely in Harriet Guest's essay "The Dream of a Common Language," *Small Change, Women Learning, Patriotism, 1750–1810* (Chicago: Chicago University Press, 2000), 275.

33. *Vindication*, 147.

34. Ibid., 212.

35. Ibid., 212.

36. Ibid., 264.

37. Ibid., 90.

38. Ibid., 92.

39. Ibid., 247.

40. *Strictures*, 3, vol. 2; emphasis added.

41. *Vindication*, 74.

42. Note the introduction to *Practical Piety*: "An eminent Professor of our time modestly declared that he taught chemistry in order that he might learn it. The writer of the following pages might, with far more justice, offer a similar declaration, as an apology for so repeatedly treating on the important topics of religion and morals." *Practical Piety*, v. vol. 1. To emphasize my suggestion on tone, note also the preface to *Thoughts on the Education of Daughters*: here Wollstonecraft argues that she has no intention of swelling the pages with apologies! (5).

43. *Strictures*, 1.

44. Ibid., 3.

45. *Vindication*, 263.

46. *Strictures*, 3–4

47. H. More, *Essays on Various Subjects Principally Designed for Young Ladies* (London: T. Cadell in the Strand, 1791), 5th ed., 13.

48. *Vindication*, 242–43.

49. H. More, *Essays*, 4–5.

50. *Strictures*, 1–2, vol. 1.

51. Ibid., 4–5, vol. 1.
52. Ibid., 61.
53. Exodus 37:1.
54. *Strictures* 34.
55. Letter from a private collection at Bristol Record Office, Ref: 26168.
56. W. Lyman, *A Virtuous Woman, the Bond of Domestic Union, and the Source of Domestic Happiness* (London: printed by S. Green, 1802), 22.
57. An address given by Stanton in 1871 confirms her admiration for Wollstonecraft: "The true nobility and virtue of Mary Wollstonecrft compelled her admission into the most aristocratic and the most moral circles in England." *Selected Papers*, 395, vol. 2.
58. *Selected Papers*, 112, vol. 1.
59. Ibid., 95.
60. Emphasis added.
61. Ibid., 96.
62. *The Works of Hannah More The White Slave Trade*, 391–405, vol. 1.
63. *Selected Papers*, 96–116, vol. 1 for the complete address.
64. Ibid., 105.
65. J. Buckminster, "A Sermon Preached before the Members of the Boston Female Asylum, September 1810." Hand-copied and bound with other printed sermons to the BFA. See "Sermons by the late Rev. Joseph S. Buckminster," www.openlibrary.org/b/OL.17872004M.
66. *Selected Papers*, 99, vol. 1.
67. *Vindication* 263
68. *Selected Papers*, 344, vol. 1.
69. This "Review" and Stanton's Article of Response are in *Selected Papers*, 297–300, vol. 1.
70. *Selected Papers*, 297.
71. Ibid., 297, 298.
72. Ibid., 298.
73. Ibid., 298, 299.
74. Ibid., 299.
75. *Selected Papers*, 299, vol. 1.
76. *Strictures*, 62–64.
77. *Vindication*, 222.
78. Exhibit No A11395. Poem *The Wife* (1848) Used by permission of The Mary Baker Eddy Collection.
79. Exhibit No L02678 Mary Baker Eddy to E. Augusta Holmes Swasey, c. 1841. Used by permission of The Mary Baker Eddy Collection.
80. Mary M. Glover (Eddy), "Odd-Fellowship" *The Covenant*, a Monthly Magazine Devoted to the cause of Odd-Fellowship. Vol V. November 1846, 582. Held at MBEL.
81. The Oddfellows was a secret benevolent and fraternal association founded in England in the eighteenth century.

82. Mary M. Glover (Eddy), *The Covenant*, a Monthly Magazine Devoted to the cause of Odd-Fellowship. August 1846. *Emma Clinton, or a Tale of the Frontiers*, 441.
83. Ibid., 441.
84. Ibid., 441.
85. *Vindication*, 243.
86. M. H. Abrams, *A Glossary of Literary Terms*, 194.
87. M. B. Eddy, *Science & Health*, 236.
88. *Emma Clinton, or a Tale of the Frontiers*, 454. Held at MBEL.
89. M. B. Eddy, *Poems*, 21.
90. *Science & Health*, 236.
91. Matthew 5:1–11. Thomas Johnson in a paper "Understanding Mary Baker Eddy" presented at a conference of the New England American Studies Association, April 28, 2002, suggests: "For Eddy, the spirituality of Jesus reflected a deepening of human sensibility, not a sentimental take on life." (24).
92. *Vindication*, 227.
93. *Science & Health*, 61.
94. *Vindication*, 226.
95. *Science & Health*, 235.
96. Ibid., 225.
97. *Science & Health*, 226–27.
98. *Vindication*, 114.

Chapter 4

1. *The Culture of Sensibility*, 68–70.
2. A. Birrell, *Collected Essays and Addresses of the Right Honourable Augustine Birrell 1880–1920* (London: Dent, 1922), 254, Vol. 11.
3. A. Birrell, *Essays about Men, Women and Books* (London: Elliot Stock, 1895), 70–72.
4. M. Twain, *Christian Science* (Buffalo, NY: Promethus Books, 1993), vi. In his paper "Understanding Mary Baker Eddy," Johnson suggested, "Mark Twain's savaging of the octogenarian in 1903 was deeply entwined with issues of both gender and class." (5).
5. *Christian Science*, 157.
6. Ibid., 60–61.
7. C. Trevett, "Woman, God and Mary Baker Eddy," *Religion* 14(1984): 143–53.
8. The Christian Romanticism that marks Wollstonecraft's writing is apparent in her emphasis on the beauty of nature and its effectiveness in mirroring the divine beauty. Her opposition to the Evangelical doctrine of original sin placed her at odds with More, who embraced this gospel-based movement. More's questioning of biblical interpretation, however, tends to unite her with liberal Protestantism. *The Encyclopedia of Religion*

explains: "Historically, the scholarly study of religion—as well as the rise of modern hermeneutics—is closely associated with the religious tradition of liberal Protestantism. Schleiermacher (1768–1834), the founder of hermeneutics as well as of liberal Protestantism, was particularly influential in articulating the outlines of this compromise. He regarded the various religions as culturally conditioned forms of an underlying and universal religious sensibility. Thus he not only moved the locus of faith from belief to experience, but also laid the foundations for a descriptive science of religion." (281). Stanton rejected both Calvinism and Evangelicalism, embracing rather a religious philosophy based on Quaker and Unitarian principles. Eddy's recognition of the absolute authority of the Bible places her in company with Evangelicalism, though her insistence on man's innate perfection collides with their creed of total depravity. Perhaps her "Science of Christianity" again positioned her toward liberal Protestantism. The foregoing leads me to conclude that ultimately each woman embraced a Religion of the Heart.

9. "Radcliffe approvingly quoted Mark Akenside's version: 'Lull'd in the countless chambers of the brain / Our thoughts are linked by many a hidden chain / Awake but one, and lo! what myriads arise!/Each stamps its image as the other flies!'" G. J. Barker-Benfield, *The Culture of Sensibility*, 18.

10. *The Encyclopedia of Religion*, 236.

11. *Letters written in Sweden, Norway and Denmark*, 289 (vol 6).

12. Ibid., 422.

13. E. C. Stanton, *As Revealed in Her Letters Diary and Reminiscences*, 344.

14. See Gillian Gill's chapter "Mark Twain Fails to Come Calling" in her biography *Mary Baker Eddy* (Reading, MA: Perseus Books, 1998).

15. The background to this lawsuit will not be examined in this work, but is fully documented in Gillian Gill's *Mary Baker Eddy* (Reading, MA: Perseus Books, 1998). Similarly, Robert Peel's biography on the life of Mary Baker Eddy gives a clear account. Through three volumes, *Mary Baker Eddy—The Years of Discovery, The Years of Trial,* and *The Years of Authority* (New York: Holt, Rinehart and Winston, 1977), Peel acquaints the reader with an appraisal of these different periods of Eddy's career.

16. G. Gill, *Mary Baker Eddy*, 439.

17. Ibid., 445.

18. Ibid., 449.

19. *Letters*, 346.

20. *Vindication*, 232.

21. *A View*, 21.

22. *The Culture of Sensibility*, 362, 364.

23. M. Wollstonecraft, "Letters to Johnson," 364 (Vol. 6).

24. *A View*, 6.

25. J. Rendall, "The grand causes which combine to carry mankind forward: Wollstonecraft, history and revolution." *Women's Writing* 4 (1997): 155.

26. *Vindication*, 231–32.

27. Thomas Paine settled in America 1774 and it is suggested that "He brought the spirit of British radicalism with him."A revolutionary pamphlet he wrote in 1776 sold 100,000 copies within three months. This confirms close philosophical links. See *From Puritanism to Postmodernism. A History of American Literature*, (Harmondsworth, England: Penguin, 1992), 56.

28. M. Wollstonecraft, *Letter on the Present Character of the French Nation*, 444, (Vol. 6).

29. *A View*, 6.

30. W. Godwin, *Memoirs of The Author of "The Rights of Woman"* (London: Penguin Books 1987), 242–43.

31. C. Tomalin, *The Life and Death of Mary Wollstonecraft* (London: Penguin Books 1985), 189.

32. The ability to envision the inherent promise within the tangible and material (nature and landscape provided a foretaste of spiritual sublimity) was what marked the romantic movement of the eighteenth century.

33. *The Life & Death of Mary Wollstonecraft*, 225.

34. *Letters*, 247.

35. Ibid., 241.

36. Letter to Johnson already referred to.

37. Ibid., 246.

38. *A View*, 22.

39. *Letters*, 287–88.

40. G. Dart. *Rousseau, Robespierre and English Romanticism* (Cambridge: Cambridge University Press, 1999), 135.

41. It is worth noting that despite her sharp censure of Rousseau, her vision of utopia coincides with his portrayal of the perfect society in *Julie or La Nouvelle Heloise*. A sentiment of virtuous republic is at the heart of the *Clarens* section in his novel: "We sing, we laugh all day long, and the work goes only the better for it . . . everyone is equal . . . but the gentle equality that prevails here re-establishes nature's order, constitutes a form of instruction for some, a consolation for others, and a bond of friendship for all." J. J. Rousseau, *Julie or La Nouvelle Heloise* (Hanover, NH: University Press of New England, 1997), 496, 497.

42. *Letters*, 307.

43. Ibid, 307.

44. J. Ruskin, *Sesame and Lilies* ((Orpington, Kent: George Allen, 1886), 135.

45. Eddy wrote, "In our immature sense of spiritual things, let us say of the beauties of the sensuous universe: 'I love your promise; and shall know, some time, the spiritual reality and substance of form, light, and color,

of what I now through you discern dimly; and knowing this, I shall be
satisfied.'" M. B. Eddy, *Prose Works* "Miscellaneous Writings," 87.

46. *Letters*, 269.
47. I. Kant, *Observations on the Feeling of the Beautiful and the Sublime*,
    trans. John T. Goldthwaite (Berkeley: University of California Press,
    1960), 78.
48. M. Wollstonecraft, "Hints" (Chiefly designed to have been incorpo-
    rated in the Second Part of Vindication) 275, (Vol. 5).
49. *Letters*, 342.
50. G. Dart, *Rousseau, Robespiere and English Romanticism* (Cambridge:
    Cambridge University Press, 1999), 138.
51. Examples being Richard Polwhele's *The Unsex'd Females* (1798); an
    anonymous poem "The Vision of Liberty," published in the *Anti-Jacobin
    Review*; *The Vagabond* by George Walker; and *The Infernal Quixote* by
    Charles Lucas.
52. *A View*, 21.
53. *Reminiscences*, 190, (Vol. 2).
54. *Eighty Years and More*, 346.
55. *Vindication*, 232.
56. M. Daly, *Beyond God the Father* (London: The Women's Press 1986),
    47.
57. The nature of Christian marriage was debated in Wollstonecraft's novel
    Maria, or The Wrongs of Woman, published posthumously in 1798.
    This text examined the position of women in society in religious and
    political terms.
58. *Selected Papers*, 246, (Vol. 1).
59. Ibid., 253.
60. Ibid., 254.
61. E. Cady Stanton, *Eighty Years and More*, vii.
62. T. Stanton and H. Stanton Blatch (eds.), *Elizabeth Cady Stanton As
    Revealed in Her Letters Diary and Reminiscences*, 120, (Vol. 2).
63. It is interesting to note that in 1868, *Revolution* serialized *Vindication*
    in an attempt to advance the feminist ideals of Wollstonecraft.
64. *Elizabeth Cady Stanton As Revealed in Her Letters Diary and Reminis-
    cences*, 117, (Vol. 2). Horace Greeley (1811–1872) was an influential
    abolitionist as well as editor of the *Tribune*.
65. Ibid., 215, (Vol. 1).
66. *Selected Papers*, 125, (Vol. 2).
67. *Reminiscences*, 215, (Vol. 1).
68. *Reminiscences*, 123, (Vol. 2).
69. Revelation 14:15 "the time is come for thee to reap; for the harvest of
    the earth is ripe."
70. *Selected Papers*, 345, (Vol. 2).
71. *Eighty Years and More*, 352.
72. Ibid., 352.

73. *Reminiscences*, 221, (Vol. 1).

74. *Selected Papers*, 113, (Vol. 1).

75. B. G. Smith, *Changing Lives—Women in European History Since 1700* (Lexington, MA: D. C. Heath and Company, 1989), 210.

76. R. Brimley Johnson (ed.), *The Letters of Hannah More* (London: John Lane, The Bodley Head Ltd., 1925), 141.

77. *Practical Piety*, 3, (Vol. 1).

78. *Memoirs of The Life and Correspondence of Mrs. Hannah More*, 147, Vol. 3.

79. An effigy of More was ceremoniously burned by male students and she was brought to a nervous breakdown.

80. This refers to the Biblical character of Rachel, who came through great tribulation to become known as the Mother of Israel. "Thus saith the Lord; Refrain they voice from weeping, and thine eyes from tears; for thy work shall be rewarded." Jeremiah 31:16.

81. *Memoirs of the Life and Correspondence of Mrs. Hannah More*, 143, (Vol. 3).

82. Ibid., 183.

83. Ibid., 213.

84. *Practical Piety*, xi, (Vol. 1).

85. Ibid., 52.

86. Part of a letter I discovered in a Hart-Davis family scrapbook at the Bristol Record Office, uncataloged and as far as I can ascertain, unpublished. Now referenced: 41593/CO/154/1.

87. *Practical Piety* 4, 5

88. *The Encyclopedia of Religion*, 236, (Vol. 6).

89. *Practical Piety*, 12.

90. Ibid., 12.

91. Ibid., 14.

92. Ibid., 8.

93. Ibid., 9.

94. The linking of the Culture of Sensibility with heart religion is expanded upon in Chapter 2 of *The Culture of Sensibility*, 65.

95. *Encyclopedia of Religion*, 237.

96. *Practical Piety* 10, 11.

97. U. King (ed.), *Women in the World's Religions Past and Present*, (New York: Paragon House Publishers, 1987) "The Feminine Aspect of God in Christianity" W. Gardini, 63.

98. *Practical Piety* 10.

99. Ibid., 11, 12.

100. See L. Mandell, *Misogynous Economies: The Business of Literature in Eighteenth-Century Britain* (Lexington, KY: University of Kentucky Press, 1999).

101. *The Culture of Sensibility*, 70.

102. Matthew 5:8 (emphasis added).

103. *Practical Piety*, 19–21.

104. *Science and Health*, 319.

105. *Practical Piety*, ix.

106. Ibid., x (emphasis added).

107. W. Wilberforce, *A Practical View of Christianity*, 2.

108. S. Gill, *Women and the Church of England: From the Eighteenth Century to the Present*, (London: SPCK, 1994), 26.

109. See J. J. Rousseau, *Emile* and G. Redmond, "The First Tom Brown's Schooldays: Origins and Evolution of 'Muscular Christianity' in Children's Literature, 1762–1857," *Quest* 30 (Summer 1978): 4–18.

110. R. W. Davis and R. J. Helmstadter (eds.), *Religion and Irreligion in Victorian Society* (London: Routledge, 1992), 102. Key texts here are Norman Vance, *The Sinews of the Spirit: The Ideal of Christian Manliness in Victorian Literature and Religious Thought* (Cambridge: Cambridge University Press, 1985) and Donald Hall (ed.), *Muscular Christianity: Embodying the Victorian Age* (Cambridge: Cambridge University Press, 1994). See also an essay by Sean Gill: "Thomas Hughes and Christian Manliness" in *Gender and Christian Religion*, R. N. Swanson (ed.), (University of Kent at Canterbury, 1996).

111. *Practical Piety*, 274 (emphasis added).

112. *Memoirs of the Life & Correspondence of Mrs. Hannah More*, 143, (Vol. 3).

113. Manuscript copy held at Bristol Record Office under Reference No 11729.

114. Signed and dated by Hannah More's own hand. Bristol Record Office Reference No 11729.

115. Emphasis added.

116. Bearing in mind that according to Morrell and Thackray, nearly all evangelicals "were hostile to science" and the religious divisions induced by the advancement of any coalition in this area, her proposal needs careful consideration. See B. Hilton, *The Age of Atonement: The Influence of Evangelicalism on Social and Economic Thought 1785–1865* (Oxford: Clarendon Press, 1988), 30.

117. M. Wollstonecraft, "Hints" (Chiefly designed to have been incorporated in the Second Part of Vindication), 375 (Vol. 5).

118. *Vindication*, 275.

119. *Strictures*, 33. This idea is expanded upon in "Doctrines on Femininity" in Leonore Davidoff and Catherine Hall, *Family Fortunes: Men and Women of the English Middle Class 1780–1850* (London: Routledge, 1987), 114–18.

120. See Ben Witherington, *Women in the Ministry of Jesus: A Study of Jesus' Attitudes to Women and Their Roles as Reflected in His Earthly Life*, (Cambridge: Cambridge University Press, 1984), 125, 127. Also, Walter Gardini's essay, "The Feminine Aspect of God in Christianity"

where he points to the feminine images that are apparent in the Old Testament but become "more explicit in the New." (58).

121. *Practical Piety*, 49.

122. *Science and Health*, 110.

123. In September, 1998, the Christian Science Board of Directors in Boston gave me permission to view an—at that time—unpublished essay written by Eddy in December 1900. Access to the archives had been granted to only a handful of scholars over the century. The essay was sent to Eddy's copyright office on December 17, 1900, but subsequently withdrawn.

124. *Human Life*, edited by Alfred Henry Lewis, carried an announcement in the February 1907, edition, "Since time was, no woman so unique. *Human Life* announces that in this issue begins a series of articles on Mary Baker G. Eddy."

125. An entry in Calvin Frye's [Eddy's secretary] diary of December 7, 1900, notes, "Judge Clarkson dined with Mrs. Eddy today & after dinner tried to convince her again that she was mistaken & the cause was going to ruin & the men were essential to take the lead of the cause of C.S. & to assert their rights without her dictation." See Robert Peel's *Mary Baker Eddy, the Years of Authority* (New York: Holt, Rinehart and Winston, 1977), 162.

126. *Prose Works*, "Miscellany," 349.

127. *Science and Health*, p. 59.

128. Exhibit No A10142B. Mary Baker Eddy, "Man and Woman" Used by permission of The Mary Baker Eddy Collection. This essay can be found in *In My True Light and Life* (Boston: The Writings of Mary Baker Eddy, 2002), 620, 621.

129. Numbers 17:5, 8.

130. While the chapter has identified feminine as well as masculine opposition, a letter Eddy wrote to Mr & Mrs. E. J. Smith in January 1884 points to the gendered nature of opposition. Judith Wellman identifies, "Working toward a transcendence of gender, Mrs. Eddy nevertheless sometimes encountered resistance based on gender. In 1884, she complained that, at the Annual Meeting of the Christian Scientist Association, 'they loaded me with praise but certain gentlemen members tried to get the paper into their hands after I had done the work for it one year with a dollar. I *beat them* as usual my lady members clapped.'" J. Wellman. "Making Connections: Mary Baker Eddy and Women's History," 16. *Roadmaps into the Mary Baker Eddy Collections*, May 2003, MBEL.

131. *Prose Works*, "Miscellaneous Writings," 363.

132. Exhibit No. A10837 Mary Baker Eddy, "Bible" undated Used by permission of The Mary Baker Eddy Collection.

133. *Science and Health*, 110.

134. Exhibit No. A10873 Mary Baker Eddy, "Woman's Bible" 1895 Used by permission of The Mary Baker Eddy Collection.
135. N. F. Cott, *The Bonds of Womanhood: "Woman's Sphere" in New England 1780–1835*, (New Haven, CT: Yale University Press, 1977), 158.

CHAPTER 5

1. *Woman's Bible*, 12. For quotations from *The Woman's Bible*, page numbers of the text only will be cited, unless it is to be found in Part 11 of *The Women's Bible*, in which case it shall be identified as such also.
2. *Science and Health*, 139.
3. Ibid., 316.
4. N. F. Cott, *The Bonds of Womanhood*, 158.
5. An article in *The Independent* newspaper, dated October 10, 1992, confirms this is still a contentious subject. Rev. Robert Law suggests, "we have not expounded the creation of Adam and Eve and the fall correctly unless we arrive at the same conclusion that Paul was moved to write for our learning, namely that women are to be submissive and not to teach or have authority over men, because of man's priority in creation and woman's priority in the transgression."
6. M. H. Abrams, *A Glossary of Literary Terms*, 145.
7. Ibid., 216.
8. Louisa May Alcott read *Science and Health*, and visited Eddy twice in 1876. See the magazine (*Quarterly Magazine THE MARY BAKER EDDY LIBRARY for the BETTERMENT of HUMANITY*) published by The Mary Baker Eddy Library, Issue No. 2, Summer, 2001. Frances Hodgson Burnett read Eddy's textbook, appearing to draw on its philosophy for her novels. She turned to its healing principles later in life. See G. Gerzina, *Frances Hodgson Burnett, The Unpredictable Life of the author of The Secret Garden* (London: Chatto & Windus, 2004).
9. Eddy's literary friends advised her against writing such a book, but she considered the book to be "the outgrowth of my whole life" and remarked in January or February 1881 "I think any one would be interested in the remarkable history of this book and the trials I have passed through since its first issue." Exhibit No LO2050. Mary Baker Eddy to Eldridge J. and Mollie Smith, c. 1881. Used by permission of The Mary Baker Eddy Collection.
10. Fee Account, see appendix.
11. A biographer, Daisette D.S.McKenzie, notes, "she often studied for months the origin and meaning of one word and its synonyms before giving it a permanent place in the text book, and in one notable instance she prayed and waited on God concerning a single word for three years." *The We Knew Mary Baker Eddy Series* (Boston: The Christian Science Publishing Society, 1953), 43,44.

12. L. P. Powell, *Mary Baker Eddy A Life Size Portrait* (London: Nisbet & Co. Ltd., 1930), 132.
13. Letter, see appendix.
14. In 1995, Eddy was inducted into the Women's Hall of Fame, where it was noted that she had made an indelible mark on religion, medicine, and journalism. In 1998, *Religion and Ethics Newsweekly* named Eddy as one of twenty individuals—and only three women—who have most influenced religious thinking in the twentieth century. M. C. Jones, "Mary Baker Eddy—Working woman," *Christian Science Sentinel* September 30, 2002, 6.
15. *Prose Works*, "Miscellany," 318.
16. *Science and Health*, 110.
17. *Eighty Years and More*, 467.
18. M. J. Selvidge, *Notorious Voices*, 97.
19. *Encyclopedia of Religion*, 280, (Vol. 6).
20. Ibid., 281, (Vol. 6).
21. Ian Finseth, "Liquid Fire Within Me: Language, Self and Society in Transcendentalism and Early Evangelicalism, 1830–1865." (MAThesis, University of Virginia, 1995).
22. *Notorious Voices*, 98.
23. *Prose Works*, "No and Yes," 11.
24. S. McFague, *Metaphorical Theology, Models of God in Religious Language* (London: SCM 1983)194.
25. Exhibit No A10320. Mary Baker Eddy/Calvin A. Frye, August 26, 1915. Used by permission of The Mary Baker Eddy Collection.
26. *The Encyclopedia of Religion*, 280, 281, Vol. 6.
27. S. McFague, *Models of God Theology for an Ecological, Nuclear Age* (London: SCM Press, 1987), 24.
28. T. Johnson, "Understanding Mary Baker Eddy," Boston: New England American Studies Association, April 2002, 18.
29. R. Peel, *Mary Baker Eddy—The Years of Discovery* (New York: Holt, Rinehart & Winston, 1977), 198.
30. *Science and Health*, 517.
31. Ibid., 517.
32. M. B. Eddy to C. E. Coate, March 15, 1882. Exhibit No. L04088 Used by permission of The Mary Baker Eddy Collection.
33. *Prose Works* "No and Yes," 45.
34. Exhibit No L04088, Mary Baker Eddy to Clara E. Choate, March 15, 1882. Used by permission of The Mary Baker Eddy Collection.
35. *Prose Works*, "No and Yes," 45,
36. Ibid., 45,
37. Exhibit No L04088, Used by permission of The Mary Baker Eddy Collection.
38. *Science and Health*, 268.
39. *Practical Piety*, 9.

40. *Science and Health*, 502.
41. Collins Dictionary and Thesaurus, HarperCollins Publishers, 2000.
42. *Science and Health*, 521.
43. Ibid., 258.
44. Ibid., 349.
45. S. Woods, *Lanyer A Renaissance Woman Poet* (New York: Oxford University Press, 1999), 139.
46. *Practical Piety*, 10.
47. *Woman's Bible*, 20, 21.
48. *Science and Health*, 501.
49. Ibid., 298.
50. Ibid., 93.
51. Ibid., 547.
52. Ibid., 516.
53. G.Gill, *Mary Baker Eddy*, 252, 253.
54. Ibid., 236.
55. Ibid., 228. This representation echoes Milton's "Last and best" theory.
56. Gillian Gill is the chief English translator of Irigaray's writing and also researches the writings of Mary Baker Eddy and Florence Nightingale. See Chapter 12 in G. Gill's *Mary Baker Eddy*.
57. *Science and Health*, 316.
58. Ibid., 85.
59. Ian Finseth, MA Thesis.
60. *Science and Health*, 173.
61. Ibid., 59.
62. Ibid., 537.
63. Ibid., 234.
64. *Woman's Bible*, 209, part 11.
65. Ibid., 13.
66. *Science and Health*, 581.
67. Ian Finseth, MA Thesis.
68. *Prose Works* "Retrospection and Introspection," 35.
69. *Science and Health*, 587.
70. Ibid., 591.
71. P. Lang (ed.), *Religions and Discourse (European Academic Publishers, Bern, Vol 9, 2001)* "God in the Feminine", A. C. Mulder 66.
72. *Science and Health*, 515.
73. Ibid., 515.
74. Ibid., 516, 517.
75. M. H. Abrams, *The Norton Anthology of English Literature*, (New York: W.W. Norton,1962) 19, (Vol. 2). See Blake's "All Religions Are One." "There is no natural religion (a and b) for his argumentative style of Divine Vision," 26.
76. S. McFague, *Metaphorical Theology Models of God in Religious Language* (London: SCM Press, 1983), 15.

77. *Prose Works*, "Miscellany," 129.
78. Genesis 1:26 (added emphasis).
79. *The Woman's Bible* also examines this particular explanation.
80. *Prose Works*, "Miscellaneous Writings," 194. The word "Science" is used in the context of "True knowledge."
81. *Science and Health*, 4.
82. Ibid., 194.
83. J. P. Heimmel, *God is Our Mother; Julian of Norwich and the Medieval Image of Christian Feminine Divinity*, (Lewiston, NY: The Edwin Mellen Press, 1982), 70–71.
84. Ibid., 55
85. A desire to show the "other, feminine side of Christ" was met with charges of heresy and blasphemy in a Passion Pageant Easter 2005. A woman was cast to play the part of Christ, bringing anathema down on the head of its director. In his defense, he pointed to the Bible: "In Christ, there is no male or female" further suggesting, "The dignity of the woman is the purposeful expression of God which she has inherited from her creator." Full text by B. Johnston, "'Heresy' of female Jesus divides Italian town," *The Sunday Telegraph*, March 13, 2005, 28.
86. *Science and Health*, 332.
87. K. Kiezeveld, "God Language as Two-Way Traffic" in P. Lang (ed.), *Religions and Discourse*, 316–18.
88. *Science and Health*, 579.
89. Ibid., 593; emphasis added.
90. *Vindication*, 232; emphasis added.
91. *Prose Works*, "No and Yes," 10.
92. Reference 11729, Bristol Record Office.
93. *Science and Health*, 585.
94. Ibid., 588.
95. Ibid., 593.
96. Ibid., 587.
97. Ibid., 171.
98. N. Neidzielska, "The rights of women sustained by divine law," *The Herald of Christian Science*, 2001, Special Issue, 4. Published by The Christian Science Publishing Society. Inside the front cover of this publication it reads "'Woman—her undeniable worth' was published in March of 2000. In honor of women's history month in the United States, we're re-publishing it in English. This special issue is about the personal and spiritual progress of women around the world." The foregoing are the only details in terms of date.
99. *Vindication*, 95.
100. *Science and Health*, 521.
101. Ibid., 525.

102. It is worth noting that this second account of creation was preceded by mist: "But there went up a mist from the earth." Genesis 2:6. Metaphorically, the mist implies the potential for obscurity.

103. Ibid., 579.

104. Ibid., 585.

105. Ibid., 338.

106. Ibid., 338.

107. Ibid., 338.

108. *Prose Works*, "Retrospection & Introspection," 27.

109. A. Day, *Romanticism* (London: Routledge, 1996), 45, 59.

110. This literary form allows Eddy to promote what John Witherspoon refers to as nature's ability to represent a "second book of Revelation." Witherspoon (1723–1794) was widely known as a leader of the evangelical or "Popular Party" in the established Church of Scotland. See *The Works of The Rev. John Witherspoon*, (Philadelphia: William W. Woodward, 1802).

111. *Prose Works*, "Miscellaneous Writings," 329–31.

112. P. Lang (ed.), *Religions and Discourse*, "Towards a Different Transcendence Feminist Findings on Subjectivity, Religion and Values," (Bern: European Academic Publishers, 2001), 62, (Vol. 9).

113. Ibid., Introduction.

114. For full text see L. Irigaray, *Divine Women*, Occasional Paper 8 (Sydney, Australia: Local Consumption Publications, April, 1986).

115. G. Gill, *Mary Baker Eddy*, 229.

116. *Prose Works*, "Pulpit and Press," 84.

117. One such acquaintance was John Greenleaf Whittier, the poet and abolitionist. "Pulpit and Press" notes, "About 1868, the author of Science and Health healed Mr. Whittier with one visit, at his home in Amesbury, of incipient pulmonary consumption." M. B. Eddy, "Pulpit and Press," 54.

118. Exhibit No A10873. Mary Baker Eddy, *Woman's Bible*, 1895. Used by permission of The Mary Baker Eddy Collection.

119. Designed to display something, especially the skill of the speaker in rhetoric.

120. A. Thorndike Rice (ed.), *North American Review* 140 (338): 389. New York: 1885.

121. C. A. Newsom, S. H. Ringe (eds.), *The Women's Bible Commentary* (London: SPCK, 1992), xiii.

122. *Woman's Bible*, 7.

123. Ibid., 12.

124. Ibid., 40.

125. Cullen Murphy suggests, "It is not going too far to say (as some have suggested) that *The Woman's Bible* is the reason that an image of Susan B. Anthony and not Elizabeth Cady Stanton graces the one-dollar coin

that was first minted in 1978." C. Murphy, *The Word According to Eve* (Harmondsworth, England: Penguin, 1998), 23.

126. E. C. Stanton, *Eighty Years and More*, 453.
127. *Woman's Bible*, viii.
128. Ibid., xxviii.
129. Ibid., 7, 8.
130. Ibid., 12.
131. C. Murphy, *The Word According to Eve*, 27.
132. *Woman's Bible*, 14, 15.
133. Ibid., 15.
134. Ibid., 15.
135. Ibid., 16.
136. Ibid., 16, 17.
137. *Science and Health with Key to the Scriptures*, 537.
138. *Woman's Bible*, 18.
139. Ibid., 19.
140. Ibid., 20.
141. Ibid., 20.
142. Ibid., 20.
143. *A Glossary of Literary Terms*, 45.
144. *Woman's Bible*, 142.
145. Ibid., 143.
146. Ibid., 144.
147. Ibid., 143.
148. T. Johnson, "Understanding Mary Baker Eddy" (Boston: *New England American Studies Association*, April 2002), 18.
149. *Woman's Bible*, 144.
150. Ibid., 144.
151. Ibid., 144.
152. Ibid., 112, part 11.
153. Ibid., 112.
154. Ibid., 113.
155. Ibid., 114.
156. Revelation 12:1.
157. Ibid., 176. It is interesting to note that the book of Revelation, according to *The Gift of Scripture* (The Catholic Truth Society, 2005) "fills us with profound hope in God." It goes on to explain "such symbolic language must be respected for what it is, and is not be interpreted literally." (48). It is interesting to note, however, that this book did not appear in the Syriac Testament as late as 1562. *The Woman's Bible* says "Neither did Luther, the great reformer of the sixteenth century, nor his co-worker, Erasmus, respect it . . . Calvin, also, had small regard for it. The first collection of the New Testament canon, decided upon by the Council of Laodicea (A.D. 364), omitted the entire book from its list of sacred works . . . The celebrated Vatican codex in the papal

library, the oldest uncial or Biblical manuscript in existence, does not contain Revelation. The canon of the New Testament was fixed as it now is by Pope Innocent I., A.D. 405, with the Book of Revelation still in dispute." (*Woman's Bible*, 177, part 11).

158. *Prose Works*, "Miscellaneous Writings," 245.
159. *The Woman's Bible*, 183.
160. See *In My True Light and Life—Mary Baker Eddy Collections* (Boston: The Writings of Mary Baker Eddy and The Mary Baker Eddy Library for the Betterment of Humanity, 2002), 636.
161. Ibid., 636.
162. *Science and Health*, 13.
163. In *My True Light and Life*, 636; emphasis added.
164. Exhibit No A10407. Mary Baker Eddy, Repaid Pages, The Interpretation of Revelation, undated. Used by permission of The Mary Baker Eddy Collection.
165. Science and Health 562
166. *Prose Works*, "The First Church of Christ, Scientist and Miscellany," 268–69.
167. *Science and Health*, vii.

CONCLUSION

1. L. Irigaray, *Divine Women*, 12.
2. C. Murphy, *The Word According to Eve*, 238.
3. M. J. Selvidge, *Notorious Voices*, 227.
4. *The Gift of Scripture* (The Catholic Truth Society, 2005), 19–25. See *The Times* of October 5, 2005, for a full review of this document.
5. A. L. Barbauld, *The Poems of Anna Letitia Barbauld*, 285.
6. M. K. Smith, *Hannah More: Sunday Schools, Education, and Youth Work*, "The Encyclopedia of Informal Education," 2002, www.infed.org/thinkers/more.htm.
7. Viola Rodgers, "Christian Science Most Potent Factor in Religious Life, Says Clara Barton." *New York American*, January 6, 1908. Reprinted in *The Christian Science Journal*, February, 1908, 696.
8. *Woman's Bible*, 183, part 11.
9. Exhibit No L04088 Mary Baker Eddy to Clara E. Choate, March 15, 1882 Used by permission of The Mary Baker Eddy Collection (emphasis added).

REFERENCES

MANUSCRIPT SOURCES

Bodleian Library: Special Collections and Western Manuscripts.
Bristol Record Office, Bristol, United Kingdom.
Brotherton Library, University of Leeds, Special Collections.
Duke Humphrey's Library, University of Oxford.
The Mary Baker Eddy Collection. The Mary Baker Eddy Library, Boston, USA.

NEWSPAPERS AND JOURNALS

The Augustan Reprint Society, facsimile of pamphlet (1979), "Women's Speaking Justified, Proved and Allowed by the Scriptures" (1666), Margaret Fell Fox.
The Christian Observer
The Christian Science Journal
The Christian Science Monitor
The Christian Science Sentinel
The Covenant, a Monthly Magazine Devoted to the cause of Odd-Fellowship
The Gentleman's Magazine
The Gift of Scripture, The Catholic Truth Society, *2005*
The Independent
Journal of Religion & Society, The Kripke Center, *Volume 7 (2005)*
Magazine of The Mary Baker Eddy Library for the Betterment of Humanity (quarterly)
The Monthly Review (London)
North American Review (1885)
Quest, 30 (Summer 1978): 4-18. G. Redmond. "The First Tom Brown's Schooldays: Origins and Evolution of 'Muscular Christianity' in Children's Literature, 1762-1857"
The Sunday Telegraph
The Times
Finseth, I. "Liquid Fire Within Me" Language, Self and Society in Transcendentalism and Early Evangelicalism, 1830-1865. MA Thesis (English University of Virginia, 1995.
Johnson, T. April 2002 "Understanding Mary Baker Eddy" Boston: New England American Studies Association.

Rendall, J. 1997 "The Grand Causes Which Combine to Carry Mankind Forward." Wollstonecraft, History and Revolution. *Women's Writing* 4 (2).

Wolosky, S. Spring 2002. "Women's Bible's Biblical Interpretation in Nineteenth-Century American Women's Poetry." *Feminist Studies* 28(1).

Websites: www.inted.org/thinkers/more.htm.

http://etcweb.Princeton.edu/cgibin/mts/05/Companion/witherspoon .joh.html.

PRIMARY SOURCES

The Holy Bible, Authorized King James Version, Printed in Great Britain at the University Press, Oxford.

Burke, E. J. T. Boulton (ed.). 1958 (1757). *A Philosophical Enquiry into the Origin of our Ideas of the Sublime and Beautiful*. London: Routledge.

Eddy, Mary Baker. 1893. *Christ and Christmas*. Boston: The First Church of Christ, Scientist.

———. 2002. *In My True Light and Life* Boston: The Writings of Mary Baker Eddy and The Mary Baker Eddy Library for the Betterment of Humanity.

———. 1923 (1895). *Manual of The Mother Church*. Boston: Trustees under the Will of Mary Baker G. Eddy.

———. 1910. *Poems*. Boston: Trustees under the Will of Mary Baker G. Eddy.

———. 1925 (1896). *Prose Works*. Boston: Trustees under the Will of Mary Baker G. Eddy. Including "Miscellaneous Writings," "Retrospection and Introspection," "Unity of Good," "Pulpit and Press," "Rudimental Divine Science," "No and Yes," "Christian Science versus Pantheism," "Message to The Mother Church, 1900," "Message to The Mother Church, 1901," "Message to The Mother Church, 1902," "Christian Healing," "The People's Idea of God," "The First Church of Christ, Scientist and Miscellany."

———.1917 (1875). *Science & Health with Key to the Scriptures*. Boston: The Writings of Mary Baker Eddy.

Gordon, Ann D. (ed.) 1997. *The Selected Papers of Elizabeth Cady Stanton and Susan B. Anthony In the School of Anti-Slavery 1840–1866*. Vol. 1. New Brunswick, NJ: Rutgers University Press

———. 2000. *The Selected Papers of Elizabeth Cady Stanton and Susan B. Anthony Against an Aristocracy of Sex 1866 to 1873*. Vol. 2. New Brunswick, NJ: Rutgers University Press

More, Hannah. 1786. *The Bas bleu; or conversation: Addressed to Mrs Vesey*. London.

———. 1798. *Cheap Repository Tracts, entertaining, moral and religious*. London: Rivington.

———. 1819. *Cheap Repository Tracts suited to the Present Times*. London: Rivington.

———. 1813. *Christian Morals*. 2nd ed., 2 vols. London: T. Cadell & W. Davies.

————. 1809 (1808). *Coelebs in search of a wife, Comprehending Observations on domestic habits and manners, religion and morals.* 3rd ed., 2 vols. London: T. Cadell.

————. 1990 (1794). *Considerations on Religion and Public Education.* Los Angeles: University of California.

————. 1815. *An Essay on The Character and Practical Writings of Saint Paul.* 3rd ed., 2 vols. London: T. Cadell & W. Davies.

————. 1791. *Essays on Various Subjects Principally Designed for Young Ladies.* 5th ed. London: T. Cadell in the Strand.

————. 1810. *Essays on Various Subjects Principally Designed for Young Ladies, with a Memoir of the Author.* Edinburgh: Oliver and Boyd.

————. 1791. *An Estimate of the Religion of the Fashionable World.* 3rd ed. Dublin: Printed for P. Wogan, P. Byrne, J. Moore, J. Jones, A. Grueber, (and five others in Dublin).

————. 1774. *The Inflexible Captive: A Tragedy.* 2nd ed. London: T. Cadell.

————. 1819. *Moral Sketches of Prevailing Opinions and Manners, Foreign and Domestic: with Reflections on Prayer.* London: T. Cadell & W. Davies.

————. 1825 (1811) *Practical Piety: or The Influence of the Religion of the Heart on the Conduct of the Life.* 14th ed., 2 vols. London: T. Cadell & W. Davies.

————. 1798. *Sacred Dramas: Chiefly intended for Young Persons, The Subjects taken from the Bible. To which is added Sensibility, a Poem.* 10th ed. London: Cadell and Davies.

————. 1788. *Slavery, A Poem.* London: T. Cadell.

————. 1825. *The Spirit of Prayer, Selected and Compiled by Herself, from Various Portions Exclusively on that Subject in Her Published Volumes.* 4th ed. London: T. Cadell.

————. 1799. *Strictures on the Modern System of Female Education, With a View of the Principles and Conduct Prevalent among Women of Rank and Fortune.* 3rd ed, 2 vols. London: Cadell and Davies.

————. 1788. *Thoughts on the Importance of the Manners of the Great to General Society,* London: T. Cadell.

————. 1818. *Thoughts on the Importance of the Manners of the Great to General Society, An Estimate of the Religion of the Fashionable World, Remarks on the Speech of M Dupont, And the Tracts Written During the Riots in 1817.* London: T. Cadell & W. Davies.

————. 1995 (1792). *Village Politics Addressed to All the Mechanics, Journeymen and Day Labourers in Great Britain, by Will Chip a Country Carpenter.* Oxford: Woodstock Books.

————. 1836. *The Works of Hannah More, Essays on Various Subjects Principally Designed for Young Ladies.* 2 vols. New York: Harper and Brothers.

————. 1818 (1819). *The Works of Hannah More, Including Several Pieces Never Before Published.* 19 vols. London: Cadell.

———. 1818. *The Works of Hannah More A New Edition in Eighteen Volumes Including Several Pieces Never Before Published.* London: T. Cadell & W. Davies.

Stanton, Elizabeth Cady. 1971 (1898). *Eighty Years and More Reminiscences 1815–1897.* New York: Schocken Books.———. 1993 (1895). *The Woman's Bible.* Boston: Northeastern University Press.

Stanton, E. C., S. B. Anthony, and M. J. Gage. (eds.). 1969. *History of Woman Suffrage.* New York: Arno and the *New York Times.*

Stanton, Theodore and Harriot Stanton Blatch (eds.). 1922. *Elizabeth Cady Stanton As Revealed in Her Letters Diary and Reminiscences.* 2 vols. New York: Harper & Brothers Publishers

Walpole, H. 1961. *Horace Walpole's Correspondence with Hannah More, Lady Browne, Lady Sufolk, Mary Hamilton (Mrs Dickenson).* Edited by W. S. Lewis, R. A. Smith and H. Bennett. London: Oxford University Press.

Wilberforce, W. 1797. *A Practical View of the Prevailing Religious System of Professed Christians in the Higher and Middle Classes in this Country Contrasted with Real Christianity.* Hull: Joseph Noble, 23 Market Place. London: Griffith, Farran, Okeden & Welsh.

Wollstonecraft, Mary. 1789. *The Female Reader: or Miscellaneous Pieces, in Prose and Verse: Selected from the Best Writers, and Disposed under Proper Heads; for the Improvement of Young Women, By Mr Creswick.* London: Joseph Johnson.

———. 1794. *An Historical and Moral View of the Origin and Progress of the French Revolution; and the Effect is has produced in Europe.* London: Joseph Johnson.

———. 1796. *Letters Written During a Short Residence in Sweden, Norway and Denmark.* London: Joseph Johnson.

———. 1788. *Mary, A Fiction.* London: Joseph Johnson.

———. 1788. *Original Stories from Real Life; with Conversations Calculated to Regulate the Affections and Form the Mind to Truth and Goodness.* London: Joseph Johnson.

———. 1798. *Posthumous Works of the Author of a Vindication of the Rights of Woman.* W. Godwin (ed.) 4 vols. London: J. Johnson, and G. G. and J. Robinson.———. 1787. *Thoughts on the Education of Daughters: with Reflections on Female Conduct, in the More Important Duties of Life.* London: Joseph Johnson.

———.1790. *A Vindication of the Rights of Men, in a letter to the Right Honourable Edmund Burke.* London: Joseph Johnson.

———. 1792. *A Vindication of the Rights of Woman with Strictures on Political and Moral Subjects.* London: Joseph Johnson.

SECONDARY SOURCES

Abrams, M. H. 1993. *A Glossary of Literary Terms.*New York: Holt, Rinehart & Winston.

———. 1962. *The Norton Anthology of English Literature.* Volumes 1 and 2, New York: W. W. Norton.

Banks, O. 1981. *Faces of Feminism: A Study of Feminism as a Social Movement.* Oxford: Martin Robertson.

Barbauld, A. L. 1994. W. McCarthy & E. Kraft (eds.). *The Poems of Anna Letitia Barbauld,* Athens: The University of Georgia Press.

Barker-Benfield, G. J. 1992. *The Culture of Sensibility: Sex & Society in Eighteenth-Century Britain.* Chicago: The University of Chicago Press.

Barrell, J. (ed.). 1992. *Painting & Politics of Culture: New Essays on British Art 1700–1850.* Oxford: Oxford University Press.

Beauvoir, S. de. 1989 (1952). *The Second Sex.* New York: Vintage.

Berglund, B. 1993. *Woman's Whole Existence: The House as an Image in the Novels of Ann Radcliffe, Mary Wollstonecraft and Jane Austen.* Lund, Sweden: Lund University Press.

Birrell, A. 1895. *Essays About Men, Women and Books.* London: Elliot Stock.

———. 1922. *Collected Essays and Addresses of the Right Honourable Augustine Birrell 1880–1920.* Vol. 11. London: Dent.

Blakemore, S. 1977. *Intertextual War: Edmund Burke and the French Revolution in the writings of Mary Wollstonecraft, Thomas Paine, and James Mackintosh.* Madison, NJ: Fairleigh Dickinson University Press.

Braude, A. 2001. *Radical Spirits: Spiritualism and Women's Rights in Nineteenth-century America.* Bloomington: Indiana University Press.

Briggs, A. 2000. *The Age of Improvement, 1783–1867.* New York: Longman.

Brimley Johnson, R. (ed.). 1925. *The Letters of Hannah More.* London: John Lane The Bodley Head.

Brown, C. G. 2001. *The Death of Christian Britain: Understanding Secularisation 1800–2000.* London: Routledge.

Buckminster, J. 1810. *A Sermon Preached before the Members of the Boston Female Asylum.* Hand-copied and bound with other printed sermons to the BFA. For copies of J. Buckminster's Sermons see www.openlibrary.org/b/OL.17872004M

Burbick, J. 1994. *Healing the Republic: The Language of Health and the Culture of Nationalism in Nineteenth-century America.* Cambridge: Cambridge University Press.

Burchfield, R. W. (ed.). 1982. *Oxford English Dictionary A Supplement to the Oxford English Dictionary.* Vols. 1–5. Oxford: Clarendon Press.

Burnett, F. H. 1993. *The Secret Garden.*Hertfordshire, England: Wordsworth Classics.

Butler, M. 1981. *Romantics, Rebels and Reactionaries: English Literature and its Background 1796–1830.* Oxford: Oxford University Press.

Cameron, K. N. (ed.). 1961. *Shelley and His Circle 1773–1822.* Cambridge, MA: Harvard University Press.

Channing, W. E. 1826. *A Discourse Preached on the evidences of revealed religion*. 2nd ed. Boston: Isaac R. Butts.

Collins, A. Y. (ed.). 1985. *Feminist Perspectives on Biblical Scholarship*. Chico, CA: Scholars Press.

Colley, L. 1992. *Britons, Forging the Nation 1707–1837*. New Haven, CT: Yale University Press.

Cott, N. F. 1977. *The Bonds of Womanhood "Woman's Sphere" in New England 1780–1835*, New Haven, CT: Yale University Press.

Cromwell, O. 1958. *Lucretia Mott*. New York: Russell & Russell.

Daly, M. 1986. *Beyond God the Father*. London: The Women's Press.

———. 1968. *The Church and the Second Sex*. New York: Harper Colophon Books.

———. 1979. *Gyn/Ecology*.London: The Women's Press.

Dart, G. 1999. *Rousseau, Robespierre and English Romanticism*. Cambridge: Cambridge University Press.

Davidoff, L. and C. Hall. 1987. *Family Fortunes: Men & Women of the English Middle-Class 1780-1850*. London: Routledge.

Davidson, C. N. 1986. *Revolution and the Word: The Rise of the Novel in America*. New York: Oxford University Press.

Davidson, C. N. (ed.). 1989. *Reading in America: Literature and Social History*. Baltimore: John Hopkins University Press.

Davis, J. 1996. *The Landscape of Belief: Encountering the Holy Land in Nineteenth-century American Art and Culture*. Princeton, NJ: Princeton University Press.

Davis, R. W. and R. J. Helmstadter. (eds.). 1992. *Religion and Irreligion in Victorian Society*. London: Routledge.

Day, A. 1996. *Romanticism*. London: Routledge.

Douglas, A. 1988. *The Feminization of American Culture*. New York: Doubleday.

Dowell, Í. and L. Hurcombe. 1981. *Dispossessed Daughters of Eve: Faith and Feminism*. London: SCM Press.

Eger, E., C. Grant, O. G. Cliona, and P. Warburton. (eds.). 2001. *Women, Writing and the Public Sphere 1700–1830*. Cambridge: Cambridge University Press.

Eliade, M. (ed.). 1987. *The Encyclopedia of Religion*. Vols 1–6. New York: Macmillan.

Eustace, H. W. 1959. *Christian Science its "Clear, Correct Teaching" and Complete Writings*. Berkeley, CA: Lederer, Street & Zeus Co.

Faust, D. G. 1981. *The Ideology of Slavery: Proslavery Thought in the Antebellum South 1830–1860*. Baton Rouge: Louisiana University Press.

Fettweis, Y. C. and R. T. Warneck. 1998. *Mary Baker Eddy—Christian Healer*. Boston: The Christian Science Publishing Society.

Fields, A. (ed.). 1898. *Life and Letters of Harriet Beecher Stowe*. London: Sampson Low, Marston & Co.

Fiorenza, E. S. 1983. *In Memory of Her: A Feminist Theological Reconstruction of Christian Origins.* London: SCM Press.

Fiorenza, E.S. (ed.). 1994. *Searching the Scriptures: A Feminist Introduction.* London: SCM Press.

Ford, B. (ed.). 1988. *The New Pelican Guide to English Literature: Volume 9: American Literature.* Harmondsworth, England:Penguin Books.

Fraser, A. 1984. *The Weaker Vessel, Woman's Lot in Seventeenth-Century England.* London: Phoenix Press.

George, M. 1970. *One Woman's "Situation": A Study of Mary Wollstonecraft.* Urbana, Illinois: University of Illinois Press.

Gerzina, G. 2004. *Frances Hodgson Burnett—The Unpredictable Life of the Author of The Secret Garden. London:* Chatto & Windus.

Gisborne, T. 1805. *An Enquiry into the Duties of the Female Sex.* 6th ed. London: T. Cadell & W. Davies.

Godwin, W. 1928. *Memoirs of Mary Wollstonecraft.* London: Constable

Godwin, W. 1969. *Memoirs of Mary Wollstonecraft.* Edited with a preface, a supplement chronologically arranged and containing hitherto unpublished or uncollected material and a bibliographical note by W. Clark Durant. New York: Haskell House.

Godwin, W. 1798 *Posthumous Works of the Author of* A Vindication of the Rights of Woman. 4 vols. London: J. Johnson, G. G. & J. Robinson.

Golby, J. M. (ed.). 1986. *Culture and Society in Britain 1850-1890: A Source Book of Contemporary Writings.* Oxford: Oxford University Press.

Gill, G. 1998. *Mary Baker Eddy.* Reading, MA: Perseus Books.

———. 2004. *Nightingales: The Story of Florence Nightingale and Her Remarkable Family.* London: Hodder & Stoughton.

Gill, S. 1994. *Women and the Church of England: From the Eighteenth Century to the Present.* London: SPCK

Green, K. 1995. *The Woman of Reason.*Cambridge: Polity Press.

Griffith, E. 1984. *In Her Own Right: The Life of Elizabeth Cady Stanton.* New York: Oxford University Press.

Grossman, M. (ed) 1998. *Aemilia Lanyer, Gender, Genre & the Canon.* Lexington: The University Press of Kentucky.

Guest, H. 2000. *Small Change, Women, Learning, Patriotism 1750–1810.* Chicago: Chicago University Press.

Hall, C. 1992. *White, Male and Middle Class: Explorations in Feminism and History.* Cambridge,: Polity Press.

Hall, D. (ed.). 1994. *Muscular Christianity: Embodying the Victorian Age.* Cambridge: Cambridge University Press.

Harding, B. 1982. *American Literature in Context 1830–1865.* London: Methuen

Hartman, M. S. and L. Banner. (eds.). 1974. *Clio's Consciousness Raised: New Perspectives on the History of Women.* New York: Harper & Row.

Hayter, M. 1987. *The New Eve in Christ—The Use and Abuse of the Bible in the Debate about Women in the Church.*London: SPCK.

Heimmel, J. P. 1982. *"God is Our Mother": Julian of Norwich and the Medieval Image of Christian Feminine Divinity.*, Lewiston, NY: The Edwin Mellen Press.

Hendler, G. 2001. *Public Sentiments: Structures of Feeling in Nineteenth-century American Literature.* Chapel Hill: University of North Carolina Press.

Hill, B. (ed.). 1986. *The First English Feminist, Reflections upon marriage and other writings by Mary Astell.* Aldershot, England: Gower/ Maurice Temple Smith.

Hilton, B. 1988. *The Age of Atonement: The Influence of Evangelicalism on Social and Economic Thought 1785–1865.* Oxford: Clarendon Press.

Hobby, E. 1988. *Virtue of Necessity: English Women's Writing 1649–99.* Ann Arbor: The University of Michigan Press.

Hobsbawn, E. J. 1962. *The Age of Revolution.* London: Weidenfeld & Nicholson

Hole, R. 1996. *Selected Writings of Hannah More.* London: William Pickering.

Hopkins, M. A. 1947. *Hannah More and Her Circle.* New York: Longmans, Green & Co.

Hufton, O. 1995. *The Prospect Before Her: A History of Women in Western Europe.* Vol. 1. London: Harper Collins.

Hurley, J. B. 1981. *Man and Woman in Biblical Perspective: A Study in Role Relationships and Authority.* Leicester, England: Inter-Varsity Press.

Irigaray, L. 1986. *Divine Women.* Sydney, Australia: This translation © Local Consumption Publications, Occasional Paper 8.

Janes-Yeo, E. 1997. *Mary Wollstonecraft and 200 Years of Feminisms.* London: Rivers Oram Press.

Jasper, D. and S. Prickett. (eds.). 1999. *The Bible and Literature, A Reader.* Oxford: Blackwell.

Jay, E. 1979. *The Religion of the Heart.* Oxford: Clarendon Press.

Johnston, J. M. 1946. *Mary Baker Eddy—Her Mission and Triumph.* Boston: The Christian Science Publishing Society.

Johnson, R. B. (ed.). 1925. *The Letters of Hannah More.* London: John Lane The Bodley Head Ltd.

Jones, M. G. 1952. *Hannah More.* Cambridge: Cambridge University Press.

Jones, V. (ed.). 1990. *Women in the Eighteenth-Century: Constructions of Femininity.* London: Routledge.

Kant, I. 1960. *Observations on the Feeling of the Beautiful and the Sublime.* Trans. John T. Goldthwait. Berkeley: University California Press.

Kelley, M. 1984. *Private Woman, Public Stage: Literary Domesticity in Nineteenth-century America.* New York: Oxford University Press.

Kelly, G. 1992. *Revolutionary Feminism: The Mind and Career of Mary Wollstonecraft.* Basingstoke: London: Macmillan.

———. 1993. *Women, Writing, and Revolution 1790–1827.* Oxford: Clarendon Press.

Kern, K. 2001. *Mrs Stanton's Bible.* Ithaca, NY: Cornell University Press.

King, U. (ed.). 1987. *Women in the World's Religions Past & Present*. New York: Paragon House Publishers.

Knight, H. C. 1851. *A New Memoir of Hannah More: or Life in Hall and Cottage*. New York: M. W. Dodd.

Knott, A.M. 1953. "Reminiscences of Mary Baker Eddy." *We Knew Mary Baker Eddy*. Third Series. Boston: The Christian Science Publishing Society.

Krueger, C. 1992. *The Reader's Repentance: Women Preachers, Women Writers and Nineteenth-Century Social Discourse*. Chicago: University of Chicago Press.

Landes, J. B. 1988. *Women and the Public Sphere in the Age of the French Revolution*. Ithaca: Cornell University Press.

Lang, P. 2001. *Religions and Discourse*. Vol. 9. "Towards a Different Transcendence—Feminist Findings on Subjectivity Religion and Values." European Academic Publishers.

Lerner, G. 1993. *The Creation of Feminist Consciousness*. New York: Oxford University Press.

Levander, C. F. 1998. *Voices of the Nation: Women and Public Speech in Nineteenth-century American Literature and Culture*. New York: Cambridge University Press.

Lewalski, B. K. 1993. *Writing Women in Jacobean England*. Cambridge, MA: Harvard University Press.

Lewis, Lady T. (ed.). 1865. *Extracts of the Journals and Correspondence of Miss Berry from the Year 1783 to 1852*. London: Longmans.

Lewis, W.S. (ed.) 1961. *The Correspondence of Horace Walpole*. London: Oxford University Press.

Lyman, W. 1802. *A Virtuous Woman the Bond of Domestic Union and the Source of Domestic Happiness*. New London, CT: Printed by S. Green.

Mack, D. 1992. *Visionary Women, Ecstatic Phrophecy in Seventeenth-Century England*. Berkeley: University of California Press.

Mandell, L. M. 1999. *Misogynous Economies: The Business of Literature in Eighteenth-Century Britain*. Lexington: University Press of Kentucky.

Marsh, J. (ed.). 1994. *Christina Rossetti Poems and Prose*. London: J. M. Dent.

Matchinske, M. 1998. *Writing, Gender and State in Early Modern England: Identity Formation and the Female Subject*. Cambridge: Cambridge University Press.

McFague, S. 1983. *Metaphorical Theology, Models of God in Religious Language*. London: SCM Press.

———. 1987. *Models of God, Theology for an Ecological Nuclear Age*. London: SCM Press.

McGrath, A. E. 1999. *Science & Religion An Introduction*. Oxford: Blackwell.

McMillen, S. 1990. *Sensibility in Transformation: Creative Resistance to Sentiment from the Augustans to the Romantics: Essays in Honor of Jean H. Hagstrum*. London: Associated University Presses.

Melnyk, J. (ed.).1998. *Women's Theology in Nineteenth-Century Britain: Transfiguring the Faith of their Fathers*. New York: Garland.

Midgley, C. 1994. *Women Against Slavery: The British Campaigns 1780–1870*. London: Routledge.

Milton, J. 1968(1667). *Paradise Lost*. London: Addison Wesley Longman.

Mitchell, W. J. T. 1986. *Iconology: Image, Text, Ideology*. Chicago: University of Chicago Press.

Moehiman, C. H. 1955. *Ordeal by Concordance: An Historical Study of a Recent Literary Invention*. New York: Longmans Green.

Moers, E. 1977. *Literary Women*. London: W. H. Allen.

Murphy, C. 1998. *The Word According to Eve*. Harmondsworth, England: Penguin.

Murray, J. A. H. (ed.) 1888. *A New English Dictionary on Historical Principles*. Vol. 8. Oxford: Clarendon Press.

Myers, M. 1982. "Reform or Ruin, 'A Revolution in Female Manners.'" H. C. Payne (ed.). *Studies in Eighteenth-Century Culture*. 11: 199–216. Published for the American Society for Eighteenth-Century Studies by The University of Wisconsin Press.

———. 1986. "Hannah More's Tracts for the Times: Social Fiction & Female Idology." Schofield, M.A. and C. Mascheski. (eds.). *Fetter'd or Free? British Women Novelists 1670–1815*. Athens, OH: Ohio University Press.

Newsom, C. A. and S. H. Ringe. (eds.). 1992. *The Women's Bible Commentary*. London: SPCK.

Neidzielska, Nadia. "The rights of women sustained by divine law." *The Herald of Christian Science*. March 2001, Special Issue, 4. Published by The Christian Science Publishing Society in honor of women's history month in the United States.

Nightingale, Florence. 1928. *Cassandra*. Reprinted in R. Strachey. 1978. *The Cause: A Short History of The Women's Movement in Great Britain*. London: Virago.

Nixon, E. 1971. *Mary Wollstonecraft Her Life and Times*. London:. Dent.

O'Grady, K., A. Gilroy, and J. Gray. (eds.). 1998. *Bodies, Lives, Voices, Gender in Theology*.Sheffield, England: Sheffield Academic Press.

Orcutt, W. D. 1950. *Mary Baker Eddy & Her Books*. Boston: The Christian Science Publishing Society.

Paine, T. 1993 (1791). *The Rights of Man*. Harmondsworth, England: Penguin.

Parton, J. 1868. *Eminent Women of the Age*. Hartford, Connecticut: S. M. Betts. Hartford, CT.

Patmore, C. 1909. *Poems by Coventry Patmore*. London: George Bell & Sons.

Paul, C. K. 1876. *William Godwin: His Friends and Contemporaries*. London: Henry S. King.

Peel, R. 1977. *Mary Baker Eddy—The Years of Authority*. New York: Holt, Rinehart & Winston.

———. 1977. *Mary Baker Eddy—The Years of Discovery*.New York: Holt, Rinehart & Winston.

———. 1977. *Mary Baker Eddy—The Years of Trial*. New York: Holt, Rinehart & Winston.

Perkin, H. 1969. *The Origins of Modern English Society 1780–1880*. London: Routledge & Kegan Paul.

Perry, R.1980. *Women, Letters and the Novel*. New York: AMS Press.

Polwhele, R. 1798. *The Unsex'd Female: A Poem*. London: Cadell and Davies.

Poston, C. H. (ed.). 1988. *A Vindication of the Rights of Woman: An Authoratitive Text, Backgrounds, the Wollstonecraft Debate, Criticism/ Mary Wollstonecraft*. New York: Norton.

Powell, L. P. 1930. *Mary Baker Eddy A Life Size Portrait*, London: Nisbet & Co., Ltd.

Pratt, R. M. M. 1961. *Mary Baker Eddy Mentioned Them*. Boston: The Christian Science Publishing Society.

Purkiss, D. 1994. *Renaissance Women: The Plays of Elizabeth Cary, the Poems of Aemilia Lanyer*. London: William Pickering.

Ramazanoglu, C. (ed.). 1993. *Up Against Foucault: Explorations of Some Tensions Between Foucault and Feminism*. London: Routledge.

Rendall, J. 1985. *The Origins of Modern Feminism: Women in Britain, France and The United States 1780–1860*. London: Macmillan.

Richardson, S. 1985 (1740). *Pamela or Virtue Rewarded*. Harmondsworth, England: Penguin.

Roberts, W. 1834. *Memoirs of the Life & Correspondence of Mrs. Hannah More*. Vols. 2–4. London: R. B. Seeley & W. Burnside.

Rousseau, J. J. 1997 (1761). *Julie or The New Heloise*. Hanover, NH: University Press of New England.

———. 1993. (1762) *Emile*. London: J. M. Dent.

Ruether, R. R. 1981. *Women and Religion in America: Vol 1 The Nineteenth-Century*. New York: Harper & Row.

———. 1983. *Sexism and God-talk: Toward a Feminist Theology*. London: SCM.

———. 1998. *Introducing Redemption in Christian Feminism*. Sheffield, England: Sheffield Academic.

———. 1998. *Women and Redemption: A Theological History*. London: SCM.

Ruland, R. and M. Bradbury. 1992. *From Puritanism to Post Modernism, A History of American Literature*. Harmondsworth, England: Penguin.

Runge, L. 1997. *Gender and Language in British Literary Criticism 1660–1790*. Cambridge: Cambridge University Press.

Ruskin, J. 1886. *Sesame and Lilies*. Orpington, Kent: George Allen.

Ryall, A. and C. Sandback-Dahlstrom. (eds.) 2003. *Mary Wollstonecraft's Journey to Scandinavia: Essays*. Stockholm: Almquist and Wiksell.

Samuels, S. (ed.). 1992. *The Culture of Sentiment: Race, Gender, and Sentimentality in Nineteenth-century America*. New York: Oxford University Press.

Sanders, V. 1996. *Eve's Renegades Victorian Anti-Feminist Women Novelists.* London: Macmillan.

Scott, S. 1766. *The History of Sir George Ellison*, London: A. Millar.

Selvidge, M. J. 1996. *Notorious Voices, Feminist Biblical Interpretation 1500–1920.* London: SCM.

Shoemaker, R. B. 1998. *Gender in English Society 1650–1850 The Emergence of Separate Spheres.* London: Longman.

Smith, B. G. 1989. *Changing Lives: Women in European History Since 1700.* Lexington, MA: D. C. Heath.

Smith-Rosenberg, C. 1985. *Disorderly Conduct: Visions of Gender in Victorian America.* Oxford: Oxford University Press.

———. 1993. "Subject Female: Authorizing American Identity." *American Literary History.* vol. 5. Oxford: Oxford University Press.

Spender, D. 1982. *Women of Ideas (And What Men Have Done to Them): From Aphra Behn to Adrienne Rich* London: Routledge & Kegan Paul.

Springborg, P. (ed.). 1996. *Mary Astell: Some Reflections upon Marriage in Political Writings.* Cambridge: Cambridge University Press.

Staveley, K. W. F. 1987. *Puritan Legacies: Paradise Lost and the New England Tradition 1630–1890.* Ithaca, NY: Cornell University Press.

Stendahl, K. 1966. *The Bible and the Role of Women. A case Study in Hermeneutics.* John Reumann, ed. Philadelphia: Fortress Press.

Sterne, L. 1968 (1768). *A Sentimental Journey Through France and Italy by Mr Yorick.* Oxford: Oxford University Press.

Stott, A. 2003. *Hannah More: The First Victorian.* Oxford: Oxford University Press.

Strachey, R. 1978 (1928). *The Cause: A Short History of The Women's Movement in Great Britain.* London: Virago.

Swanson, R.N. (ed.) 1998. *Gender and Christian Religion.* Studies in Church History 34. Suffolk: Boydell and Brewer.

Taylor, B. J. 1983. *Eve and the New Jerusalem: Socialism and Feminism in the Nineteenth-Century.* London: Virago.

———. 2003. *Mary Wollstonecraft and the Feminist Imagination.* Cambridge: Cambridge University Press.

Thompson, H. 1838. *The life of Hannah More: With Notices of Her Sisters.* London: T. Cadell.

Tobin, B. F. 1994. *History, Gender and Eighteenth-century Literature.* Athens GA,: University of Georgia Press.

Todd, J. 1994. *Mary Wollstonecraft Political Writings.* Oxford: Oxford University Press.

———. 1977. *A Wollstonecraft Anthology.* Bloomington: Indiana University Press.

———. 2000. *Mary Wollstonecraft: A Revolutionary Life.* London: Weidenfeld and Nicolson.

Todd, J. and M. Butler. (eds.). 1989. *The Works of Mary Wollstonecraft.* Vols. 1–7. London: William Pickering.

Tomalin, C. 1974. *The Life and Death of Mary Wollstonecraft*. London: Weidenfeld and Nicolson.

Tomlinson, I. C. 1945. *Twelve Years with Mary Baker Eddy*. Boston: The Christian Science Publishing Society.

Twain, M. 1993 (1907). *Christian Science*. Buffalo, NY: Promethus Books.

———. 1923. *What is Man?: And Other Essays*. New York: G. Wells.

Valenze, D. M. 1985. *Prophetic Sons and Daughters: Female Preaching and Popular Religion in Industrial England*. Princeton, NJ: Princeton University Press.

Vance, N. 1985. *The Sinews of the Spirit: The Ideal of Christian Manliness in Victorian Literature and Religious Thought. Cambridge*: Cambridge University Press.

Wagner-Martin, L., and C. N. Davidson, eds. 1995. *The Oxford Book of Women's Writing in the United States*. Oxford: Oxford University Press.

Wardle, R. M., ed. 1951. *Mary Wollstonecraft: A Critical Biography*. London: Richards Press.

———. 1966. *Godwin and Mary: Letters of William Godwin and Mary Wollstonecraft*. Lawrence, KS: University of Kansas Press.

———. 1979. *Collected Letters of Mary Wollstonecraft*. Ithaca, NY: Cornell University Press.

Welter, B. 1973. *The Woman Question in American History*. Hinsdale, IL: Dryden Press.

Wilber, S. 1907. *The Life of Mary Baker Eddy*. Boston: The Christian Science Publishing Society.

Wilberforce, R. I. and S. Wilberforce, eds. 1840. *The Correspondence of William Wilberforce*. London: John Murray.

Witherington, B. 1984. *Women in the Ministry of Jesus: A Study of Jesus' Attitudes to Women and their Roles as Reflected in His Earthly Life*. Cambridge: Cambridge University Press.

Woods, S 1999. *Lanyer A Renaissance Woman Poet*. New York: Oxford University Press.

Wu, D. 1994. *Romanticism: AnAnthology*. Oxford, UK: Blackwell.

Yellin, J. F. 1989. *Women & Sisters; The Antislavery Feminists in American Culture*. New Haven, CT: Yale University Press.

Yonge, C. M. 1888. *Hannah More*. London: W. H. Allen & Co.

INDEX